ROCK AND ROLL

EXPLORER GUIDE TO SAN FRANCISCO AND THE BAY AREA

MIKE KATZ AND CRISPIN KOTT

FOREWORD BY JOEL GION

Pe...

Guilford

D1292604

Globe
Pequot

An imprint of The Rowman & Littlefield Publishing Group, Inc.
4501 Forbes Blvd., Ste. 200
Lanham, MD 20706
www.rowman.com

Distributed by NATIONAL BOOK NETWORK

British Library Cataloguing in Publication Information available

Library of Congress Control Number: 2021933104

ISBN 978-1-4930-4173-2 (paper : alk. paper)
ISBN 978-1-4930-4174-9 (electronic)

∞™ The paper used in this publication meets the minimum requirements of American National Standard for Information Sciences—Permanence of Paper for Printed Library Materials, ANSI/NISO Z39.48-1992.

Contents

Introduction

San Francisco's rich and unique cultural history since its time as a gold rush frontier town has long made it a bastion of forward thinking and freedom of expression. It makes perfect sense, then, that both it and the surrounding Bay Area should prove to be a crucible for some of the most enduring and influential music of the rock and roll era.

Perhaps best known for the '60s psychedelic scene which included the Grateful Dead, Jefferson Airplane, Creedence Clearwater Revival, Santana, the Steve Miller Band, Sly and the Family Stone, and Janis Joplin, the Bay Area's rock and roll history twists and turns like Lombard Street itself. The first wave San Francisco punks wrought the Avengers and Dead Kennedys; punk later gripped the East Bay, giving us Green Day and Rancid. From the folk and blues eras through the chart-topping sounds of Journey and Huey Lewis and the News. The rock equivalent of Manifest Destiny carried wave upon wave of young musicians in search of fame, fortune, and the great lost chord to the Golden Gate. San Francisco and the surrounding Bay Area have collectively produced countless key figures in rock and roll, from musicians to journalists to entrepreneurs. The modern concept of the vast outdoor rock festival took root in and around San Francisco.

The Bay Area is also where music history happened to artists from almost everywhere else: San Francisco is where the Beatles played their final concert and where the Sex Pistols fell apart; where the Clash recorded much of their second album; where a drug-addled Keith Moon passed out during a concert by the Who only to be replaced behind the drum kit by an eager fan.

From the heady days of Haight-Ashbury in the '60s to today, the Bay Area has provided a distinctive soundtrack to the American experience that has often been confrontational, controversial, enlightening, and always entertaining. *Rock and Roll Explorer Guide to San Francisco and the Bay Area* restores a sense of time and place to music history by identifying and documenting critical points of interest spanning genres and eras, and delineating the places in San Francisco, Berkeley, Oakland, and the surrounding Bay Area critical to its musical development and ultimate triumphs and tragedies. In this way we can see and understand how bands came together, scenes developed, and classic songs were written. In some cases, the buildings are still there as they once were; in others only the address remains, but perhaps you can still get a sense of the history that happened there.

Among the many locations in this book are addresses where musicians and other key rock and roll figures once called home, but we consciously left their current residences out. *Rock and Roll Explorer Guide to San Francisco and the Bay Area* is intended as a fun and informative field guide through music history rather than a star map for locating famous musicians.

For the sake of continuity and clarity, we've opted to stick with the original name of some of the Bay Area's larger arenas and stadiums, most of which are referenced in multiple chapters and across different eras. In the modern age, corporate naming rights have muddied the waters and made it difficult to find firm footing in describing venues which have had numerous sponsors. Where

applicable we've also included a venue's name at the time of any specific events referenced in a particular entry.

Look for the no-access symbol ⊘ to indicate buildings that have been demolished. The structures are no longer there, but the stories remain.

Though rock and roll is baked into the Bay Area's cultural fabric, the *Rock and Roll Explorer Guide to San Francisco and the Bay Area* is not a comprehensive encyclopedia of music, rock venues, or the music industry; nor does it present the definitive biographies of the musicians included. The artists and locations chosen represent a sometimes broad look at the history of rock and roll in the Bay Area, with an eye on those who either grew up or spent their formative years here. But there's so much more we couldn't include, and we hope readers will be inspired to go even further, whether they're hitting the streets themselves or experiencing the city vicariously from afar. Artists come and go, neighborhoods change, venues open and close, but the music lives on.

Author's note:

The majority of this book was researched and written prior to the 2020 COVID-19 pandemic. Unfortunately, some of the locations we describe herein have closed permanently, and it's possible that others may yet follow.

We have made every effort to update and correct information that has changed due to the outbreak and its after-effects up to the time of publication.

San Francisco City Hall

Foreword

These days there's more people than ever leaving their hearts in San Francisco, and more times than not they are left broken. Much has changed since Tony Bennett first vowed to return to retrieve his own heart in his career defining tune. The modern-day reality is that the majority of those hearts are now left behind unwillingly, then mass-buried underneath soulless multimillion dollar furnished condos.

This is a city that traditionally has served 57 varieties of rebellion before even having to go off menu and so maybe it's time to once again remember what the dormouse said, "We built this city on rock and roll." Hmm, maybe I should Google it.

Even stranger days indeed as the idea of obligated-to-be-here money implant people embracing a sense of indigenous "freaky San Francisco" abandon seems to be not only unrequired, but an unnecessary effort altogether. Where's a nice 6.0 earthquake when you need one? Get enough *Shake Rattle and Roll* to scare off the strictly breadheaded yawner sect, but still not big enough to knock anything important over. Maybe a nice 'n' breezy 5.0'r.

Harsh realities but that's just the nature of change and especially when it's on a hypersonic explosion level then it's do or bye-bye in figuring out how to not only just stay present, but get on the floor and *swing* with it.

This city is built from the underground up with survivor stories of the downtrodden uprisings and it's never been all that easy to navigate for any of the decades-long Fellini-esque parade of artist rebels. Even the most fabled odor-seasoned outlaw biker occasionally took a spill on rain-slicked grooves of the cable car tracks and at the end of the day, it's not SF's individual fault or any other one place for that matter, but a sign of the times. You can see it overly represented now in every desirable city in the modern world, but if any of them are gonna pull off the ultimate Hail-Mary WTF artistic comeback, San Francisco has been time tested and proven to come through over and over again all on down the timeline. The beats, flower power, none of that was invited to happen here— until it was "a happening."

As a child growing up, San Francisco had not only qualified as one of those "somewhere over the rainbow" locales, but had more character than anywhere else over even the most entangled butterfly junction of rainbows. There is a dreamlike cinematic quality to the colorful streets in North Beach and its canopy of abstract patterned electrical cable spider webs. Its high-rolling hills covered with European style flush, old-world Victorian splendor, and Art Deco class comingling with new modernist architecture. Nob Hill casting its huge affluent shadows down long steep hills running all the way down to the downtrodden Tenderloin. The Mission's vibrant and strong spirit of Latino community and culture. The Broadway strip's rainy night wet streets reflecting all the neon back up to the would-be's while the won't-be's little by little disappear into the city's thick fog of illusions. The Haight-Ashbury, where the magic of the '60s music revolution has left an eternal psychedelic varnish over everything (that is as long as you're wearing the right glasses). Lower Haight's rows of Victorian apartments with their decorative architecture looking like a giant display of elongated turn-of-the century wedding cakes.

These steep San Francisco hills are also alive with the sound of film music. I often put on my headphones and listen to Lalo Schiffirin's *Bullitt* soundtrack, where I become Steve McQueen barreling (or perhaps just strolling) down the slopes of Nob Hill into North Beach. Then it's back up the other side of Telegraph Hill as John Barry's 1968 *Petulia* score eerily guides my inner Julie Christie through the fog and lush foliage. If you take this excursion, make sure to stop and listen out for the real flocks of wild parrots flying overhead.

From there, head back down to Vesuvio while averting your eyes from the modern cars on the streets to be back in 1977, '67, '57, '47—pick your era of footprints from punk, psychedelic rock, be-bop jazz and on down. Once at Vesuvio, you can drink where the beats drank and even take home a beat poet souvenir by peeling off one of the many decade-spanning pieces of chewed gum from underneath one of the upstairs tables. Do your gum research and maybe you'll even excavate a Kerouac.

For now, all of that timelessness that's been laid all over this land can be traveled back to and made real again with this guidebook you are holding. I'm not going to go deep music history here because it's all laid out and then some for you on every page after this one.

My birth certificate states time of birth at 4:20 in the afternoon, so let this new weed's baby leave you with one more bit of advice on starting your first trip. We legalized it here so stock up accordingly, then let the Jefferson Airplane, Moby Grape, Sly and the Family Stone, and all your personal favorites from the "San Francisco sound" double as your audio guide while you read your way through the Haight-Ashbury, but keep in mind: the Lower Haight belongs to the Brian Jonestown Massacre.

— Joel Gion, percussionist, The Brian Jonestown Massacre

SAN FRANCISCO

NORTH BEACH— FISHERMAN'S WHARF

HUNGRY-I
599 Jackson St.

Founded in 1950 and primarily known as a comedy and folk venue, the hungry-i ushered in a new era of the former when social satirist Mort Sahl became a regular performer in the late '50s. The response was immediate, and soon the hungry-i would host Dick Gregory, Lenny Bruce, Tom Lehrer, Bob Newhart, and May & Nichols. Musically the venue was primarily folky, with the Kingston Trio recording an album there, and performers like Miriam Makeba, the Limelighters, the Gateway Singers, and the Smothers Brothers all making the scene. But a few rock groups did hit the stage at the hungry-i, including the Lovin' Spoonful, in town in 1966 to play the second Family Dog concert at Longshoremen's Hall.

ORPHANAGE
870 Montgomery St.

Originally a topless club called the Roaring Twenties, which itself had a brief, strained relationship with rock and roll during a 1966 engagement by the Charlatans; an audience member preferring topless women to folk rock hurled a glass ashtray at the band, hitting then-drummer Dan Hicks in the head. Renamed the Orphanage in the early '70s, the club featured eclectic offerings, including Graham Central Station; the Tubes; and Toots and the Maytals, who were seen by Mick Jagger and Keith Richards during a 1975 appearance.

THE SENTINEL BUILDING—COLUMBUS TOWER
916 Kearny St.

Originally completed just after the earthquake in 1907, this designated landmark structure at the corner of Columbus Avenue has seen its share of musical and entertainment history. The original hungry-i was located in the basement in the early '50s, and in the '60s it served as the headquarters of San Francisco's popular folk group the Kingston Trio, who built a recording studio, Columbus Recorders, in that same subterranean space. It was utilized by a variety of artists, most notably the Grateful Dead, who in 1968 assembled the myriad pieces of their jigsaw puzzle of a second album, *Anthem of the Sun*. The album was cobbled together from

Sentinel Building

material recorded in several studios in Los Angeles and New York City, as well as a handful of live shows across California, Oregon, and Washington. Since 1972 the Sentinel Building has housed the offices of filmmaker Francis Ford Coppola's American Zoetrope.

THE PURPLE ONION
140 Columbus Ave.
Similar to the hungry-i, the Purple Onion was mostly a folk and comedy spot, with everyone from the Kingston Trio to Phyllis Diller playing the small stage. The Smothers Brothers recorded an album at The Purple Onion, and Maya Angelou sang and danced there before becoming a respected poet. In the '90s, under the guidance of club manager Tom Guido, the Purple Onion began hosting rock shows, with the Brian Jonestown Massacre, the Rip Offs, the Trashwomen, and the 5.6.7.8's playing its intimate room.

NORTH BEACH REVIVAL/MORTY'S
1024 Kearny St.
Once known as the Off Broadway, a jazz and comedy club which showcased everyone from Stan Kenton to Lenny Bruce, the spot didn't host rock bands until its name was changed to the North Beach Revival in the early '70s. A pre-fame Dr. Hook and the Medicine Show used to be regulars in the early days of this incarnation. By the '80s, the club was renamed Morty's, hosting alternative rock groups like the Himalayans, which featured a pre-Counting Crows' Adam Duritz on vocals.

CITY LIGHTS BOOKSTORE
261 Columbus Ave.
City Lights has been a focal point for San Francisco's intellectual community since its establishment in 1953 by poet Lawrence Ferlinghetti. Initially a haunt as well as publisher of the Beat Generation, it enthusiastically embraced the counterculture of the '60s as a

City Lights Bookstore

natural extension of its own founding ethos. Countless important rock and roll figures, including Bob Dylan, Janis Joplin, and Paul Kantner have explored its shelves seeking inspiration. Additionally, it was an important ticket outlet to many of the shows at the Avalon, Fillmore, and other iconic destinations. City Lights has continued moving forward with the times and remains an important part of the cultural life of the city to this day.

VESUVIO CAFE
255 Columbus Ave.
A classic beatnik hangout, Vesuvio Cafe was where Francis Ford Coppola wrote huge swathes

Vesuvio Café

of the script for the original *Godfather* flick. Vesuvio even used to sell a "Beatnik Kit," which included a poem called "How Are You Going to Keep Them Down on the Farm After They've Seen North Beach?" Both Dylan Thomas and Jack Kerouac used to frequent Vesuvio, and many years later so too did Paul Kantner of the Jefferson Airplane, who treated the place as his local watering hole.

TOSCA CAFE
242 Columbus Ave.
A celebrated and timeless local bar, Cafe Tosca was famous with filmmakers, actors, and writers. U2 have frequently visited Tosca during stays in San Francisco, and many years earlier a rowdy party comprised of Bob Dylan, Allen Ginsberg, Lawrence Ferlinghetti, and Peter Orlovsky was thrown out.

Cafe Tosca

SUGAR HILL: HOME OF THE BLUES
430 Broadway
Opened in 1961 by folk and blues singer Barbara Dane, it featured some of the top

names in jazz and blues during its five year run, including Carmen McRae and John Lee Hooker, both of whom recorded live albums here.

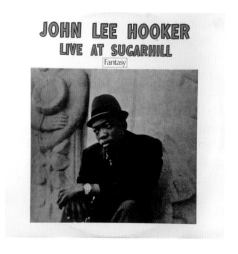

VELVET UNDERGROUND
471 Broadway
Lesley Kamstra's boutique was the fashion choice of stylish women of means in the late '60s, including Janis Joplin and Grace Slick. The young Stevie Nicks visited occasionally to

admire the garments she couldn't afford. She memorialized the shop in her 1982 Fleetwood Mac song "Gypsy."

PEPPERMINT TREE
660 Broadway
Formerly known as The Celebrity, the Peppermint Tree opened as a rock and roll spot in 1964 with Paul Revere and the Raiders as their first headlining act. Briefly struggling as a topless venue in a neighborhood lousy with them, The Celebrity bounced back in 1967 with high-profile bookings like Little Richard. By 1975 they'd stopped hosting live music altogether.

THE CONDOR
300 Columbus Ave./560 Broadway
Perhaps the most celebrated topless club in the country in the '50s and '60s, the Condor's superstar Carol Doda turned up toward the tail end of her long career as the moll to mobster Mike Nesmith in the boxing scene in the Monkees' 1968 film *Head*. Bobby Freeman, the city's first rock and roll star who topped the charts in 1958 with "Do You Want to Dance," used to spell Doda with amped-up singing performances in the Condor. Freeman's 1964 smash "C'mon and Swim" was built around moves by go-go dancer Judy Mac (the Galaxy Club) and was cowritten and produced by Sly Stone.

ANN'S 440
440 Broadway
Known for launching the careers of both Johnny Mathis and Lenny Bruce, Ann's 440 was renamed the Chi-Chi Theater in the '80s, hosting punk and new wave shows in a tinseled room.

MOTHER'S BLUES CLUB
430 Broadway
Among the groups who played here during its brief mid-'60s run as a rock venue were the Grateful Dead, the Great Society, and New York City's the Lovin' Spoonful, who were on the verge of superstardom with their first hit "Do You Believe in Magic" climbing the charts.

THE STONE
412 Broadway
Originally opened by singer Tony Bennett as an opulent supper club The Stone in 1967, by 1969 it was briefly known as Mr. D's, where it hosted the first headlining shows in the Bay Area by Three Dog Night in November 1969. By 1972 the address was briefly the second location of folk rock club The Matrix. The following year the venue featured Bob Marley and the Wailers, who'd been stranded in Las Vegas after being dumped as a support act for Sly and the Family Stone. In the mid-'70s it was called The Soul Train, hosting stars like Harold Melvin and the Blue Notes; Richard Pryor recorded his live album, *That Nigger's Crazy*, there. After briefly being known as The Hippodrome in the late '70s, the venue was renamed The Stone in 1980, hosting shows by the Jerry Garcia Band, James Brown, the Temptations, and Robert Cray. Prince played The Stone in 1982, as did numerous metal bands, including Metallica. The Stone was part of a trio of related Bay Area clubs alongside the Keystone Berkeley (2119 University Ave., Berkeley) and the Keystone Palo Alto (260 California Ave., Palo Alto). All three clubs were closed by the '90s.

ANXIOUS ASP
528 Green St.
Several years before Janis Joplin hung out here, the Anxious Asp was a bustling beatnik club where Jack Kerouac read poetry and the walls were lined with pages from the Kinsey Reports

on *Sexual Behavior in the Human Male* and *Sexual Behavior in the Human Female*.

EL CID
1203 Grant Ave.

Local group the Beau Brummels cut their teeth playing the El Cid, one of the most famous topless joints in the city. The group was discovered by DJ and promoter Tom Donahue, who legend has it heard about them from a prostitute. Beau Brummels vocalist, Sal Valentino, grew up in North Beach, his father having played stickball on the streets with the DiMaggio brothers.

WOLFGANG'S
901 Columbus Ave.

Previous incarnations saw this venue try to capitalize on era-specific dance crazes, like the Twist and disco (during which it was named Dance Yer Ass Off). Reopened in 1983 by Bill Graham (his real first name was Wulf, but his family called him Wolfgang), the 600-seat club became popular by hosting everyone from U2 to Midnight Oil, Big Country to John Hiatt, Spinal Tap to Pee Wee Herman. A fire ravaged the building in 1987 and Wolfgang's never reopened.

Mike Katz

901 Columbus Avenue

BIMBO'S 365 CLUB
1025 Columbus Ave.

Initially opened as Bal Tabarin in 1931, the club was sold to Agostino "Bimbo" Giuntoli in 1951. Giuntoli moved his own establishment, 365 Club (365 Market St., San Francisco), to North Beach. The luxurious Bal Tabarin was the first local nightclub issued a liquor license after the repeal of prohibition, and it still retained its extravagance two decades later when it was renamed Bimbo's 365 Club.

For his first fifteen years on Columbus, Giuntoli booked numerous popular nightclub acts across various disciplines, like Louis Prima, Esquivel, and Sid Caesar. Prior to its renowned owner's retirement the palette expanded further, with soul acts like Smokey Robinson and the Miracles, the Fifth Dimension, and Marvin Gaye—who stayed for an extensive residency in the spring of 1966—taking the stage.

Through the '70s and '80s, Bimbo's 365 was primarily available as a banquet hall, occasionally opening its doors to rock music,

Bimbo's 365 Club

most notably a vastly undersold performance by Iggy and the Stooges in 1974.

Bimbo's 365 Club has since reestablished itself as a live music venue, hosting in recent years gigs by Guided By Voices, Adele, Manic Street Preachers, Cate Le Bon, and Beck.

LONGSHOREMEN'S HALL
400 North Point St.
The site of numerous crucial concerts promoted by the Family Dog starting in 1965, Longshoremen's Hall was built in 1959 as a sailor's union hall.

The Trips Festival, held from January 21–23, 1966 and organized as part of the ongoing Acid Tests by writers Ken Kesey and Stewart Brand, was billed as "a JUBILANT occasion where the audience PARTICIPATES because it's more fun to do so than not."

The Trips Festival's Acid Test was held on Saturday, January 22, with thousands of attendees drinking LSD-infused fruit punch. In *The Electric Kool-Aid Acid Test*, author Tom Wolfe wrote of "Lights and movies sweeping around the hall; five movie projectors going and God knows how many light machines, interferrometrics, the intergalactic science-fiction seas all over the walls, loudspeakers studding the hall all the way around like flaming chandeliers, strobes exploding, black lights with Day-Glo objects under them and Day-Glo paint to play with, street lights at every entrance flashing red and yellow, two bands, the Grateful Dead and Big Brother and the Holding Company and a troop of weird girls in leotards leaping around the edges blowing dog whistles."

JANIS JOPLIN

Trinity Mirror/Mirrorpix/Alamy

"Maybe I won't last as long as other singers, but I think you can destroy your now by worrying about tomorrow. If I hold back, I'm no good now, and I'd rather be good sometimes than holding back all the time. I'm 25 and, like others of my generation, and younger, we look back at our parents and see how they gave up and compromised and wound up with very little. So the kids want a lot of something now rather than a little of hardly anything spread over 70 years."
—JANIS JOPLIN, *NEW YORK TIMES*, APRIL 21, 1968

The most indelible image of Janis Joplin is probably her 1967 performance in the film *Monterey Pop*. An incandescent Janis roaring through a mind-blowing performance of "Ball and Chain" with Big Brother and the Holding Company. Mama Cass Elliott and the rest of the audience with mouths agape, exploding into rapturous applause. Janis skipping off in delight. She knows she's triumphed on the biggest stage of her young career. The future is limitless.

It is now more than 50 years since that moment, and it bears reminding just how revolutionary a figure Janis Joplin was for mainstream America in the 1960s. The image of a white woman fronting a rock band, belting out the blues, and baring her soul was akin to a fiery meteorite landing in the middle of main street. What she represented, in an era of reexamined values and self-discovery, meant

as much as the songs she sang. As Ellen Willis astutely observed for *Rolling Stone* in 1976, "Joplin belonged to that select group of pop figures who matter as much for themselves as for their music." Her story has taken on a heroic, mythic quality in the ensuing years, and, as we know, it has a tragic, unhappy ending. Her journey, however, is still worth examining and continues to fascinate.

Janis Joplin grew up in Port Arthur, an oil town on the Texas Gulf Coast. By the time she reached high school, she had become something of a misfit. A serious reader and aspiring painter with a fascination for Black music, she grew increasingly frustrated with the conservatism and casual bigotry of her surroundings. "Texas is OK if you want to settle down and do your own thing quietly," she told Nat Hentoff of the *New York Times* in 1968, "but it's not for outrageous people, and I was always outrageous." After graduation she spent some time at a local college, but leapt at the opportunity to move in with a relative in Los Angeles, where she found work as a keypunch operator for General Telephone in Santa Monica. Enamored of the Beat Generation and their rejection of American conformity, she eventually settled in Venice, where she fell in with a beatnik crowd. Here she experimented with her sexuality and various drugs. By 1961 she'd saved a few thousand dollars, quit her job, and ventured north to San Francisco. She was drawn to North Beach and made her camp there, exploring Beat hangouts like **City Lights Bookstore (261 Columbus Ave., San Francisco)**, the **Co-Existence Bagel Shop (1398 Grant Ave., San Francisco),** and the **Vesuvio Cafe (255 Columbus Ave., San Francisco).** When she could, Janis sang in coffee houses like the **Fox & Hound (1339 Grant Ave., San Francisco).** The scruffy Texan with the big, gritty voice invariably made an impression, but wasn't everyone's cup of tea in a Joan Baez era. Eventually the money ran out and she was forced to retreat back to Port Arthur, her perspective of what she could and should be irrevocably changed.

Once back home she enrolled at the University of Texas in Austin and more aggressively devoted herself to art and music. She found a community of like-minded types at the Ghetto, a bohemian hangout near campus. She joined her first musical group, the Waller Creek Boys, and refined her singing skills. One night at the Ghetto she met Chet Helms, a UT dropout who was hitchhiking around the country. He would eventually play a pivotal role in her life and career.

In early 1963 Helms encouraged her to come back with him to San Francisco, where a burgeoning folk music scene would properly welcome her. Janis agreed and the pair eventually made it out West, initially crashing on the living room floor of David Freiberg (later

of Quicksilver Messenger Service and Jefferson Starship). Her old haunt, the Fox & Hound, had new ownership and had been renamed **Coffee and Confusion (1339 Grant Ave., San Francisco),** and she was able to raise some cash singing there and at the nearby **Coffee Gallery (1353 Grant Ave., San Francisco),** where she gained a fan in bartender Howard Hesseman (later the star of WKRP in Cincinnati). She formed friendships with a variety of folk performers on the scene, and played different gigs with several of them. She played in a trio with Larry Hanks and Roger Perkins, and later in a quartet when they added Billy Roberts, who wrote "Hey Joe." She frequented other folk dens in the surrounding Bay Area as well, including San Jose's **Folk Theater (970 South 1st St., San Jose)** and the **Top of the Tangent (117 University Ave., Palo Alto).**

Another local musician she occasionally appeared with was guitarist Jorma Kaukonen, then known as "Jerry." To rehearse for a benefit gig at the Coffee Gallery she trekked out to Kaukonen's home **(1174 Fremont Ave., Santa Clara)**, where he made several recordings of the duo playing old blues standards, but the tape recorder picked up the sound of Jorma's wife Margareta typing a letter in the next room. Years later these recordings were recognized for their historical importance when they emerged on the bootleg market as *The Typewriter Tapes*. As Jorma recalled to KQED in 2016, "The Janis that I knew was that Bessie Smith bluesy Janis—and to be honest with you, that's my favorite Janis."

When she wasn't singing or drinking or couch surfing, Janis could often be found hustling pool at either **Gino & Carlo (548 Green St., San Francisco)** or the **Anxious Asp (528 Green St., San Francisco)** down the block, where she met Jae Whitaker, a young African-American girl she fell for almost immediately. Not long after, she moved into Jae's home at

Gino & Carlo

Village and Lower East Side. Whether she actually performed publicly is uncertain, but later confessions to friends suggest she mostly drank and downed amphetamines. She stopped again in Port Arthur on the way back to the West Coast. When she arrived in San Francisco a friend hooked her up with a tiny apartment in the **Goodman Building (1117 Geary St., San Francisco),** and she soon took up where she left off, picking up gigs in the various folk establishments in the Bay Area.

Goodman Building

186 States Street, which she shared with four housemates. The couple drove down to Monterey in May for the **1963 Folk Festival (2004 Fairground Rd., Monterey),** where Janis won an open-mic competition and reportedly met one of her heroes, Bob Dylan.

In San Francisco, she began to develop a modest reputation, but continued drug and alcohol use was beginning to make her unreliable. She was a no-show at a couple of gigs, and in the fall, hitchhiked to Port Arthur, and then New York for a few weeks, where she explored Dylan's old stomping grounds in Greenwich Village. She had broken things off with Jae, so upon her return to San Francisco she resumed sleeping on floors and couches.

In the Spring of 1964 she acquired a used car and, after making a few stops in Texas, returned to New York for four months, where she crashed at various places in the East

In one of the odder twists in Janis's story, she performed a few times with Dick Oxtot, a traditional jazz bandleader, and even made a handful of recordings, both at his house and at various gigs. She first approached him at the **Blind Lemon (2362 San Pablo Ave., Berkeley),** and as Oxtot describes in his memoir, *Jazz Scrapbook,* "She introduced herself as Janis Joplin, from Texas, and said she loved 'singin' the blues,' and she would like to sing some with us. I was somewhat skeptical, since she resembled a strange street urchin more than a singer. . . . Not only did she knock me out, but also everyone in the room. Her voice was rasping, but beautiful and powerful. No one could fail to be impressed. Before she left, all of us in the band urged her to come back and sing with us 'any time.'" Oxtot even tried to get her a job with

Turk Murphy at **Earthquake McGoon's (630 Clay St., San Francisco ⊘).** Turk had been impressed by her voice on tape, and offered to let her sit in with the band. Oxtot's wife got Janis properly dolled up for the occasion, but Murphy refused to let her sing as promised. As Oxtot recounts, Turk claimed "I can't have her sing, she's a beatnik!" Thus ended Janis's trad jazz career. Some of the Oxtot recordings were edited and included on the double LP *Janis* in 1975, a quasi-soundtrack to the documentary film of the same name.

Janis descended further into drugs. The substance of choice then was methamphetamine, and the best place to get it was a North Beach fast food joint, the **Hot Dog Palace (348 Columbus Ave., San Francisco),** known locally as "the Amp Palace." Janis and her friend Linda Gottfried became steady customers, and soon the coffee houses that she depended on for her meager income would no longer book her. At the same time, Janis fell hard for a new guy, Peter de Blanc, a good-looking sophisticated college grad. Before long both of them were hooked on speed, with Janis's health deteriorating ever further. Chet Helms, hearing of her situation, stopped by to check on her, and was horrified by what he found. Janis was practically a zombie, barely functional, and under 100 pounds. Helms and some friends threw a party to raise bus fare and in May 1965 sent her back to Port Arthur. Peter, pledging to marry her, promised to clean himself up and come for her in Texas as soon as possible.

Janis's brush with death produced the most unexpected transformation yet. As her younger sister Laura recounts in her memoir *Love, Janis*, "Janis returned home convinced that her past ways were wrong. For the first time, she was asking for advice from our parents and listening to their replies. . . . She had come home to recoup and repair. Her attitude brought a wonderful, pleasing peacefulness to the family." Janis bought new clothes and enrolled in college again at nearby Lamar Tech. She studied British Literature and history, getting good grades, and even took up swimming. She wrote repeatedly to Peter in San Francisco, still fully expecting to get married. In August, Peter de Blanc finally arrived in Port Arthur and easily ingratiated himself to the Joplin family, formally asking Janis's father for her hand in marriage. Shortly thereafter, he left suddenly, due to a death in the family, he claimed. His excuses over the next three months grew more elaborate as Janis did her best to stay focused on college. Out of anxiety or restlessness, she turned once again to music, playing gigs at a cafe in nearby Beaumont. Eventually it was discovered that de Blanc had been playing a cruel sort of sociopathic game. He was already married to a woman he abandoned, and was currently living with another woman who was pregnant. Janis's dreams of a happy conventional life disintegrated, and she coped by deepening her commitment to music, adding more gigs in Houston and Austin.

In May 1966 word reached Janis that Chet Helms wanted her to join a rock band he was managing back in San Francisco. Since she'd seen him last Helms had begun promoting concerts for the Family Dog, a hippie collective, at the **Avalon Ballroom (1244 Sutter St., San Francisco)**. Telling her parents she was off to Austin for the weekend, Janis packed the car and ventured west for a third time, reaching San Francisco on June 4.

Big Brother and the Holding Company had formed the year before and consisted of James Gurley (guitar), Peter Albin (bass, vocals), Sam Andrew (guitar, vocals), and Dave Getz (drums). They had seen the success of Jefferson Airplane, the first local band to score a major record deal with its male and female vocalists, and sought to emulate that formula. When Janis met them a few days after her arrival they were rehearsing in an old Victorian carriage house they shared with artists Alton Kelley and Stanley "Mouse" Miller at **74 Henry Street**. Janis remembered Albin and Andrew from her folkie days, when they held jam sessions at their **1090 Page Street** headquarters. They remembered Janis as well, and after rehearsing with her that day, accepted her into the group. Playing with a loud amplified band was a new experience for Janis, but she rapidly adapted by increasing her own volume and developing her distinctive howls and screams.

Helms had secured Janis an apartment at **1947 Pine Street**, right near where she had once regularly shopped for drugs. She was terrified of descending once again into that lifestyle, and insisted that her new bandmates not partake of them in her presence. She was also afraid of being recognized by former dealers and often stayed indoors.

Poster by Stanley Mouse, 1967

For her first gig with Big Brother at the Avalon on June 10, Janis only joined the band onstage midway through the performance. She made a good impression, however, and her role increased dramatically in the ensuing months. Soon it was clear that Janis, as her confidence and stage presence grew, was becoming the main draw, much to the consternation of some of the group.

Helms began to receive interest from a few smaller record labels looking to cash in on the emerging San Francisco sound. In July the group auditioned for Bob Shad's Mainstream, a jazz label, at a recording studio in the old Spreckels mansion near Buena Vista Park **(737 Buena Vista Ave. West, San Francisco)**. The band had run through three songs before Helms pulled the plug, convinced that Shad was up to no good. His impression would prove prescient.

Also in July, Big Brother moved en masse, including their families, to a big house near Lagunitas **(1 Spring Rd., Forest Knolls)** they named Argentina. Other San Francisco musicians, including Quicksilver Messenger Service, lived in the area as well, which was a quiet retreat from the city. They lived, rehearsed, and partied in the house, often with their

Mike Katz

1947 Pine Street

illustrious Marin neighbors. They would stay here until the end of 1966.

Even at this relatively early stage, the first pangs of dissension began to emerge, largely due to the attention Janis began to receive. After an August gig at the Avalon, Paul Rothschild from Elektra Records approached her about forming a new group with several other notable performers. She was flattered by the offer, but when she told the band about it they were deeply resentful. Her departure would be perceived as a serious betrayal; a violation of their sense of family. Janis passed on the offer. Later that month, the group parted ways with Chet Helms, feeling his Family Dog commitments were not leaving him enough time to properly manage the group.

A late August residency in Chicago proved to be a disaster on multiple levels. Mother's Blues Club stopped paying the group two weeks into their three week gig, leaving them with virtually no money to get home, and no manager to look after their interests. Bob Shad learned the group was in town, and offered the now-desperate musicians a contract and recording session. Not laden with options, they accepted the poor arrangement and made the best of it. In December they recorded more material in Los Angeles. Most of the tracks would not be heard for several months. Years later, members of Big Brother acknowledged that signing with Mainstream was in some respects an oblique way of keep Janis tied to the group. As Sam Andrew stated in the documentary film *Janis: Little Girl Blue*: "It was good that she stayed with us 'cause we let her alone. . . . We weren't talented enough to get in her way."

Early 1967 looked more promising for Big Brother. They hired a new manager, Julius Karpen, and a couple of their Mainstream singles were released. The band was unhappy with the sound of the records, which included "Down On Me" and "Bye Bye Baby," but they

did get some airplay on the newly emerging FM radio station KMPX. Still, they wanted badly to get out of the deal, but felt powerless to do anything about it. They were booked solid for the first few months of the year, often sharing the bill with groups like the Grateful Dead and Jefferson Airplane, despite their lack of a major record deal. One of the most significant events of the early part of the year, the "Human Be-In" at **Golden Gate Park** on January 14 featured just about every important band in San Francisco, along with a whole host of poets and activists. The media coverage it generated played no small part in the massive convergence of young people on San Francisco in the coming months, culminating in the legendary Summer of Love.

Julius Karpen secured Janis a new apartment at **122 Lyon Street**, adjacent to the Panhandle. It would be her main pad for the next year or so. An elaborate television

122 Lyon Street

production featuring Big Brother in live performance was filmed at **KQED studios (525 4th St., San Francisco)** and aired on the April 25 episode of *Come Up the Years.* Big Brother also secured a new rehearsal space, which they nicknamed "the Warehouse" in an old three-story industrial building at the corner of **Golden Gate Avenue and Van Ness Avenue**. A live performance of "Down On Me," and an interview with a supremely square gentleman from KTVU were recorded there sometime in late 1967. The site is now the location of Opera Plaza.

All of this continuing notoriety and momentum led to their now-legendary performance at Monterey. It was very nearly a moment lost to history.

Several weeks earlier, organizers started planning what became the **Monterey Pop Festival (Monterey County Fairgrounds, 2004 Fairground Rd., Monterey),** as a showcase for the new generation of musical artists. Ralph Gleason, the respected San Francisco critic had been brought on board as an advisor and strongly suggested adding some of the groundbreaking bands he knew from up north, including Big Brother and the Holding Company. Outside of the Bay Area, most of these groups were relatively unknown, save the Jefferson Airplane. At the same time, D. A. Pennebaker was enlisted to film a documentary about the event. As acts were taking the stage, they were asked to sign a document allowing themselves to be filmed. Several of the San Francisco bands refused, seeing this as a violation of their communal anti-commercial ethos. They had only participated because no one was being paid an appearance fee, and the proceeds were intended for charity. Why should they allow themselves to be exploited so the organizers could sell a film? Julius Karpen, on behalf of the band, also adamantly refused to sign as the group took the stage on Saturday afternoon. The group,

completely unaware, blasted through their set, bringing down the house. When Janis learned immediately afterward that the performance wasn't filmed, she was apoplectic. So was Pennebaker, who demanded that the problem be resolved so he could get another chance to film her. A deal was brought to them: Agree to be filmed and get another slot. Karpen again refused, but at Janis's insistence the band reconsidered. Eventually Albert Grossman, the mastermind who managed Bob Dylan; Peter, Paul, and Mary; and several others was brought in to mediate, and advised them to take the deal. He, too, had been blown away by Janis, and saw an opportunity. Not long after, he displaced Karpen as the group's manager. Big Brother played a second, abbreviated set on Sunday night, and it is this performance we see in the film *Monterey Pop.*

The momentum that Big Brother and Janis had been building went into overdrive after Monterey. Despite all the established stars present, the breakout performances of the event were turned in by Janis and Jimi Hendrix, two relative unknowns at that time. Clive Davis, the new president of CBS Records, was in the audience and moved to sign Big Brother immediately. "I knew I was in the midst of something unique and profoundly deep and I acted on that instinct," he told *Rolling Stone* in 2017. "There's no doubt it was the Monterey Festival that started it all. What would have happened if I had not been there? Would I have recognized how deep and profound it all was? . . . But it is, in retrospect, a once-in-a-lifetime epiphany and a profoundly impacting and effecting event." Davis would have to work things out with Bob Shad at Mainstream before he could bring the group to CBS, however. In the wake of the festival, Mainstream released a collection of the tracks they had recorded in Los Angeles the previous December. Clocking in at just under 24 minutes, *Big Brother and the*

Cheap Thrills album cover by Robert Crumb, 1968

time away from the rest of the group at the Chelsea Hotel, it presented a quandary, and she was getting mixed messages from friends and management. The pent-up demand for the new album *Cheap Thrills* was so high that it went gold within days of its release in August and hit #1 on the Billboard album chart. Later that month she told the rest of the band that she would complete the current tour, which ended in December, before going her own way. Their final concert together was on December 1, 1968, at the Avalon, a benefit for the Family Dog.

Holding Company wasn't exactly a disgrace, but in no way was it a fair representation of what the band could do.

Ultimately Davis and CBS had the funds and clout to get what they wanted, and in early 1968 brought the group to New York City to begin work on a new album. On March 8, they opened Bill Graham's Fillmore East, an event nearly as important as Monterey in that the cream of the Big Apple's entertainment media was there to witness Janis and the group for the first time. An anonymous critic in the March 23rd issue of *Cash Box* described the band thusly: "Big Brother and the Holding Company don't really have much to offer except Janice (sic) Joplin, who is the group's lead vocalist. She's kind of a mixture of Leadbelly, a steam engine, Calamity Jane, Bessie Smith, an oil derrick, and rot-gut bourbon funneled into the 20th century somewhere between El Paso and San Francisco. She must be seen, or more precisely, heard to be believed but, if you like the Blues, you'll love Janice Joplin." This bad rap on the band became a common refrain and a conventional wisdom among some critics and fans, and it began to wear on all of them. For Janis, who was spending considerably more

Poster by Rick Griffin with photo by Bob Seidemann, 1967

Janis salved her feelings of remorse at leaving Big Brother by descending further into drug use, including heroin. Meanwhile, to add insult to injury, she recruited Sam Andrew to help her assemble a new backing group, the Kozmic Blues Band. The resulting tour and album, *I Got Dem Ol' Kozmic Blues Again Mama!* was seen as something of a disappointment. Some of the same people who insisted she ditch Big Brother criticized this new band as well, claiming she was abandoning psychedelic rock for a more traditional soul/R&B sound and diluting her delivery. Her shows at the **Winterland Ballroom (2000 Post St., San Francisco ⊘) and Fillmore West (10 South Van Ness Ave., San Francisco)** in late March of 1969 were not received warmly by fans or critics. Even Ralph Gleason, ever the staunch defender of San Francisco rock, proclaimed the band "a drag" in the *Chronicle*.

Dave Getz reflected in the documentary *Janis: Little Girl Blue*: "She started to become something people expected of her—a caricature of who she was, and play it for people, and I think that hurt her in some way."

Janis's final San Francisco performance was a reunion with Big Brother (minus James Gurley) at the **Fillmore West** on April 4, 1970. Six months later she died of an accidental heroin overdose in Los Angeles just as she was finishing her final album, *Pearl*.

MORE JANIS JOPLIN

NOTEWORTHY LIVE PERFORMANCES

Saint Francis Hotel (335 Powell St., San Francisco): On June 19, 1966 Big Brother played a benefit for Timothy Leary's defense fund.

California Hall (625 Polk St., San Francisco): On July 28, 1966, Big Brother, the Great Society, and the Charlatans performed at "Bilbo's Birthday," a celebration of J.R.R. Tolkien. Janis was reportedly a serious Tolkien enthusiast, so she must have loved this.

Both/And (350 Divisadero St., San Francisco): On May 22, 1966, Janis came here with Sam Andrew and James Gurley to see one of Janis's heroes, Big Mama Thornton. Janis was especially impressed with her rendition of "Ball and Chain," and asked for permission to cover it backstage after the gig. Big Brother would share a bill with her at **California Hall** the following April.

Panhandle, Golden Gate Park, San Francisco: Big Brother participated in the Love Pageant Rally, led by the Merry Pranksters and Ken Kesey, a protest of the criminalization of LSD on October 6, 1966.

Avalon Ballroom (1244 Sutter St., San Francisco): Big Brother, along with the Grateful Dead and Quicksilver Messenger Service played a "Zenefit" for the San Francisco Zen Mountain Center on November 13, 1966. On August 13 the following year, Janis made a special arrangement with Moby Grape to give up part of their set so that Big Brother could perform for her family, who were in town. Janis's younger sister and brother enjoyed the show more than her parents, apparently.

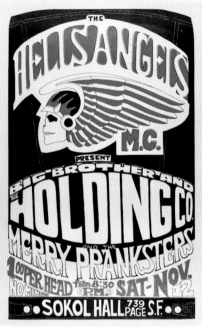

Poster by Alan "Gut" Terk, 1966

Sokol Hall (739 Page St., San Francisco): Big Brother played a Hells Angels party with the Merry Pranksters on November 12, 1966. Janis maintained a cordial, if occasionally disruptive relationship with the Angels throughout her career.

Fillmore Auditorium (1805 Geary Blvd., San Francisco): Janis played her first show here with Big Brother on July 1, 1966. Like many, she had a tempestuous professional relationship with Bill Graham. He reportedly once had her physically thrown out of the building for saying in an interview that the Avalon was her favorite place to play.

Carousel Ballroom (10 S. Van Ness Ave., San Francisco): Big Brother played here on June 23, 1968, not long before it became Bill Graham's

Fillmore West. The concert was recorded by Owsley "Bear" Stanley and released officially in 2012.

1837 Alcatraz Avenue, Berkeley: The band played February 10–11, 1967, as promoted by Golden Sheaf Bakery, with Country Joe and the Fish. Janis and Country Joe, after meeting, began a brief romance.

Pepperland Dance Hall (737 East Francisco Blvd., San Rafael): Janis played her second to last Bay Area performance here, at a Hells Angels party, with Full Tilt Boogie on May 15, 1970. Also on the bill was Big Brother and the Holding Company with new singer Nick Gravenites.

Santa Clara County Fairgrounds (344 Tully Rd., San Jose): Janis Joplin's last ever performance in the Bay Area took place here on July 12, 1970. The opening act on the bill was a local San Jose group, Fritz, which featured a young Lindsey Buckingham and Stevie Nicks.

Monterey County Fairgrounds (2004 Fairground Rd., Monterey): Just a little less than a year before their fateful performance at Monterey Pop, Big Brother and Quicksilver Messenger Service shared the bill at this two-day "Independence Dance" event on July 2–3, 1966.

OTHER NOTEWORTHY LOCATIONS

1515 Gough Street, San Francisco: Janis is reported to have lived here for a few months in 1965.

635 Ashbury St., San Francisco: Janis lived here for a time in 1967 in a second-floor apartment with Peggy Caserta.

Mnasidika (1510 Haight St., San Francisco): One of the first hip women's apparel and leather

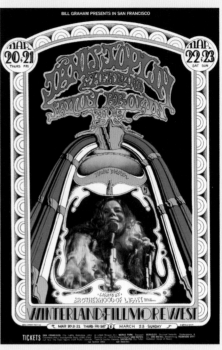

Poster by Bill Bostedt and Randy Tuten with photo by Jim Marshall, 1969

goods stores in the city, it was owned by Peggy Caserta, who met Janis here. The two became close friends and occasional lovers until Janis's death. In operation from 1965–1968. Mnasidika is a character from Sapphic poetry.

541 8th St., San Francisco: Photographer Bill Brach took several early publicity shots of Big Brother with Janis Joplin here in 1966 at what was then the Anchor Steam Brewery.

892 Noe Street, San Francisco: Janis moved to a third floor apartment here in 1968 after she lost the lease on her Lyon Street apartment because of her dog George.

Fairmont Hotel (950 Mason St., San Francisco): Big Brother and the Holding Company appear in the film *Petulia* (1968)

performing at a fundraiser in the lobby of this landmark hotel. The scene features actors George C. Scott, Julie Christie, and Richard Chamberlain.

380 West Baltimore Avenue, Larkspur: Janis moved here to Marin County in 1969, in what became her final home.

The Lion's Share (60 Red Hill Ave., San Anselmo): When Janis Joplin died, she left money in her will to host a party in her honor at this one-time music spot. The event was held on October 26, 1970, with a live performance by the Grateful Dead. Invitations are said to have read "The drinks are on Pearl." An estimated 200 people attended with a tab of $1,600.00.

Andi Sumpter

Masonic Auditorium

MASONIC AUDITORIUM
1111 California St.

Long a venue of rock renown, Masonic Auditorium has hosted everyone from Bob Dylan to Van Morrison, Ravi Shankar to Frank Sinatra.

BOARDING HOUSE
960 Bush St.

Opened by former hungry-i manager David Allen and perhaps as well known for comedy—Robert Klein, Lily Tomlin, Billy Crystal, Albert Brooks, and Steve Martin (who made a name for himself during a two-week stint)—the Boarding House was also a key rock venue during the second half of the '70s, with Talking Heads, Patti Smith, Bob Marley and the Wailers, and many other playing the space. Neil Young played a five-night engagement at the Boarding House in 1978, running through material that would eventually morph into *Rust Never Sleeps*. The

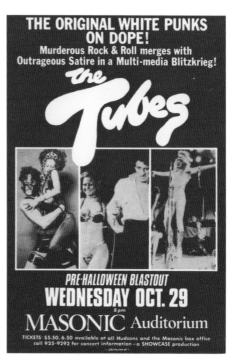

address was home to a variety of clubs for decades prior to the opening of the Boarding House, including a period for most of 1970 when Los Angeles club owner Doug Weston tried to extend his reach with the Troubadour North.

Poster by Randy Tuten

After a fire gutted 960 Bush Street, the building was torn down and condominiums were built in its place. The Boarding House made a brief return in the early '80s, opening at 901 Columbus Avenue in North Beach, but by 1982 it was closed for good. Allen died in 1984.

960 Bush was also the home of Coast Recorders, an important recording studio in the '60s, which itself moved around the city a few times over the years.

AVALON BALLROOM

1268 Sutter St.

Built in 1911 as the Puckett Academy of Dance, the Avalon Ballroom was for a brief time in the

1268 Sutter Street

Poster by B. Kliban

mid-'60s run by Chet Helms of the Family Dog. Helms was a friend of Janis Joplin's back in Texas, and his popular Avalon Ballroom hosted her first show with Big Brother and the Holding Company in June 1966. After a run of legendary shows, Helms lost his permits over noise complaints and the Avalon Ballroom was shut down as a rock venue in November 1968.

HEMLOCK TAVERN

1131 Polk St. ⊘

Opened as a rock venue in 2001 on the site of former gay bar the Giraffe, the Hemlock hosted thousands of touring groups before its closure in 2018. Animal Collective, Parquet Courts, Joanna Newsom, Beach House, Ty Segall, Cat Power, and local hero Kelley Stoltz are among the indie acts who've graced the stage at the Hemlock. The Hemlock closed in 2018, when the building was razed for a 54-unit residential development.

CHET HELMS

United Archives GmbH/Alamy

Chet Helms with Janis Joplin, 1967

It's no exaggeration to state that without Chet Helms, the classic era of psychedelic rock in San Francisco might never have happened. It was Helms who first embraced and absorbed the early pangs of the counterculture movement and had the vision and resourcefulness to find creative ways of showcasing the emerging musical talent of the Bay Area. He was more than a promoter; he was one of them. Unlike his counterpart Bill Graham, he lived the life and espoused the values of the new culture, earning the respect and loyalty of many important artists of the era on their own terms. His time as an impresario was relatively brief, but he played an inexorable role in creating the musical landscape of San Francisco and delivering its message to the world.

After dropping out of the University of Texas, Helms, like many, hitchhiked around the country in search of a more meaningful existence, growing his hair long and rejecting the conventional American lifestyle. He arrived in San Francisco in 1962 and scraped by for a couple of years before falling in with the crowd at **1090 Page Street** ⊘, a boarding house popular with San Francisco State students and creative types where jam sessions were often held in the basement, attracting a wide variety of early hippies and freaks. Helms took to organizing and promoting these events, transforming the basement into a popular destination with an admission of 50 cents. Eventually it all got too crowded and too loud, but one of the participating groups evolved

Poster by Stanley Mouse, 1966

into Big Brother and the Holding Company, and made Chet their manager. On a return trip to Texas Helms met up with his friend Janis Joplin, ultimately encouraging her to come back with him and join the group.

By 1965 Helms had forged an alliance with the Family Dog, a hippie commune residing at **2125 Pine Street** ⊘. He helped them promote a few events before establishing **Family Dog Productions (639 Gough St., San Francisco)** to organize and promote concerts by the new generation of performers, including Jefferson Airplane, the Great Society, Big Brother, and the Charlatans, first at the **Longshoremen's Hall (400 North Point St., San Francisco), California Hall (600 Turk St., San Francisco)**, the **Open Theater (2976 College Ave., Berkeley)**, and eventually the **Fillmore**

Auditorium **(1805 Geary Blvd., San Francisco)**, where he alternated events with another young and enterprising promoter, Bill Graham. He and Graham were initially allies, but soon became serious competitors and adversaries. Their contrasting styles and personalities made for an interesting and fruitful dichotomy in the nascent scene.

From 1966–1968, Helms hosted events at the **Avalon Ballroom (1244 Sutter St., San Francisco)** featuring every important band of the area, including the Grateful Dead, Jefferson Airplane, Big Brother, Moby Grape, Santana, Steve Miller Blues Band, Creedence Clearwater Revival, Quicksilver Messenger Service, and Country Joe and the Fish, as well as many influential touring groups such as Buffalo Springfield, the Doors, Van Morrison, Canned Heat, the Byrds, Love, and the Velvet Underground. Additionally, Helms pioneered the use of light shows, and first employed artists like Wes Wilson, Alton Kelley, and others to create colorfully innovative posters to publicize Family Dog events.

After losing the lease at the Avalon, Helms decamped to **Family Dog on the Great Highway (660 Great Highway, San Francisco ⊘)**, but the new spot was far from the scene he had helped create and it only lasted until the summer of 1970. Chet Helms largely withdrew from concert promotion after that and eventually became a highly respected art dealer as proprietor of the **Atelier Doré (771 Bush St., San Francisco)** from 1980 until shortly before his death in 2005.

Poster by Victor Moscoso, 1966

SAN FRANCISCO PUNK

Avengers onstage, 1978

If the San Francisco punk scene had a single watershed moment, one where it fully came into its own, it was at **Winterland Ballroom (2000 Post St., San Francisco ⊘)** on the night of January 14, 1978. The show, promoted by Bill Graham, quickly passed into legend as the last ever (until their inevitable reunion two decades later) played by the Sex Pistols, England's notorious shit-stirrers, who'd spent the previous week-and-a-half making few friends but many headlines across the deep south with shambolic gigs in cities like Atlanta, San Antonio, Baton Rouge, and Tulsa. San Francisco, still perceived around the world as the universal hippie mecca, would be their final stop, and the only show along the West Coast.

"Everywhere else they'd avoided regular rock clubs and were doing crazy things, and I'm sure the band is just like, what the fuck?" said Penelope Houston, singer of the Avengers, who along with the Nuns, were the two local punk bands who opened the Winterland show. "And they skipped L.A.; L.A. was very pissed off."

In early 1978, the San Francisco punk scene was still coalescing. And while local punk shows might take place in clubs or parties, none of those came close to approaching the capacity of Winterland, a cavernous indoor ice arena opened in 1928, which as a live music venue held around 5,400 people.

"It was way more than any of us had ever played for before," said Houston in 2019. "They were punks from the whole West Coast basically, but also a lot of people who just came to see it as the spectacle of punk."

The spectacle of punk had been covered ad nauseam by the mainstream press in predictably hyperbolic terms, with reports focusing little on the music and primarily on the clothes, haircuts, and nihilism. It's unclear how many in the sold-out crowd at Winterland were there for the circus, but that's at least partly what they got, with a mad crush at the front of the stage engaging in the British punk fan's favorite pastime: Gobbing.

"The Nuns going out there first had probably the most shit thrown at them and the most loogies, spit, that stuff," said Houston. "Then when we were out on stage I slipped in some."

"I Believe in Me," the Avengers' turbo-charged anthem of DIY self-reliance, has always had a malleable verse, with Houston singing about what's happening in the moment or what's on her mind, which at Winterland was the Sex Pistols. Houston's voice is shaky as she introduces the song, which fizzles out seconds later. The band resets and explodes, a unified force led by a suddenly hyper-confident Houston.

"You can hear this fear in my voice, but then by the end of that, we've kind of conquered that fear," she said.

After watching some of the Sex Pistols set from behind the stage, Houston said she decided to head into the crowd to see what it felt like.

"I noticed when I was up there singing, I would see a friend of mine for a second and then I'd look back and they were lost in a sea of faces," she said. "It was just jammed and I was just drenched in sweat, and it's not my own sweat. And you could lift your feet off the floor and still be there. It was just insane. I was like, 'Okay, so I went out there and experienced that; I'm going to go watch it from backstage.'"

Winterland was a long way away from the earliest San Francisco punk shows less than two years earlier, some of which didn't even happen. Crime, the first West Coast punk band to release a single ("Hot Wire My Heart," 1976), saw their February 1976 live debut at **The Stud (1533 Folsom St., San Francisco)** thwarted after the band created a flyer featuring an image of Adolf Hitler; Crime's actual first show took place at a "Gay Halloween" costume celebration at **The Old Waldorf (444 Battery St., San Francisco)** on October 31, 1976, but they only lasted five songs before the plug was pulled. The Nuns, who'd already performed a few times in Marin County, actually arrived at **McGowan's Wharf Tavern (101 Jefferson St., San Francisco)** for a late 1976 gig before being tossed out without having played a single note.

Of course the San Francisco punk scene's nerve center wasn't the vast, decaying Winterland Ballroom, which after its closure later in 1978 was eventually razed to make way for apartments; it was **Mabuhay Gardens (443 Broadway, San Francisco)**, a Filipino restaurant and club in the shadow of North Beach's glittering striptease joints. Owned by Ness Aquino, Mabuhay was already hosting Filipino artists in the basement lounge when

The former Mabuhay Gardens

THERE'S ALWAYS ROOM FOR JELLO

In 1979, Dead Kennedys frontman and chief provocateur **Jello Biafra** ran for mayor of San Francisco, using the **Target Video Warehouse (678 South Van Ness Ave., San Francisco)** as his campaign headquarters. Biafra decided to run after finding himself dissatisfied with the announced candidates, including incumbent Mayor Dianne Feinstein.

"I think if you look around you'll find my candidacy is no more of a joke and no less of a joke than anyone else running you care to name," said Biafra on a local television news hour.

Dead Kennedys emerged from the San Francisco punk scene as one of its most politically vitriolic and musically explosive bands, with Biafra's erudite observations delivered with an almost histrionic yawp. They courted controversy on both sides of the aisle and were fully tapped into the world around them and their perception of its ills. Anyone surprised by Biafra's decision to run for mayor

hadn't been paying attention to the Dead Kennedys.

Among the items on Biafra's mayoral platform were legalized squatting in vacant buildings; banning all cars from the city streets; requiring police officers to run for reelection every four years; forcing businesspeople to wear clown suits; and erecting in public parks statues of Dan White, the former member of the Board of Supervisors who'd assassinated Mayor George Moscone and Supervisor Harvey Milk in November 1978. San Franciscans would be encouraged to deface the statues with eggs sold by the Parks Department.

A Labor Day "Biafra for Mayor" fundraiser was held at **Mabuhay Gardens (443**

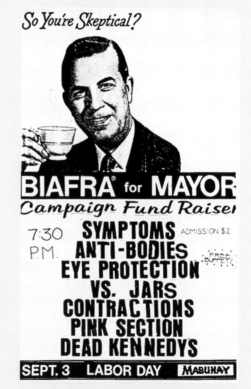

Broadway, San Francisco), with bands like Symptoms, Anti-Bodies, Eye Protection, and Dead Kennedys playing. Biafra raised the filing fees and obtained enough signatures to ensure he would receive equal news coverage to other candidates. He appeared in local news broadcasts during a rally on the steps of **City Hall (1 Dr. Carlton B. Goodlett Pl., San Francisco)**, leading a whistle-stop tour along the BART stations on Market Street, and matching a publicity stunt which saw Feinstein sweep the streets of the Tenderloin by using a vacuum cleaner on the sidewalks of Pacific Heights.

"My views are my own," said Biafra on a news report as he walked along Market Street prior to the election. "I don't have, like, 20 years of special interests slowly buying me off."

Biafra finished third out of seven candidates in the November election, receiving 6,591 votes, 3.79 percent of the total cast. Feinstein, a Democrat, ultimately won reelection in a runoff vote against second-place finisher Quentin Kopp, who ran as an Independent.

Biafra's activism has continued over the years, including a bid to win the Green Party nomination in the 2000 presidential election; he threw his full support behind the party's candidate Ralph Nader in the general election.

After the Dead Kennedys split in 1986, Biafra—born Eric Reed Boucher—continued creating music, as well as releasing spoken word albums. He continues to run Alternative Tentacles, the independent label founded by Biafra and Dead Kennedys guitarist East Bay Ray in 1979 in part to release the band's own music. His most recent musical projects include Jello Biafra and the Guantanamo School of Medicine.

Jerry Paulson of *Psyclone Magazine* began booking bands on Monday and Tuesday nights in 1976. Dirk Dirksen was already entrenched at Mabuhay, presenting events like comedians Les Nickelettes, and Rick & Ruby, and cabaret nights as early as 1974. Dirksen quickly caught on to the theatricality of punk, positioning himself as the premier promoter of the burgeoning scene.

"The Mab," as it was commonly known, began increasing its number of all-ages punk shows through 1977 to meet demand.

"The sprouting of the scene to come was really around the Mabuhay," said Houston, who went to shows there before joining what would eventually become the Avengers. Crime, the Nuns, Psycotic Pineapple, Negative Trend, Avengers, and the Dead Kennedys were among the local bands who played numerous nights at the Mab, augmented occasionally by touring punk acts like Blondie, Devo, the Screamers, and the Ramones.

Period photos of shows at the Mabuhay Gardens invariably show a short stage, in front of which are assembled several small tables, large enough for only two chairs beside them;

sometimes the tables and chairs are upturned, and almost always there is popcorn. Popcorn everywhere.

"I think that was salty popcorn to get people to buy drinks," said Houston. "And the popcorn always got thrown. People would throw it and then it would get swept up at the end of the night, and it was like, no big deal. People have to throw something: Better they throw a little basket with popcorn in it than a pint glass."

Punk shows at the "Fab Mab" were often raucous affairs, with the lines inexorably blurred between band and crowd.

"There were people that were famous for jumping into the audience," said Houston. "Rozz (Rezabek, Negative Trend), he would jump up and grab whatever pipes were up there, because he's super tall, and swing way out over the audience."

But the Mab was about more than three chords and chaos; many of the bands who played there had a social conscience, none more famously than Dead Kennedys, who through the lyrics of frontman Jello Biafra lambasted mainstream politics on both sides of the aisle with songs like "California Über Alles" and "When Ya Get Drafted." Mabuhay Gardens also played host to punk benefit shows, including New Wave Against Blk Lung, with the Avengers, the Dils, Negative Trend, Psycotic Pineapple, and others showing support for striking coal miners.

The Fab Mab's link to the counterculture was set earlier than punk's arrival, with the venue sharing the building with the former **Garibaldi Hall (439 Broadway),** originally Dimas-Alang Hall, where numerous poetry readings were held in the late '50s. Allen Ginsberg read "Kaddish" there in 1959 at a benefit for John Wiener's *Measure* magazine. Later that year, Lawrence Ferlinghetti, Ray Bremser, Michael McClure, David Meltzer and others participated in the "Mad Monster Mammoth Poets' Reading," a benefit for Auerbahn Press.

Mabuhay Gardens closed in 1987, but its legacy lives on, not only through the bands who played there, but also its enigmatic chief promoter: The alley just to the right of the building has since been renamed Dirk Dirksen Place.

Years after the Avengers split in 1979, Houston went on to have a successful career as a singer-songwriter, playing folk music, which isn't necessarily the jarring transition early Avengers fans might have believed.

"I remember telling people probably in '78 or '79, 'It's like we make folk music,' and they'd be like, 'What are you talking about?'" Houston said. "And I'd say, 'People sit on their porch, they play for themselves and other people; we are playing just for our friends, and the people in the audience can get up on stage and sing with us. It was like I saw this really, which is funny because I had no idea I was going to end up making folk music later.'"

The Avengers are still playing shows around the Bay Area and around the world; Houston had a longtime day job as an archivist with the San Francisco History Center and Marjorie G. and Carl W. Stern Book Arts & Special Collections department at the main branch of the **San Francisco Public Library (100 Larkin St., San Francisco),** and she still works there on the official **San Francisco Punk Archive.**

"I think we did feel like we were creating something new and we were trying to wash away the rock and roll that had come before," said Houston in 2019. "It started out as something kind of pure and it turned into this, you know, dinosaur rock, with Boston, UFO, these huge, huge spectacles where they would have to bring in, you know, three semi trucks full of gear for their show. We wanted to bring it back to the people and have the interaction between band and audience be extremely connected."

MORE SAN FRANCISCO PUNK

NOTEWORTHY LIVE PERFORMANCES

Deaf Club (530 Valencia St., San Francisco):
Open for just 18 months, the Deaf Club was
a club for deaf people that held its first punk
show on December 9, 1978, featuring the
Mutants, On the Rag, and the Offs, whose
manager Robert Hanrahan booked the shows.
Dead Kennedys, Flipper, the Zeros, Crime, the
Dils, and the Avengers were among the many
bands who played here during its brief time as
a club.

"The Deaf Club was great," said Houston.
"It was basically this big room with a bar at one
end and a stage at the other. You just went in
and there were these just regular working class
deaf people drinking beers and stuff, and then
all the punks. The people were super nice to us
and they were entertained by our antics, and
they never complained about the noise. Deaf
Club was cool."

330 Grove Street (San Francisco) ⊘: From
1969–1977, 330 Grove Street was the home of
People's Press, one of dozens of underground
print shops across the Bay Area, which produced
movement materials like *The Black Panther
Primer*, *The Ecology Primer*, and *Vietnam: A
Thousand Years of Struggle*. In 1978, 330 Grove
is where Gilbert Baker reportedly worked with a
collective to create the rainbow flag as a symbol
of LGBTQ pride. Later that year, a punk show
featuring Dead Kennedys, the Avengers, and
the Mutants took place there, with Avengers
guitarist Greg Ingraham quitting the band. The
Dils, Negative Trend, and the Controllers would
also play at 330 Grove. The footprint of the since

demolished building is now a small part of a large parking garage

San Francisco Art Institute (800 Chestnut St., San Francisco): Penelope Houston moved to San Francisco on New Year's Eve 1976 to study at the Art Institute, lasting two semesters before dropping out.

"At the end of one of the semesters I handed in for my painting class an 85 page xerox booklet," she said. "I made five of these booklets and they were all the Avengers and punk and the Mabuhay and stuff. Just xeroxes, no text. And I handed that in and got an F."

The Art Institute hosted numerous punk shows in the late '70s, with bands like the Dead Kennedys, the Dils, and the Avengers. In 2017, Houston was invited to participate in the Art Institute's annual fundraising gala, where 12 different artists created art bars for partygoers. Houston's installation was the backstage of a fictitious punk club called **Hinckley's (1111 Polk St., San Francisco)**, which she decorated with flyers and other artwork, and which also included an interactive graffiti-strewn couch and a live band.

"I created the history of Hinckley's, which had been a gay club, then it turned into a gay disco, then they started having punk dates. Everybody started going there. Then after two years it got shut down because of noise complaints and underage drinking and it just turned either back into a gay disco or disappeared."

Elite Club (1805 Geary St., San Francisco): After the closure of Fillmore Auditorium in 1968, the hall was renamed the Elite Club, serving as a rock venue until the early '80s. Its most fertile period was its last few years, when punk bands

like Dead Kennedys, Flipper, Meat Puppets, and Bad Brains played shows there.

Temple Beautiful (1839 Geary St., San Francisco ⃠): Built in the early 20th century as a synagogue for Temple Beth Israel, the building was briefly used as a rehearsal space by the Grateful Dead after the congregation relocated several miles south to 625 Brotherhood Way. By the time it began being used as a punk venue in 1979, the building, sandwiched between the then-former Fillmore Auditorium and the former San Francisco headquarters of Jim Jones' Peoples Temple, had lost some of its luster. Sometimes informally called by its address on punk flyers, local punk bands like the Dead Kennedys, the Avengers, the Dils, and many others played the temple.

Also playing 1839 Geary were the Clash; due to a dustup related to the Bill Graham-promoted show in Berkeley planned for one night earlier, the group was called "The Only English Band that Matters" alongside a clear photo on the flyers, and word of mouth assured fans that it was indeed them. The gig, on February 8, 1979, was held as a benefit for New Youth Productions, a punk collective which sought to create a more equitable environment for punk

performers. Also on the bill were Negative Trend and the Zeros.

The temple was left derelict until the late '80s when it was purchased by designer Tony Duquette, who restored the building to its former grandeur as an art gallery, in which he premiered Canticle of the Sun of St. Francis of Assisi, the patron saint of San Francisco. The building was burned beyond repair due to an electrical fire in early 1989, and has since been replaced by a branch of the United States Postal Service.

On Broadway (435 Broadway, San Francisco): Opened in the early '80s by punk promoter Dirk Dirksen directly next door to Mabuhay Gardens, On Broadway was a theater and nightclub where Dirksen could indulge in his fondness for theater of various types. This included punk shows by Dead Kennedys, Circle Jerks, Fang, Fear, and Black Flag. On Broadway closed in the mid-'90s.

Savoy-Tivoli (1434 Grant Ave., San Francisco): During its brief time as a live music venue in the mid-'70s, the Savoy-Tivoli squeezed a lot of history through a small window, booking everyone from the Ramones to Graham Parker to Southside Johnny and the Asbury Jukes to Crime in a single week. Blues singer Jimmy Reed died in his sleep in 1976 after playing the club.

Valencia Tool & Die (974 Valencia St., San Francisco): A ground floor art gallery with a basement performance space accessed through a trap door, Valencia Tool & Die was a punk venue from 1980–1983, featuring shows by Dead Kennedys, Flipper, Black Flag, Hüsker Dü, and Faith No Man, an early incarnation of Faith No More.

California Hall (625 Polk St., San Francisco): Occasionally the site of rock shows over the years, punk came to California Hall on August 28, 1977, when the Avengers, the Nuns, and Mary Monday played the venerable hall.

Sound of Music (162 Turk St., San Francisco): Even by punk standards, the Sound of Music was reportedly a dump. Opened by Celso Roberto, the Sound of Music rode the punk wave in the late '70s, augmenting its regular drag shows with the new sound. Flipper, Toiling Midgets, Gun Club, Faith No More, Frightwig, and Romeo Void.

American Can Company (2301 3rd St., San Francisco): A former warehouse where guitarist Greg Ingraham and drummer Danny Furious were living, the American Can Company is where the Avengers not only formed, but also played their first show in early June 1977.

Mike Katz

"Huge, gigantically tall loft spaces and they had a PA set up there for their rehearsals," said Houston. "And I was in there one day when nobody was around, and I dropped the needle on a Patti Smith album. I started singing along into the PA and I was just like, 'Whoa, I'm so loud!' They came back from wherever they were, and I was like, 'I'm going to be your vocalist!'"

The Avengers debuted during a party in the loft, playing covers by the likes of Patti Smith, Iggy Pop, and Lou Reed. By the end of the month they'd written a few original numbers and played four gigs at Mabuhay Gardens.

Kezar Pavilion (755 Stanyan St., San Francisco): Traditionally used for basketball, Kezar Pavilion has periodically opened its doors to rock shows. On October 13, 1979, something of a worldwide punk summit was held at Kezar, with local favorites Dead Kennedys supporting headliners the Clash (London) and the second-billed Cramps (New York City).

The Old Waldorf (444 Battery St., San Francisco): Opened by Jeffrey Pollack in 1976, the Old Waldorf hosted punk shows by Dead Kennedys, Television, and the Avengers, who played there on June 13, 1979, one of their final shows before splitting later that month. Pollack sold the club to impresario Bill Graham, who kept it open for three more years.

"They had tables and you were forced to have a two-drink minimum, and we always thought that was fucked up," said Houston. "And then we had to do two sets and were playing with Penetration, which was kind of exciting cause they were from out of town, we'd heard of them. But we almost never did two sets. And I used to drink gin and tonics to get me warmed up for my set, so by the time we got

to the second set, I was really drunk, probably one of the drunkest performances I ever did, and somebody recorded that show."

The Stone (412 Broadway, San Francisco)/ Keystone Berkeley (2119 University Ave., Berkeley)/Keystone Palo Alto (260 California Ave., Palo Alto): A trio of sister clubs, local San Francisco punk bands at various times played them all, sometimes moving from one to the next. Such was the case in December 1977, when the Avengers opened for Talking Heads in Berkeley one night and Palo Alto the next. In February 1986, Dead Kennedys played two of their final shows at the Stone. They would split that summer following the recording of *Bedtime for Democracy*, but would reunite—without singer Jello Biafra—in 2001.

Aitos (1920 San Pablo Ave., Berkeley): Sometimes using the less-provocative "New Wave" on flyers, Aitos nevertheless hosted late '70s punk shows by Dead Kennedys, the Avengers, the Dils, Mutants, and Sudden Fun.

Ruthie's Inn (2618 San Pablo Ave., Berkeley): Promoter Wes Robinson saw the potential in punk, staging most of his East Bay shows at Ruthie's Inn. Dead Kennedys, Bad Brains, Social Distortion, Flipper, Fang, D.R.I., and Black Flag are among the punk bands who played Ruthie's between 1983–1987, though it became even better known as a thrash metal club during that same period.

Longbranch Saloon (2504 San Pablo Ave., Berkeley): Among the punks and new wavers who played the Longbranch were the Avengers, Psycotic Pineapple, the Tubes, and the Patti Smith Group.

The Rio Theatre (140 Parker Ave., Rodeo): On June 18, 1977, the Nuns and the Avengers

headed out to Rodeo to play the Rio. It was the third gig for the latter, and singer Penelope Houston said it was an eye-opening experience.

"Rodeo is even further than any place we'd ever heard of or gone to," she said. "It was really like we were on tour. It was this big, big old theater, really beautiful place that at that time seemed like it was completely run by hippies and nobody had ever heard of punk. . . . The sound was totally weird and there was some crazy buzzing coming through all the amps because of the wiring in the building. I just remember thinking, 'Are we going to get out of here alive?'... We just felt like we were totally out of our element and since we'd only been a band for like a couple of weeks, we barely knew what our element was."

NOTEWORTHY RECORDING LOCATIONS

Bear West Recording Studio (915 Howard St., San Francisco): In mid-1976, Crime turned up at Bear West to record the two songs that would comprise their crucial debut single, "Hotwire My Heart" and "Baby You're So Repulsive." According to legend, the group could not afford the extra studio time required to rerecord the A-side after drummer Ricky Tractor fumbled the intro.

Mills College (5000 MacArthur Blvd., Oakland): For their second single, Crime headed to the recording studio at Mills College, where they cut "Frustration" b/w "Murder By Guitar" in early 1977.

Wally Heider Studios/Hyde Street Studios (245 Hyde St., San Francisco): Renowned as one of San Francisco's first recording studios to lure business away from Los Angeles and New York City in the late '60s, Wally Heider also saw a

few punks come through the doors between sessions by popular rock artists like Jefferson Starship; Crosby, Stills, Nash & Young; and Hot Tuna. Avengers cut a few tracks, including "No Martyr" and "Desperation," there on February 8, 1978, thanks to the largesse of an engineer.

"He was like, 'We can get you in in the middle of the night.' It didn't cost us anything. I don't think there was ever a time where we were like, 'Let's make a record.' It was like, 'Let's record some stuff because we've got more songs.'"

The facility was sold in 1980 and renamed Hyde Street Studios. Dead Kennedys recorded their third studio album, *Frankenchrist*, there in mid-1985, along with some of their second album (*Plastic Surgery Disasters*) and their fourth and final album (*Bedtime for Democracy*) in 1982 and 1986 respectively.

Record Plant (2200 Bridgeway, Sausalito): In another instance where the Avengers were given an opportunity to cut a few tracks, the band traveled on March 28, 1978, to Sausalito to a studio that was seemingly the living embodiment of the decade's excess.

"It was just like total '70s coked out," said Houston. "The walls were covered in wood and it was amazing looking."

"Open Your Eyes," "This White Line," and a cover of the Rolling Stones' "Paint it, Black" emerged from this session.

Mobius Music (1583 Sanchez St., San Francisco): This longtime studio is most notable among fans of San Francisco punk as the facility where Dead Kennedys recorded their seminal debut album, *Fresh Fruit for Rotting Vegetables*, along with its followup, the *In God We Trust, Inc.* EP.

Peter Miller Studios (2258a Union St., San Francisco): Christ on Parade, Samiam, and the Avengers have all recorded at Peter Miller.

Different Fur Studios (3470 19th St., San Francisco): On October 12, 1978, the Avengers headed into Different Fur with former Sex Pistols guitarist Steve Jones in the producer's chair, cutting four tracks.

"I remember Steve had lots of opinions about guitar sound and zero opinions about vocals," said Houston, who would return to Different Fur in 1992–1993 to record her solo album, *The Whole World.*

Devo, Jonathan Richman and the Modern Lovers, and Primus are among the other artists who've worked at Different Fur.

Iguana Rehearsal Studios (1527 Folsom St., San Francisco): An Avengers rehearsal space, Iguana also saw the group record a few demos, which later appeared on a two-disc compilation alongside various other recordings called *Avengers,* but informally referred to as *The Pink Album.*

THE MATRIX
3138 Fillmore St.

Opened in 1965 as a showcase for the city's emerging folk-rock scene, the club became a launching pad for the Jefferson Airplane, whose cofounder Marty Balin was an original investor. It nurtured the nascent San Francisco sound by featuring influential acts like the Great Society, Big Brother and the Holding Company, and Quicksilver Messenger Service, among many others.

It eventually closed in 1972, but has had a few reincarnations since, including a new stint as The Matrix that closed in 2018.

KABUKI THEATER
1881 Post St.

Originally built as a dinner theater in 1960, the Kabuki attracted promoter Bill Graham

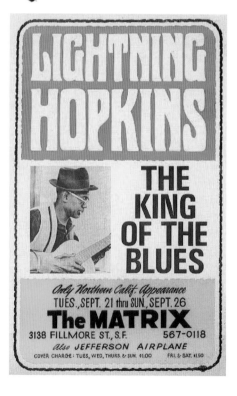

in 1981, when he began throwing around 60 shows a year there. It became de rigeur for the era's MTV stars to play the Kabuki, with the theater hosting everyone from Duran Duran, Eurhythmics, ABC, Dexy's Midnight Runners, Fun Boy Three, Frankie Goes to Hollywood, and local heroes Huey Lewis and the News, who celebrated the success of *Sports* with a jubilant run of shows in December 1983. The Kabuki's time as a live music venue ended the following year when the building sold for $3.5 million, half a million bucks less than the cost of opening the dinner theater 24 years earlier.

WINTERLAND BALLROOM
2000 Post St. ⊘
Opened in 1928 as an ice rink, Winterland was first used by Bill Graham when he booked a gig by Jefferson Airplane and the Paul Butterfield Blues Band in 1966. Graham increasingly booked shows here as the space was

Poster by Bob Cato, Michael Manoogian, and Georges Hugnet, 1976

considerably larger than the Fillmore West, and it became his primary venue after the Fillmore's 1971 closure. The Grateful Dead filmed a five-night run at Winterland in 1975, performances of which became *The Grateful Dead Movie*. The Jimi Hendrix Experience, the Rolling Stones, Aerosmith, Mott the Hoople, Janis Joplin, David Bowie, and many others played Winterland. The Band made their public debut at Winterland in 1969, with an ill Robbie Robertson only able to play the gig after the intervention of a hypnotist. The Band would return here on Thanksgiving 1976 for *The Last Waltz*, which was recorded and released as a live album, and a concert film and documentary.

Winterland opened 1978 with what turned out to be the final show by the Sex Pistols on January 14; the venue closed for good later that year with a run of shows by Bruce Springsteen and the E Street Band, Tom Petty and the Heartbreakers, Ramones, and Smokey Robinson. The Grateful Dead headlined the final night on

Poster by Randy Tuten, 1970

New Year's Eve 1978, with support from the Blues Brothers. Bill Graham flew in astride a massive joint from which he tossed regular-size joints into the crowd. Attendees and performers were treated to a hot breakfast the morning after. The shuttered theater was eventually leveled in 1985.

MELVIN BELLI OFFICES
722-728 Montgomery St.
Melvin Belli was one of the great blustering self-promoting celebrity lawyers of his age, representing everyone from Muhammad Ali to Zsa Zsa Gabor, Chuck Berry to Errol Flynn. He represented Dallas nightclub owner Jack Ruby, who famously shot Lee Harvey Oswald. Belli's offices turned up in a pivotal scene in both rock history and the Rolling Stones film *Gimme Shelter*. The Stones were struggling to find a place to put on a free concert in the spirit of Woodstock when Belli received a call from Dick Carter, owner of a financially strapped raceway in Altamont. The conversation set in motion the ill-fated show, and after a violent death at the hands of a member of the Hells Angels, the Stones gig at Altamont has often been cited as the end of the '60s.

BOTTOM OF THE HILL
1233 17th St.
Opened by Tim Benetti in 1991, this intimate all-ages Portrero Hill mainstay has hosted early gigs by the Strokes, Oasis, Arcade Fire, the White Stripes, and Queens of the Stone Age, all of whom went on to fill stadiums. With its tiny stage, small back room, and outdoor patio, Bottom of the Hill remains a popular favorite for music fans hoping to catch the next big thing.

Crispin Kott

WHISKY A GO GO
568 Sacramento St.
A short-lived satellite location of the famous West Hollywood club opened in 1965, the

discotheque atmosphere of the Whisky a Go Go, which advertised "topless fencing" and "topless fashion" in its newspaper ads, ran counter to the loose vibe in more popular clubs that began popping up across San Francisco in the next couple of years. The Doors, Grateful Dead, and Johnny Rivers were among those who played the San Francisco Whisky before it closed its doors sometime in 1967.

THE TOWN SQUIRE
1318 Polk St.
This stylishly hip men's apparel store was popular with the gay community as well as several of San Francisco's rock stars in the '60s, including members of Jefferson Airplane.

CHASE CENTER
1 Warriors Way
After spending the past few decades in the East Bay, the Golden State Warriors returned to San Francisco for the first time since the 1965–1966 NBA season. Chase Center officially opened its doors with a pair of dates by Metallica performing with the San Francisco Symphony on September 6, 2019. Other early live music performances at Chase Center have included Elton John, the Who, Liam Gallagher, Janet Jackson, Santana, Eric Clapton, and the Dave Matthews Band.

MediaPunch Inc./Alamy

"San Francisco, it's my favorite place in the world. I wish they would fix the roads and a few other things for the amount of taxes that we pay, but all in all it's a beautiful place to live."

—NEAL SCHON, JOURNEY, 2019

Throughout the '80s, San Francisco-based Journey were one of the biggest bands on the planet, playing sold-out shows to screaming fans in arenas and stadiums and busting the charts with several multiplatinum albums. But their lineup from that era—vocalist Steve Perry; guitarist Neal Schon; bass guitarist Ross Valory; drummer Steve Smith; and keyboardist Gregg Rolie, who left in 1980 and was replaced by Jonathan Cain—began to coalesce in significantly more humble settings.

Initially dubbed the Golden Gate Rhythm Section, Journey was founded in 1973 by former Santana bandmates Schon and Rolie, who enlisted Valory and guitarist George Tickner, formerly of local psych-rock band Frumious Bandersnatch; along with Tubes drummer Prairie Prince, later replaced by Aynsley Dunbar. The collective was signed to Columbia Records and released three albums—only the first featuring Tickner—in a jazz-inflected prog rock vein, and though the group was a popular live act in the Bay Area, their studio efforts failed to meet sales expectations. By 1977, Journey was faced with either pursuing a new direction or possibly losing their record deal. They chose the former, and after briefly adding Robert Fleischman as lead vocalist, the group hired Perry.

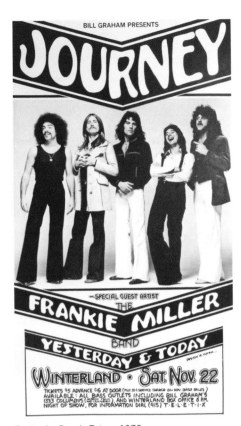

Poster by Randy Tuten, 1975

Perry's introduction to Journey audiences came on October 27, 1977, at **The Old Waldorf (444 Battery St., San Francisco),** a 600-seat nightclub on the second floor of a building a few blocks west of the Ferry Building and the San Francisco Bay. Journey fans were perplexed.

"We were like killing it, and then we introduced Steve and he came onstage and the audience kind of like, they went, 'What is *that*?'" said Schon. "Little did they know that it was going to turn into a monster worldwide after that. But at the time they were going, 'Oh man, you just messed up this jam band!'"

In the fall of 1977, the newly configured Journey convened at **His Master's Wheels (60 Brady St., San Francisco),** where they'd cut their previous album *Next.*

"It wasn't like the gem studio of all time, but it did have great sounding rooms and (owner Elliot Mazer) did have great equipment," said Schon. "But it wasn't aesthetically like, 'Oh shit, look at this place!'"

To produce *Infinity*, Journey manager Herbie Herbert brought in Roy Thomas Baker, known for his deftly polished work on numerous albums by Queen and Nazareth. The group began cutting the album at His Master's Wheels that October, but thanks to an incident involving their producer and a fire extinguisher, Journey were forced to finish the record in Los Angeles.

"The story is true," said Schon, confirming the rumor in 2019. "I don't know where you heard it, but it is definitely true. It was like nothing I'd ever seen before. They were all drunk, drinking a lot and all kinds of other shit. And Baker just decided to go off and spray the fire extinguisher all over the Neve board, and all over the equipment. And it was a frickin' mess, man. Someone called Elliot Mazer and said, 'Man, you better get down here. I'm not sure you're going to like what you see going on.' And so he calmly came into the studio and asked to see Roy, that he wanted to speak to him outside. And then he took him in this room and we heard him starting to raise his voice, yelling and

Escape album cover by Stanley Mouse

screaming, and then he just fucking went off on the guy. Like, 'How dare you come in here and do this to my place?!?' Basically, 'I don't care who you are!'"

The figurative conflagration failed to upend Journey's trajectory, and *Infinity* would rise to #21 on the *Billboard 200* on May 6, 1978. The follow-up, *Evolution*, would go one better, hitting #20 on May 5, 1979. It was a sign of things to come for Journey, who would dominate the charts and airwaves in the '80s, with *Escape,* their first album with Cain, topping the *Billboard 200* on September 12, 1981, and remaining on the chart for an astounding 152 weeks.

Journey are still thrilling fans around the world, though as of 2020 their lineup is in a state of flux. The '80s-era band of Schon, Cain, Valory, and Smith were fully reunited in 2015, augmented by Arnel Pineda, a dynamic Filipino singer who came to Schon's attention and joined Journey in 2007 through a series of YouTube clips that showed he had the vocal range of Steve Perry. But in early 2020, legal troubles fractured Journey again, with Schon and Cain firing Valory and Smith and announcing former bass guitarist Randy Jackson and drummer Narada Michael Walden as their replacements. As of October 2020 the legal dispute is still ongoing.

MORE JOURNEY

NOTEWORTHY LIVE PERFORMANCES

Winterland Ballroom (2000 Post St., San Francisco ⊘): Journey made their live debut at Winterland on New Year's Eve in 1973, supporting Santana. They would return to Winterland numerous times between then and November 22, 1977, but for Schon the first time was perhaps the most memorable.

"It was amazing," he said. "We had a great night. And then we jumped on a flight and went to Hawaii. (Winterland) was kind of our home ground stomping area. At that point, San Francisco and us had made a huge connection together, and it was obvious. The audience always went nuts when we played, especially Winterland."

Great American Music Hall (859 O'Farrell St., San Francisco): Journey's second gig in their hometown took place here on February 5, 1974. It marked the live debut of drummer Dunbar.

"It was great, but the place was really not set up for rock and roll," said Schon. "We weren't even close to the decibels bands had gotten to, and I thought it was just too loud for the place. It sounded good, but at the breaking point where you thought some of the paint was going to come off the walls once they plugged in the PA."

The Warfield Theatre (982 Market St., San Francisco): Journey played the Warfield only once, as part of the 1981 Bammies, an annual award show organized by *BAM (Bay Area Music)*, a free biweekly music magazine. Perry played a solo show in the former vaudeville theater, but when Cain showed up to show his support, he found he wasn't on the guest list and left.

"I did know one thing," wrote Cain in his 2018 memoir, *Don't Stop Believin'*, "I wasn't going to buy a ticket."

Cow Palace (2600 Geneva Ave., Daly City): Journey first played the Cow Palace on New Year's Eve in 1974, returning a handful of times over the years, including a New Year's Eve gig sharing the bill with Blondie in 1978; and a three night stand from November 30 through December 2, 1981, with the last night a benefit to save San Francisco's cable cars.

"That was probably one of the worst-sounding buildings ever," said Schon. "It was a fun place, but just terrible-sounding."

Laughter, Love & Music (Polo Fields, Golden Gate Park, San Francisco): After a split in 1987, Journey members Perry, Schon, and Cain briefly reunited on November 3, 1991, for a massive tribute concert in the memory of legendary promoter Bill Graham, Melissa Gold, and Steve Kahn, who'd died in a helicopter crash a week earlier. Also on the bill were the Grateful Dead; Crosby, Stills & Nash; Santana; John Fogerty; and many others.

Oakland-Alameda County Coliseum (7000 Coliseum Way, Oakland): While this multipurpose baseball-football stadium has had numerous official names over the years, locals often ignore the current naming rights and simply call it Oakland Coliseum or Oakland Stadium. Journey played the Coliseum as part of Bill Graham's Day on the Green series each year between 1977–1980, and again in 1982 and 1983.

Oakland-Alameda County Arena (7000 Coliseum Way, Oakland): Like its bigger sibling, this former home to the Golden State Warriors has had a few different names over the years, but is often simply called Oakland

Arena. Journey played here a handful of times, including a performance on March 28, 1980, with soon-to-be keyboard player Cain, a member of support group the Babys.

Concord Pavilion (2000 Kirker Pass Rd., Concord): Journey played this then-new Bay Area amphitheater on August 7, 1976, with Sons of Champlin and Earthquake.

Fox Theater (1807 Telegraph Ave., Oakland): Neal Schon's Journey Through Time made its Bay Area debut at Oakland's grandiose Fox Theater on February 23, 2019. A supergroup which counts among its members Gregg Rolie, bass guitarist Marco Mendoza, and drummer Deen Castronovo, Neal Schon's Journey Through Time deftly performs songs from across the Journey catalog, covering the early prog-jazz rock era, through the radio and MTV smash hits of the Steve Perry years and beyond.

NOTEWORTHY RECORDING LOCATIONS

CBS Studios/The Automatt (827 Folsom St., San Francisco ⊘): Journey recorded their first two albums—*Journey* (1975) and *Look Into the Future* (1976)—at CBS Studios. They returned in October 1978 to record a live session at the Automatt, a popular leased studio space within the CBS facility. Intended as part of the King Biscuit Flower Hour, the session, which featured Journey alongside a number of guests, included a few of the band's own songs augmented by a selection of cover songs. Notable as the first appearance of Smith on drums, the session also featured Stoneground singers Annie Sampson and Jo Baker; Doobie Brothers guitarist Tom Johnston; and Oakland-based horn section Tower of Power. For legal reasons the sessions were not broadcast as intended, and were

traded as a bootleg for many years before seeing an official release as a download via Wolfgang's.

"It was awesome," said Schon. "About a year ago somebody played that for me for the first time since we did it, and I thought, wow, we sounded pretty good."

Fantasy Studios (2600 Tenth St., Berkeley): Journey recorded two worldwide smashes at this now-closed studio, *Escape* (1981) and *Frontiers* (1983). They returned to Fantasy for some of *Raised on the Radio* (1986) and *Eclipse* (2011), and it always remained a favorite of Schon's.

"I worked there for years," Schon said. "They let me store equipment over there. Every time I had an itch to go into the studio, they'd be kind enough and I'd just say, 'Block out some time,' and they'd set up my stuff and then rip it down and put it in storage for me. I think that the rooms sounded good for the band. We used the bigger room, and at that time too they had a huge Neve board in there. Nothing was digital yet, everything was analog. They had all the best equipment. Everything kind of clicked, and everybody felt really comfortable in there."

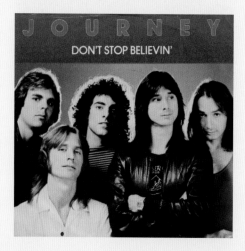

JOURNEY

DON'T STOP BELIEVIN'

OTHER NOTEWORTHY LOCATIONS

Journey HQ (1111 Columbus Ave., San Francisco): After *Escape* launched them into the stratosphere, Journey and their management bought this unique building, once a showroom for the trade association of the redwood industry, with different paneling on each floor. Journey ran their '80s empire from here, later selling the building for a tidy profit.

1111 Columbus Avenue

"Amazing piece of property," said Schon. "Every time I drive by it I'm always pissed off that we had to sell it, you know? It was very incredible. Every floor there was something different going on."

Jonathan Cain Home Studio (25 Saddle Lane, Novato): Cain's longtime home had a recording studio he called Wildhorse, where Journey cut some of their reunion album, *Trial by Fire* (1996), as well as Journey's *Red 13* EP (2002) and Cain's 1995 solo album, *Beyond the Thunder*. As early as *Frontiers* (1983), Cain and Perry would meet here to work on songs together. Cain sold the home in 2010 and moved to Nashville.

Aragon High School (900 Alameda de las Pulgas, San Mateo): Neal Schon dropped out of Aragon High to pursue music in the late '60s.

"I really did not like school at all," Schon said. "I just felt like I was somewhere else. I knew what my niche was going to be. I kind of made up my mind what I wanted to do early in life, and I just wasn't interested in getting a high school diploma or going through college. I kind of wanted to get out in the world and do what I wanted to do. And I'm still doing it."

Ellwood P. Cubberley High School (4000 Middlefield Rd., Palo Alto): Rolie was a member of the Cubberley High Class of 1965. The high school closed in 1979, with the building eventually being converted into the Cubberley Community Center, which is still there today.

Blackie's Pasture (654 Tiburon Blvd., Tiburon): In 1988, Perry broke it to Schon and Cain in this otherwise tranquil setting overlooking Richardson Bay that his time in Journey was over. The group would reunite in 1995, recording the *Trial by Fire* album, but Perry left again in 1997.

While today's Fillmore is a gentrified, boutique-laden district, it was in the early 20th century, an ethnically and racially diverse working-class neighborhood. A significant portion of the district was Japantown (Nihonmachi), a bustling enclave of Japanese-American families and businesses. On February 19, 1942, shortly after the outbreak of World War II, President Franklin D. Roosevelt signed Executive Order 9066, which enabled the government to designate certain "military areas" and exclude from them people perceived as a threat for sabotage or espionage.

San Francisco was designated as such an area, and by April, its Japanese-American inhabitants, many of whom were US citizens, were made to give up their homes, businesses, and belongings and were forcibly relocated to regional internment camps for the duration of the war.

At the same time, a massive influx of African Americans migrated to the Bay Area as labor to support the war effort and found the recently vacated Fillmore was, in an era of legal housing discrimination, one of the very few areas available to rent. Those new San Franciscans brought their music and entrepreneurship with them, and the Fillmore rapidly became an exciting destination for African American entertainment, with clubs, bars, music halls, and other assorted venues established by Black proprietors scattered throughout the district. It became a "Harlem of the West."

After the war, some of the Japanese-Americans returned, but many found places to live elsewhere throughout the Bay Area. The Fillmore by then had been thoroughly transformed into a thriving enclave of Black music and nightlife. By the '50s, however, the clubs, hotels, and most importantly the people of the Fillmore began to face the full frontal assault of Urban Renewal, as the city embarked on an aggressive campaign to redevelop what it considered a crime and poverty-ridden blight, ultimately displacing many thousands of people and demolishing a large percentage of the old buildings. By the mid '60s, the Fillmore's era as a Black music mecca was over, but a new era had begun. In tribute to its historic musical past, the free two-day Fillmore Jazz Festival is held outdoors each summer.

JACK'S TAVERN
1931 Sutter St. ⊘

The club generally credited with igniting the music boom in the district was Jack's, opened just as prohibition was repealed in 1933. Even though there were only about 5,000 African Americans living in all of San Francisco at the time, it found its audience in the racially diverse district. Within a few years, other establishments, including **Club Alabam (1820A Post St. ⊘)**, and the **Town Club (1963 Sutter St. ⊘)**, were catering to Black patrons and offering first-rate live entertainment. Jack's bounced around the neighborhood a few times until it succumbed to redevelopment in the early '70s. A later incarnation at **1601 Fillmore St.** ultimately became the **Boom Boom Room.**

PRIMALON BALLROOM
1223 Fillmore St. ⊘

For a while in the '50s, the Primalon rivaled the nearby **Fillmore Auditorium (1805 Geary St.)** as a high-capacity venue for top flight jazz and R&B. Having previously been a roller rink, indoor golf course, and dance hall in its lifetime, it was rebranded as the Primalon in 1949. In addition to Fillmore locals, it attracted a significant white clientele that embraced jazz, beat poetry, and the emerging postwar proto-counterculture. World class jazz musicians such as Dizzy Gillespie, important R&B performers like Percy Mayfield, T-Bone Walker, and Amos Milburn, as well as Bay Area standouts Johnny Otis and Pee Wee Crayton held court here. The Primalon eventually closed in 1961.

BLUE MIRROR COCKTAIL LOUNGE
935 Fillmore St. ⊘

Leola King's small club was something of an R&B stronghold, known to have featured important and influential performers such as Lowell Fulson, T-Bone Walker, and Little Willie John.

MELROSE RECORD SHOP
1236 Fillmore St. ⊘

Proprietor Dave Rosenbaum was well known as an aficionado of jazz and blues, and Melrose, along with its sister shop **Rhythm Records (1980 Sutter St. ⊘)** were well stocked with the best selection in San Francisco. Rosenbaum even created his own Rhythm label, which is notable for issuing Saunders King's "S.K. Blues," in 1942, the first Bay Area blues record to become a national hit. Marguerite Johnson, later known as Maya Angelou, worked for a time during her tenure at Washington High School as a shop assistant at Melrose.

THE BOOM BOOM ROOM
1601 Fillmore St.

In 1988 the last incarnation of Jack's Tavern settled in this location before changing ownership not long afterward and reinventing itself as a tribute to blues legend John Lee Hooker, who was known to frequent the place until his death in 2001. It remains a stylish place to drink, dance, and hear a wide variety of live music, from rock to hip-hop and everything in between.

The Boom Boom Room

BOP CITY
1690 Post St.—1712 Fillmore St.

Originally established as Vout City by the colorfully eclectic Slim Gaillard in the late '40s ("Vout" being a play on his trademark invented language "Vout-o-Reenee") the club quickly failed, leaving the landlord, Charles Sullivan to pick up the pieces and find a new tenant. He found one in Jimbo Edwards, a prominent car dealer, who opened Jimbo's Waffle Shop. The spot became popular with musicians who helped Edwards convert a large back room into an informal after-hours hangout for all-star jam sessions and partying. It was christened "Bop City" in honor of the recently closed club in New York. Many of the top Black musicians of the day, such as Charlie Parker, Johnny Hodges, Milt Jackson, Miles Davis, and Art Tatum made a point of stopping by when their gigs were over for the evening, and occasionally young wannabes would join them. Visiting celebrities in the know, like Marilyn Monroe, Joe Louis, Jack Kerouac, and Sammy

Davis Jr. would also make the scene. Some of the other performers known to have graced the makeshift stage include Billie Holiday, T-Bone Walker, Arthur Prysock, Lionel Hampton, Sarah Vaughn, Stan Getz, Louis Jordan, Billy Eckstine, Dinah Washington, and Louis Armstrong, who reportedly met Charlie Parker there. Jimbo hung on until 1965, as the clubs disappeared and the wrecking ball of urban renewal approached. Thanks to community activists, the building survived, but was moved around the block to **1712 Fillmore Street**, where it rests today. For many years, Marcus Books, an historic Black interest specialty shop occupied the former waffle emporium until it moved out in 2014.

MANOR PLAZA HOTEL
930 Fillmore St. ⊘

This stylish hotel featured a nightclub that hosted stars such as Dinah Washington and Ike and Tina Turner, and once employed Flip Wilson as a doorman. R&B bandleader Johnny Otis made the Manor Plaza his San Francisco headquarters, and it was here that he first met and auditioned the young Etta James, hiring her on the spot.

BOOKER T. WASHINGTON HOTEL
1540 Ellis St. ⊘

Originally a rooming house, and later known as the somewhat disreputable Hotel Edison, the building was renovated and renamed the Booker T. Washington in 1951. It rapidly became the most fashionable place in town for traveling Black musicians and celebrities, with a cocktail lounge featuring talent booked by Charles Sullivan, who had an interest in the hotel and was the owner of nearby Bop City.

SUGAR PIE DESANTO'S CHILDHOOD HOME
1131 Buchanan St. ⊘

One of ten children in what must have been an extremely lively household, Umpeylia Balinton

Mike Katz

The former Bop City, now at 1712 Fillmore Street

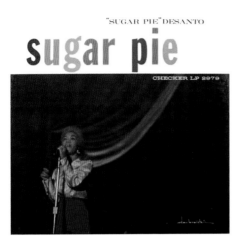

"SUGAR PIE" DESANTO

sugar pie

CHECKER LP 2973

was the daughter of a Filipino father and an African American mother who had been a concert pianist. She attended both **Galileo High School (1150 Francisco St.)** and **Girls High School (1430 Scott St.)** and, like her neighborhood friend Jamesetta Hawkins (later Etta James), was introduced by Johnny Otis. Otis, who had a gift for inventing new names for his discoveries (he reinvented himself, after all), rechristened her Sugar Pie. He can only have been referring to her diminutive (4'11") size, because she could belt out a tune with a tough bluesy bravado few others could match. After Otis, she toured with James Brown for two years. Sugar Pie recorded extensively with Bob Geddins in Oakland, including her first hit "I Want to Know," in 1960, and later recorded for Chess in Chicago. She is still going strong today, well into her 80s.

FILLMORE AUDITORIUM
1805 Geary Blvd.
In the Fillmore's heyday as the jazz and blues capital of San Francisco, Charles Sullivan was its supreme impresario. He handled the top talent in the city and was generally believed to be one of the wealthiest Black men on the West Coast. The Majestic Hall was originally built in 1912, and by 1952 it had spent the last 15 years as a dance hall and roller skating rink. After securing the lease he transformed it into the Fillmore Auditorium and made it the top venue for jazz, blues, and R&B in the Bay Area well into the 1960s. James Brown, Little Richard, Ike and Tina Turner, Bobby "Blue" Bland, Otis Redding, the Temptations, and many others played the Fillmore. By the mid '60s, however, the area's transformation made the Fillmore's run as an exclusively Black entertainment venue increasingly difficult, and Sullivan made it available for sublet to a young promoter named Bill Graham who booked rock and roll acts for the emerging Haight-Ashbury scene. On August 2, 1966, Sullivan was discovered fatally shot in an industrial area south of Market on Bluxome Street, in what was controversially ruled a suicide. It proved to be a tragic but fateful passing of the torch.

Mike Katz

ETTA JAMES

"I guess you'd call me cocky. My cockiness got me in trouble. My rebelliousness was deep-rooted and long-lasting. Some people go through a period—maybe a year or two or three—where they rail against authority. In my case the rebel period lasted for what seemed like several lifetimes."

ETTA JAMES, *RAGE TO SURVIVE* (W/DAVID RITZ), 1995

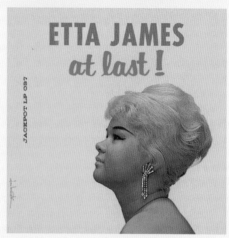

By the time she recorded her signature tune, "At Last" in 1960, Etta James was already, at 21, a six-year show business veteran. Recruited by Johnny Otis at 15, she forged her imprisoned mother's signature on a permission form to hit the road with the pioneering bandleader, enduring a grueling and decidedly unglamorous few years traveling the "chitlin circuit," a network of African American entertainment venues scattered throughout the East Coast, Midwest, and especially the Deep South. Her tumultuous upbringing in San Francisco's Fillmore District and Hunters Point projects had conditioned her for much, but the unruly caravan of performers she toured with, and the often turbulent adventures they shared was something she could not possibly have prepared for.

Jamesetta Hawkins was born in Los Angeles to a 14-year-old mother who would bounce in and out of her life for many years to come, often with tempestuous results. When her foster mother died in 1950, her true mother Dorothy reappeared and dragged her up to San Francisco, where she was promptly deposited with relatives in Hunters Point. Dorothy lived primarily in and around the Fillmore, typically staying in cheap rooming houses. One of her longest residences during this time was **1137 Folsom Street**, which Etta remembers in her 1995 memoir as "white trash skid row." Jamesetta spent part of her time with her mother, and attended **Girls High School (1430 Scott St.)**. She was insolent and delinquent, often skipping school to run with a local girl gang, the Lucky 20's. They committed petty crimes and harassed other kids, so eventually she was remanded to the **Continuation High School (1099 Hayes St.)**, considered a last resort for troubled students. The fact that Jamesetta was very light skinned often made her the target of both derision and harassment from all sides. That her father's identity was a mystery only heightened her insecurity.

Back in the projects, she teamed up with a couple of sisters, Jean and Abye Mitchell, and formed a vocal group the Creolettes. Jamesetta had enjoyed singing in church back in L.A., and this gave her an opportunity to exercise those creative passions once again. The name was

inspired by the fact that all three girls were of light complexion.

Soon the Creolettes were building a reputation playing amateur nights and sock hops around town. The eldest of the Mitchell sisters, Abye, was old enough to get in to the **Primalon Ballroom (1223 Fillmore St. ⊘)** and met Johnny Otis, who was always on the lookout for new talent. Jean called late one night and implored the girls to come to the Primalon and sing for him, but Etta adamantly refused. It was only when Otis himself got on the line and convinced her that it truly was about singing did Etta agree to meet at his hotel. The impromptu audition was held at 2 a.m. in Otis's rooms at the **Manor Plaza Hotel (930 Fillmore St.)**. Etta, who hated having to perform on demand, insisted on singing her part from the bathroom. The Creolettes ran through a few standards in harmony, including "How Deep Is the Ocean" and "Street of Dreams," all while Etta sat on the edge of the tub. Otis was astounded and insisted on hiring the girls immediately. That, of course, had to wait until Etta, only 15, could bring him that forged parental permission. Dorothy was currently doing time in the joint for buying weed in a house of ill repute. It was Otis who renamed her Etta James and remade the Creolettes as her backing group the Peaches.

With Johnny Otis's guidance, Etta secured a deal with Modern Records in Los Angeles, one of the premier R&B labels on the West Coast. In November of 1953 she recorded her first sides, "Roll With Me Henry," an answer song to Hank Ballard's "Work With Me Annie,"and "Good Rockin' Daddy." Otis played "Henry" repeatedly on his radio show in L.A. to generate sales, but other stations refused, thinking the title too

suggestive, so it was renamed "Wallflower." James had written the words to the song, but in typical business fashion of the day, her slice of the royalty pie was reduced to near-nothingness, a harbinger of troubles to come. The single was a modest R&B hit, but white pop singer Georgia Gibbs, who covered it as "Dance With Me Henry" gave it the Pat Boone treatment and sold infinitely more. Etta seethed.

It was while on the road touring with stars like Little Willie John, Jackie Wilson, Little Richard, and Johnny "Guitar" Watson that she settled on the look that would define her career. Embracing her racial ambiguity, she bleached her hair and emulated the strippers, prostitutes, and drag queens she encountered. "The bad girls were the whores who had the look

Poster by Maro Spusta

I liked . . ." she recounted in her 1995 memoir, "I wanted to be rare, I wanted to be noticed, I wanted to be glamorous, I wanted to be exotic as a Cotton Club chorus girl, and I wanted to be obvious as the most flamboyant hooker on the street. I just wanted to *be*."

She would eventually leave Otis and move to Chess Records which sat near the top of the R&B recording hierarchy, but spent her life and career struggling with a maddening assortment of crises and maladies. Heartache, drug addiction, domestic violence, and money trouble plagued her throughout various stages of her life. She even served several stints in prison for a multitude of crimes, including theft and writing bad checks. The same rebellious, stubborn resolve that got her into so much

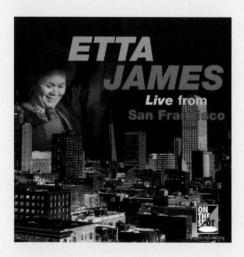

trouble seems to have helped her survive as well, and somehow, she managed to keep working and recording through the next four decades. "At Last" reached #2 on the Billboard R&B chart, and only #47 on the pop chart in 1960, but her soulful take on the Mack Gordon/ Harry Warren standard brought her to the attention of an entirely new audience. Her 1968 recording of "I'd Rather Go Blind," another song that has similarly become a classic, reportedly left Leonard Chess in tears when he first heard it.

Etta James mastered many forms of music in her career, including ballads, blues, R&B, soul, funk, and jazz, only sporadically crossing over to the white audience. Her 1994 album *Live from San Francisco*, recorded at **The Boarding House (901 Columbus Ave.)** in 1981, is especially notable for a moving rendition of the Eagles' "Take It to the Limit," demonstrating her ability to handle a contemporary rock ballad as well. Rock fandom, on the other hand, in its obsessive propensity for categorization, has sometimes found her hard to classify, muting Etta James's true influence on American music of the second half of the 20th century. Meanwhile, many of the leading female vocalists of the rock era, including Janis Joplin, idolized her. Wherever she resides in the American musical pantheon, her legacy is most assuredly incontestable.

WALLY HEIDER STUDIOS/HYDE STREET STUDIOS
245 Hyde St.

Though San Francisco had secured a place at the forefront of American music, it didn't have a top-flight rock recording studio of its own until veteran engineer Wally Heider set up shop here in 1969. Jefferson Airplane, the Grateful Dead, Creedence Clearwater Revival, Van Morrison, Neil Young, and many others recorded landmark albums here. Crosby, Stills, Nash & Young cut their wildly successful 1970 album *Déjà Vu* here, and Crosby returned the following year for his first solo album *If I Could Only Remember My Name* with a revolving all-star cast of San Francisco rock musicians. In 1978, Heider sold the operation and by 1980 it had been renamed Hyde Street Studios, which continues to produce great music to this day.

Andi Sumpter

gigs until Bill Graham booked the theater in 1979 for a run of Bob Dylan's gospel shows. The Warfield has since gone on to host many memorable shows, with the Grateful Dead recording a live album there in 1980, Elvis Costello playing a spinning-wheel show there in 1986, Prince playing a late night set there after a show at Oakland-Alameda County Arena in 1987, and Guns N' Roses playing a "public rehearsal" there ahead of the *Use Your Illusion* tour in 1991.

ORPHEUM THEATRE
1192 Market St.

Opened as a cinema in 1926 after the Orpheum served as a vaudeville house on O'Farrell, the building spent the next 50 years simply showing movies. But in 1977, the theater underwent a $2 million renovation and saw the Civic Light Opera set up shop there. The Orpheum has periodically hosted spillover shows when the Warfield was unavailable, with Tom Waits, Jerry Garcia, and Erasure all playing there.

Crispin Kott

THE WARFIELD THEATRE
982 Market St.

Originally opened in 1922 as an opulent movie house for the then-exorbitant sum of $3.5 million, the Warfield didn't host its first rock

PACIFIC HIGH STUDIOS/HIS MASTER'S WHEELS
60 Brady St.

With Richard Olsen of the Charlatans serving as the studio's manager, many San Francisco bands came through Pacific High Studios in the late '60s and early '70s. The Grateful Dead spent nine days here in 1969 recording

60 Brady Street

Workingman's Dead. After the studio was renamed His Master's Wheels, Journey recorded much of *Infinity*, their first album with vocalist Steve Perry, here, in 1977. During the sessions, producer Roy Thomas Baker decided to relieve some tension by spraying a fire extinguisher all over the studio and the musicians. The chemicals in the spray ruined the expensive mixing board and other studio equipment, and the band finished the album in a studio in Los Angeles.

LOUISE M. DAVIES SYMPHONY HALL
201 Van Ness Ave.
Though it only opened in 1980, Davis Symphony Hall shares with the War Memorial Opera House a focus on classical and opera, and is the home of the San Francisco Symphony. But it too has hosted rock concerts, including a 1982 double-bill headlined by Joan Baez and Paul Simon.

BILL GRAHAM CIVIC AUDITORIUM
99 Grove St.
Originally built in 1915 for the Panama Pacific Exposition, the Bill Graham Civic Auditorium was during the late promoter's lifetime called the San Francisco Civic Auditorium, but was renamed in his honor after his death in 1992. It was extensively renovated twice, the first in 1964, and a year later it felt the power of the British Invasion with a concert by the Rolling Stones, who played there on May 14, 1965. It has gone on to host numerous rock acts like U2, the Verve, Beastie Boys, and David Byrne. It's also been the site of the annual Bay Area Music Awards, as well as the Hookers Ball throughout the '70s.

Bill Graham Civic Auditorium

WAR MEMORIAL OPERA HOUSE
301 Van Ness Ave.
More opulently appointed than other local venues, the War Memorial Opera House has primarily hosted jazz, classical, and operatic performances. But it's also had the odd rock or folk star—Carole King played a sold-out show here in the early '70s during the height of her initial solo fame—as well as a performance by disco star Sylvester later in the decade. But the building is perhaps most historically significant as the place where Japan signed the final article of surrender following World War II, and where

Andi Sumpter

War Memorial Opera House

the charter for the United Nations was ratified in 1945.

RALPH RECORDS, HOME OF THE RESIDENTS
444 Grove St.
Originally formed in Shreveport, Louisiana, the Residents had a brief stay in San Mateo before making their way to San Francisco, where they rented an industrial space used for their DIY record label Ralph, their Buy or Die mail order operation, and other Residents-related endeavors. Many of their albums were also recorded here.

CALIFORNIA HALL
625 Polk St.
Modeled after a Heidelberg Castle and opened in 1912, California Hall hosted two key Family Dog-promoted shows in 1965, including one headlined by the Charlatans on the same night as one of the Acid Tests at the Fillmore

Mike Katz

California Hall

Auditorium: A bus ran between the two venues all night. Most active as a concert venue from 1966–1967, California Hall also hosted shows by the Jefferson Airplane, Moby Grape, the Grateful Dead, Quicksilver Messenger Service, and Big Brother and the Holding Company. California Hall can be seen in the 1971 film *Dirty Harry* as Harry Callahan and Chico Gonzalez respond to an "804 in progress" and find atop the building a man contemplating suicide.

AUGUST HALL
420 Mason St.
Built in the late 19th century as a Victorian playhouse by architect August Headman, this building would later become a cinema as Stage Door Theatre, where on May 9, 1958, it hosted the premiere of Alfred Hitchcock's film *Vertigo*. After nearly two decades as Ruby Skye, primarily showcasing EDM with visits from many of dance music's premier DJs, the theater reopened in 2018 as August Hall. Courtney Barnett, Jay Som, Johnny Marr, and Black Moth Super Rainbow are among the artists who've played August Hall.

GREAT AMERICAN MUSIC HALL
859 O'Farrell St.
Saved from possible demolition in 1972 when purchased by Tom Bradshaw, the Great American Music Hall was in its early years of operation best known for jazz, though it eventually capitulated to the times. On August 13, 1975, the Grateful Dead performed a concert there that 16 years later would be officially released as *One from the Vault*. An intimate room with ornate balconies and frescoes, the Great American Music Hall remains a popular venue, hosting everyone from Van Morrison and David Crosby to Sleater-Kinney and the Breeders with gigs most nights of the week.

In 2019, Journey cofounder Neal Schon said the Great American Music Hall wasn't initially equipped to handle amplified rock music.

Crispin Kott

"I thought it was just too loud for the place," he said of Journey's 1974 appearance there, which was only the band's second time playing San Francisco. "It sounded good, but at the breaking point where you thought some of the paint was going to come off the walls once they plugged in the P.A."

Years later, Schon and Journey keyboardist Jonathan Cain ran into former Led Zeppelin singer Robert Plant at a Paul Young gig elsewhere in town.

"And he said, 'Do you know anything to do after this? I'd like to hear some music,'" Schon recalled. "And we said, 'Well, Buddy Rich is playing down at the Great American Music Hall.' So he hopped in the limo with us and we went down there and checked him out. And Buddy sounded phenomenal in there."

THE REGENCY BALLROOM
1300 Van Ness Ave.

Built over a century ago as a masonic lodge, the Scottish Rites Bodies Regency Center is a multiuse events space which includes a grand ballroom that has long served as a live music venue. The Dandy Warhols, John Fogerty, Parliament-Funkadelic, Counting Crows, Rancid, and many other have played the Regency Ballroom.

VAILLANCOURT FOUNTAIN
Embarcadero Plaza

Just across the Embarcadero from the Ferry Building sits the former Justin Herman Plaza, within which is a fountain designed and completed in 1971 by Quebecois artist Armand Vaillancourt. Constructed out of square precast concrete tubes, the fountain was the backdrop and eventual unwitting participant during a free concert on November 11, 1987, by U2, unofficially dubbed "Save the Yuppies." During the instrumental break in the band's performance, frontman Bono climbed on the structure and spray-painted "Rock N Roll Stops the Traffic," an act which he later said the artist would have approved of (at the original dedication in 1971, Vaillancourt painted "Quebec Libre" in as many places as he could reach after a single act of vandalism reading those words painted the night before had been painted over.)

U2 weren't the first band to play before Vaillancourt Fountain: Flamin' Groovies performed there on September 19, 1979, with audio of the show broadcast live on KSAN.

BILL GRAHAM

Pictorial Press Ltd./Alamy

"I don't know if I could have ever found another place. Why would I have even tried? That was the place."

—BILL GRAHAM ON FILLMORE AUDITORIUM, *BILL GRAHAM PRESENTS: MY LIFE INSIDE ROCK AND OUT*

Born Wulf Wolodia Grajonca in Berlin in 1931, legendary promoter Bill Graham did nothing if not intensely. At the age of 8, "Wolfgang" as he was nicknamed by his family, escaped Nazi Germany in 1939 after first being put into a local orphanage by his mother to protect him from anti-Semitic violence. By the age of 10, Grajonca had been placed in foster care in the Bronx, and he stayed in New York City through college.

Taunted by classmates for his German accent shortly after arriving in America, he not only trained himself to speak with a New York accent, he also took on a name that allowed him to be like the other kids: Bill Graham. . . . In his 20s, Graham bounced around the United States and beyond, serving in the US Army during the Korean War and working as a waiter in a Catskills resort. Graham's travels occasionally took him to San Francisco after he reconnected with one of his older sisters, Rita. In the early '60s, Graham went out to San Francisco and never left. But not before trying his hand at acting.

Graham reportedly had talent as an actor, and in the early '60s he hoped to make a Hollywood connection by driving Buddy

Poster by Wes Wilson with photo by Herb Greene, 1966

Hackett's Mercedes and golf clubs from New York to Los Angeles in three days; when Graham arrived and was told he wouldn't be handing the car off to Hackett directly, he and a friend drove the car to hang out in Carmel for a couple of days, then continued on to San Francisco and spent the night at Rita's house before heading back to Los Angeles, where he left Hackett's car in a lot near 20th Century Fox. Graham's acting career went about as well, though the story is illustrative of two important facets of Graham's personality: Grim determination and a short fuse.

Graham is of course best known as the impresario behind Bill Graham Presents, which produced shows in legendary halls in the Bay Area and beyond, especially during the second half of the '60s, when his name was synonymous with the San Francisco Sound. Graham's reach extended beyond that fabled era and those storied halls; in the early '70s, sensing the tectonic shift in how the premier bands were presenting themselves, Graham shuttered the **Fillmore West (10 South Van Ness Ave., San Francisco)** in favor of the much larger **Winterland Ballroom (2000 Post St., San Francisco).** He also began producing a series of large scale outdoor concerts at **Oakland-Alameda County Coliseum (7000 Coliseum Way, Oakland)** in 1973, which ran nearly every year through 1992, the year after Graham's death. But Graham might never have gotten into concert promotion if not for his involvement with the San Francisco Mime Troupe (SFMT).

The SFMT which celebrated its 60th anniversary in 2019, mounts annual productions of political satire, which it performs for free in various city parks. From the beginning, the SFMT didn't actually perform mime, using elements of Commedia dell'arte and other forms of theater to create something new and radical. The SFMT began running into trouble with the Department of Recreation & Parks in 1962 after just two performances of The Dowry in Washington Square Park, a production directed by the troupe's founder, R. G. Davis. The following year, the city ruled that permits to perform in its parks could be revoked if a performance was deemed offensive or unsuitable for children. On August 7, 1965, Davis was arrested by police at the beginning of the fourth performance of Il Candelaio by Giordano Bruno; Davis was charged with performing without a park permit. The fracas received considerable press coverage. Music promoter Chet Helms said the arrest followed a meeting of the SFMT about their financial issues and was instigated by the troupe's then-business manager, Bill Graham.

S.F. MIME TROUPE
APPEAL II
FOR CONTINUED ARTISTIC FREEDOM IN THE PARKS
DANCE-CONCERT
═══ WITH ═══
JEFFERSON AIRPLANE   JOHN HANDY QUINTET   SAM THOMAS & THE GENTLEMEN'S BAND

THE MYSTERY TREND   THE GREAT SOCIETY
AND MANY OTHER FRIENDS

FRIDAY, DECEMBER 10
9 P.M. TILL ?
FILLMORE AUDITORIUM
FILLMORE & GEARY STREETS
DONATIONS - $1.50   INFORMATION: GA 1-1984

"I felt that it was wrong to provoke a political confrontation for purely financial reasons," said Helms in *Bill Graham: My Life Inside Rock and Out.* "But it did get attention."

Held in the **San Francisco Mime Troupe's loft (924 Howard St., San Francisco)** on November 6, 1965, the first benefit, called an "Appeal Party," included appearances by Jefferson Airplane, the Fugs, Lawrence Ferlinghetti, the John Handy Quintet, and "others who care," and was a smash, with lines to get in encircling the block. Graham quickly began devising a second appeal party, which he booked for December 10 at **Fillmore Auditorium (1805 Geary Blvd., San Francisco).** This time around it was called a "Dance-Concert," with a repeat performance by Jefferson Airplane, the Great Society, Sam Thomas and the Gentlemen's Band, the Mystery Trend, and the newly rechristened Grateful Dead, who'd played their first gig since dumping "the Warlocks" less than a week earlier. A third and final Graham-produced SFMT appeal party was held, again at Fillmore Auditorium, on January 14, 1966. Many

of the same artists from the second fundraiser performed at the third, only this time the top of the poster read "Bill Graham Presents," a clear sign that he'd already set himself on a course he would follow for the rest of his life.

Graham's decision to establish his own production outfit and theater proved prescient; the growing local rock scene was fractured, playing wherever and whenever they could. With Fillmore Auditorium the scene had its own temple, one which at least at first was shared with the Family Dog, a much looser collective who were also producing shows. Graham splintered the relationship following a three-night stand at the Fillmore by the Paul Butterfield Blues Band on March 25–27, 1966. After witnessing the impact of the performances, Graham contacted the group's manager Albert Grossman to make a deal to promote the next Paul Butterfield Blues Band performances in San Francisco. Helms of the Family Dog accused Graham of going behind their back, but Graham—who viewed the Family Dog as too loose and unprofessional—retorted with a piece of advice: "Get up early."

"He never forgot that," said Graham in his memoir. "I never forgot it. Chet *never* got up early. And what I really meant had nothing to do with *when* you got up. It really meant, no matter what time you get up, use your time to work."

Graham employed a similar tactic when racial tensions rose across the city and the nation following the assassination of Dr. Martin Luther King, Jr., on April 4, 1968, literally going the extra mile over concerns about maintaining a business in an auditorium located in a largely Black neighborhood that catered to a predominately white clientele. Around that time, a six-month experiment involving a self-run venue by a collective including the Grateful Dead, Jefferson Airplane, Quicksilver Messenger Service, and Big Brother and the Holding Company was limping to an end. **The**

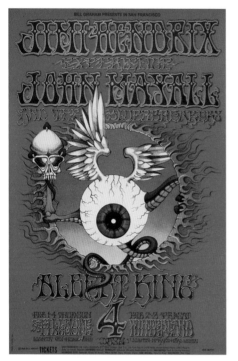

Poster by Rick Griffin, 1968

Carousel Ballroom (10 South Van Ness Ave., San Francisco) was about to become available. Worried he might not be able to make a profit at the Fillmore Auditorium any longer, Graham got up early.

Graham was already bicoastal by then, having opened the Fillmore East in New York City with a concert by Big Brother and the Holding Company, Tim Buckley, and Albert King on March 8, 1968. He knew the competition would be fierce for the lease on the Carousel Ballroom, so Graham flew to Ireland to meet with its owner, Bill Fuller. According to Graham, the pair came to an agreement on the terms of a three-year lease while downing a bottle of bourbon. Graham closed Fillmore Auditorium with a run of shows by Creedence Clearwater Revival, Steppenwolf, and It's a Beautiful Day on July 4, 1968, and he opened the Fillmore West the next night with the start of a three-

night stand by the Butterfield Blues Band, Ten Years After, and Truth.

Graham never attempted to renew the lease on the Fillmore West; by mid-1971 he'd already been hosting larger shows at Winterland for years and sensed that popular bands had begun realizing they could make more money with fewer gigs in bigger halls. The Fillmore West closed on July 4, 1971, with performances by Creedence Clearwater Revival, Santana, and Tower of Power.

Graham closed Winterland with a marathon show on New Year's Eve 1978, which he opened by flying in on a gigantic joint suspended by wires from which he threw actual joints into the crowd below. The concert was headlined by the Grateful Dead, the Blues Brothers, and New Riders of the Purple Sage. That year

Poster by Wes Wilson, 1966

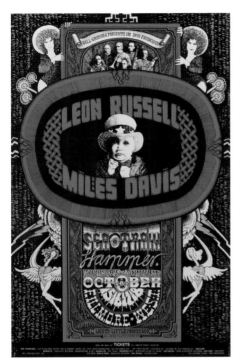

Poster by Norman Orr, 1970

Winterland had already seen the new rock begin supplanting the '60s San Francisco Sound, with shows by the Sex Pistols, Tom Petty and the Heartbreakers, Elvis Costello and the Attractions, Patti Smith, Ramones, and Bruce Springsteen.

While Bill Graham Productions remained active in the 13 years before Graham's tragic death in a helicopter crash on October 25, 1991, he no longer had a clear base of operations. In the early '80s, Graham bought the **Old Waldorf (444 Battery St., San Francisco)** and **Wolfgang's (901 Columbus Ave., San Francisco)**, and he booked regular gigs elsewhere, like the **Kabuki (1881 Post St., San Francisco)**, but for many the period between his start at the Fillmore Auditorium and his closing Winterland is viewed as his heyday.

Over the course of his professional career, Graham butted heads with performers over perceived unprofessionalism. He was sometimes viewed as a greedy square and stuffed shirt in the late '60s by musicians and music lovers, most of whom he was at least a decade older than. Graham was sometimes knocked as a monopolist throughout his life by business rivals and others. But Laughter, Love and Music, a free tribute concert to his life held in Golden Gate Park on November 3, 1991, drew hundreds of thousands of people with a bill including many performers who cut their teeth at the Fillmore and other Graham-linked venues.

The City of San Francisco paid Graham the ultimate tribute in 1992, renaming San Francisco Civic Auditorium the **Bill Graham Civic Auditorium (99 Grove St., Pacific Motor Trucking Company San Francisco)**. Graham had never produced a show there.

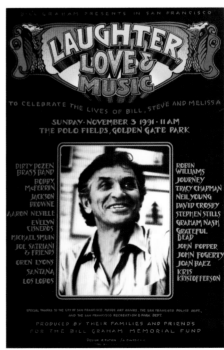

Poster by Randy Tuten and Arlene Owseichik, 1991

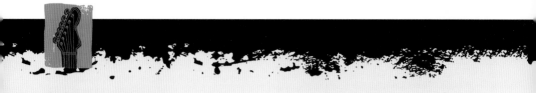

MORE BILL GRAHAM

323 Locust St., San Francisco: Prior to relocating to San Francisco for good in the early '60s, Graham would rent a guest house at 323 Locust.

Pacific Motor Trucking Company (110 Market St., San Francisco): During one of his early months-long visits to San Francisco, Graham worked as a statistician and timekeeper for Pacific Motor Trucking. When he wasn't in the field dealing with payroll matters, Graham spent his time in the company's Market Street office.

Mel's Drive In (3355 Geary Blvd., San Francisco): During the early Fillmore Auditorium days, Graham and some of his associates would stop by Mel's on Geary for a late night bite.

Fillmore Records Office (1550 Market St., San Francisco): Bill Graham set up shop on the third floor of this building where he ran Fillmore Records and San Francisco Records, which were cofounded with Brian Rohan and David Rubinson.

Bill Graham Presents Offices (201 11th St., San Francisco): In the '80s, Bill Graham Presents was headquartered in a building at 201 11th Street. In late April 1985, Graham penned an open letter opposing President Ronald Reagan's planned visit to a military cemetery in Bitburg, Germany, which counted among its interred members of the Waffen-SS. By then, Reagan had responded to worldwide criticism by adding a visit to the Bergen-Belsen concentration camp, but not canceling the trip to Bitburg ensured the criticism would continue. Graham's letter, which also announced a rally in Union Square, closed with the address of Bill Graham Presents. A fire which subsequently gutted the 11th Street offices, burning up much of Graham's saved memorabilia, was deemed arson by investigators.

Bill Graham's 1333 Columbus (1333 Columbus Ave., San Francisco): Opened in the midst of Graham's Winterland era, Bill Graham's 1333 Columbus was a T-shirt and poster store that also sold tickets to all Graham-promoted events.

Masada (800 Corte Madera Ave., Corte Madera): Home from 1978 until his death. Named Masada after the Israeli mountain fort. The house has since been razed and a new home built on the property.

HAIGHT-ASHBURY

BIRTH OF BLUE CHEER
369 Haight St.

Partly named after a potent form of LSD, Blue Cheer's loud, feedback-filled blues came together in 1967 in bass guitarist and vocalist Dickie Peterson's Lower Haight apartment. Perhaps best known as a power trio after being whittled down from a six-piece ahead of their combustible 1968 debut album *Vincebus Eruptum*, which included a fiery cover of Eddie Cochran's "Summertime Blues," Blue Cheer have often been cited as forebears of heavy metal. Though not as widely reported, the Blue Cheer apartment was raided by police on October 2, 1967, the same day members of the Grateful Dead were busted in their house at 710 Ashbury Street.

Before moving out to Novato after their bust, Blue Cheer rehearsed at **Joynt Ventures**, a head shop on **24th Street** in the Mission run by poster artist and former Hells Angel Allan "Gut" Terk, who also managed the group.

GROOVE MERCHANT RECORDS
687 Haight St.

Longtime Lower Haight record shop Groove Merchant specializes in new and used soul, funk, hip-hop, rock, and jazz vinyl, but owner Chris Veltri is also a connoisseur of historic music ephemera, frequently trading in posters, flyers, books, buttons, and other sought-after promotional materials from bygone eras. Groove Merchant opened in 1989 within Dick Vivian's **Rooky Ricardo's (448 Haight St.)**, another longtime destination for vinyl heads which originally stocked only 45s, but has since expanded to include LPs. Both shops are still going strong and are essential stops for record lovers.

THE INDEPENDENT/THE HALF NOTE CLUB/THE VIS/ THE KENNEL CLUB/CRASH PALACE/THE JUSTICE LEAGUE
628 Divisadero St.

Few local venues have had a history as convoluted as The Independent, which celebrated its 15th year of existence in 2019. Owned by Allen Scott, The Independent is one of the most popular music spots in San Francisco, hosting a wide range of genres in a space that for many years focused more specifically on one style of music or another.

The Half Note Club was opened in 1967 by San Francisco 49er Kermit Alexander and local businessman Herman Warren, primarily showcasing jazz artists, including Miles Davis and Thelonious Monk. After Warren sold the property in the '80s, it had a brief life as The Vis before opening as The Kennel Club in 1987, with bands like Nirvana, Dinosaur Jr., and Jane's.

QUICKSILVER MESSENGER SERVICE

They may not have fared as well commercially as some of their '60s compatriots, but Quicksilver Messenger Service were an essential contributor to the San Francisco scene, and for many, a defining band of the psychedelic era. Intertwining eclectic elements of rock, jazz, blues, and even classical, they were known throughout the Bay Area for their blistering live performances highlighted by the guitar interplay of Gary Duncan and John Cipollina.

Formed in the summer of 1965 and forged in a series of intense rehearsals over the ensuing months at **The Matrix (3138 Fillmore St., San Francisco)**, QMS had its public debut on January 15, 1966, at the fabled **Muir Beach Tavern and Lodge (Muir Beach, Marin ⊘)**. By the following month they'd become regulars at the **Fillmore (1805 Geary Blvd., San Francisco)** sharing the bill with the likes of Jefferson Airplane, Big Brother and the Holding Company, the Charlatans, and the Great Society.

Like several others in the scene, a performance at the 1967 Monterey Pop Festival (2004 Fairground Rd., Monterey) led to a record deal and their debut album *Quicksilver Messenger Service*, was released in 1968. By then, their lineup consisted of Cipollina (guitar), Duncan (guitar, vocals), David Freiberg (bass, vocals), and Greg Elmore (drums). Their follow-up, *Happy Trails*, released the following year and considered by many to be the group's masterpiece, consisted of live performances collected from the **Fillmore West (10 S. Van Ness Ave., San Francisco)**, the Fillmore East in New York, and live in-studio at **Golden State Recorders (665 Harrison St., San Francisco)**.

Nicky Hopkins, the melodic pianist known largely for his work with the Rolling Stones,

Poster by Wes Wilson, 1966

Poster by Victor Moscoso, 1966

Poster by Victor Moscoso, 1966

joined them for their third album, *Shady Grove*, recorded at **Wally Heider Studios (245 Hyde St., San Francisco)** and released in December 1969. They were joined in 1970 by Dino Valenti, who assumed the lead vocals and wrote most of the material for their fourth album *Just for Love*, released that summer, including "Fresh Air," their most successful single.

Valenti had rehearsed with the group early on, but was busted for drug possession and did a stretch in Folsom State Prison. He attempted a solo career and tried forming another group upon his release, but ultimately threw in with QMS instead. He is typically credited with corralling the group's jam-band proclivities and transitioning them toward a more classic rock sound. The band also relocated to Hawaii, and

Cipollina and Hopkins left the group not long afterward. Quicksilver soldiered on for several more years before folding in 1979. Freiberg, who became a member of Jefferson Starship, reunited with Duncan in 2009 and toured again as QMS with a squad of backing musicians.

Addiction, and the Jesus Lizard all taking the stage. In 1993, The Kennel Club hosted the first-ever Noise Pop Festival, founded by Kevin Arnold and Jordan Kurland; Noise Pop remains one of the Bay Area's most popular festivals, taking place in numerous venues across the city.

The Kennel Club shut down in 1994, and the space was briefly known as the Crash Palace, with only a handful of shows including the Brian Jonestown Massacre happening before it too went under.

628 Divisadero had a three-year break from presenting live music before Michael O'Connor reestablished the space as the Justice League, which largely focused on hip-hop and electronica and featured performances by De La Soul, the Jungle Brothers, The Streets, and Fatboy Slim.

The Independent is the first venue at 628 Divisadero since the Half Note to survive more than a few years, and it's still going strong. Artists like Sonic Youth, LCD Soundsystem, Beck, Green Day, and The National are among those who've played the Independent over the past 15 years.

UNIVERSITY OF SAN FRANCISCO
2130 Fulton St.
On April 7, 1967, Jefferson Airplane and Buffalo Springfield played the gymnasium at the University of San Francisco as a fundraiser for nearby **St. Ignatius High School (222 Stanyan St., San Francisco)**. Two years later, the freshly renamed St. Ignatius College Preparatory moved to its current location, 2001 37th Avenue in San Francisco's Sunset District.

FUNKY JACK'S
142 Central Ave.
"Funky Jack" Leahy opened a recording studio in the basement here in 1969. Steve Miller recorded vocals for "Fly Like an Eagle" here. Closed in 1979 a few years after Leahy and his

wife were attacked in their bed by an axe-wielding handyman who they let sleep in the basement; Leahy's secretary was stabbed to death moments earlier. The building was briefly taken over by the Jimi Hendrix Electric Church in the '70s, a short-lived museum run by a fan.

HERB GREENE'S STUDIO
828 Baker St.
Photographer Herb Greene took many iconic photographs of San Francisco musicians here in his third floor apartment, including the Grateful Dead and Jefferson Airplane. Several of the photos, including the album cover for *Surrealistic Pillow*, feature an odd hieroglyphic mural which was drawn on the wall in felt-tip pen by roommate Bill Brach, who studied Egyptology at San Francisco State. When Brach moved out Greene left the mural intact and used the room as a studio.

828 Baker Street

COUNTRY JOE AND THE FISH

THE FISH TANK
612 Ashbury St.

By the time Country Joe and the Fish made their way across the Bay to Haight-Ashbury, they'd already established themselves back in Berkeley with a wild, fiercely political, embryonic jug-punk sound, first as the duo of Country Joe McDonald and Barry "the Fish" Melton, and then as a fully fledged electric band. Members of the group would settle in the heart of the scene at **612 Ashbury**, in a house that became known as "The Fish Tank."

Country Joe and the Fish stuck around in Berkeley long enough to record an eponymous EP and a debut LP, *Electric Music for the Mind and Body*, at **Sierra Sound Laboratories (1741 Alcatraz Ave., Berkeley)**; the latter, and its followup, *I-Feel-Like-I'm-Fixin'-to-Die*, were released in 1967, the year Country Joe and other members of the group moved into the Fish Tank. McDonald reportedly settled in San Francisco a year earlier at **1101 Masonic Street**.

Back in Berkeley, Country Joe and the Fish had carved out their sound playing numerous shows at clubs like the **Questing Beast (previously the Cabale) (2504 San Pablo Ave.)** and the **Jabberwock (2901 Telegraph Ave.)**, playing for $5 and food. Members of the group possibly lived above the Jabberwock in the mid-'60s before resettling

in San Francisco. The building that housed the Jabberwock was demolished in 1967.

Beset by a fractured lineup and on the verge of a split, Country Joe and the Fish closed out the '60s with one of the era's most iconic

performances at the Woodstock Music & Art Fair in Bethel, New York. Though the full band played, it was McDonald's solo performance of "The Fish Cheer/I-Feel-Like-I'm-Fixin'-to-Die Rag," with its timely anti-war message and reworked opening ("F-I-S-H" became "F-U-C-K") that left a lasting impression. Country Joe and the Fish split less than a year later.

McDonald, Melton, and various other members of the group would go on to play together in various configurations, with the celebrated 1967 lineup reuniting in 1977 to record the aptly titled *Reunion* in the studios at **Fantasy Records (2600 Tenth St., Berkeley)**, their first time recording in their hometown since their debut album. Melton carved out a career in law, working in the Mendocino County Public Defender's Office, the Office of the (California) State Public Defender, eventually serving as the public defender of Yolo County, California. McDonald continued playing live and releasing records, culminating in a celebratory farewell performance at **The Chapel (777 Valencia St., San Francisco)** on December 22, 2017.

THE SPRECKELS MANSION
737 Buena Vista Ave. West
Built in 1897 by Richard Spreckels, the nephew of sugar magnate Adolph Spreckels, former residents included journalist Ambrose Bierce and writer Jack London, who wrote *White Fang* here. In the mid-'60s, Gene Estabrook ran a small 8-track recording studio here. Quicksilver Messenger Service and the Steve Miller Band recorded material for the film *Revolution* in Estabrook's studio. It was later owned by actor and activist Danny Glover.

GRAHAM NASH HOUSE
731 Buena Vista Ave. West
Former Hollies guitarist and singer Graham Nash owned this house in the early '70s, a fertile period where he was making beautiful music within and without Crosby, Stills, Nash & Young. Singer Bobby McFerrin later owned the house.

BIRTHPLACE OF THE ACE OF CUPS
1480 Waller St.
Legendary all-female psych-rock group the Ace of Cups came together in a second floor apartment at **1480 Waller Street**, where bass guitarist Mary Gannon and keyboardist Marla Hunt lived. The group's "Waller Street Blues" told a tale of bohemian squalor within these walls. The Ace of Cups drifted apart into the early '70s, but they reunited nearly 50 years after they began, releasing their first-ever album, *Ace of Cups*, in 2018.

JAX MUSIC
1458 Haight St.
The Jacksons made an in-store appearance here on Saturday afternoon, December 18, 1976, to promote their eponymous new album *The Jacksons*, their first after leaving Motown and the name Jackson 5 behind. Hundreds of fans turned up and some reportedly shattered the storefront glass in their zeal to meet the visiting superstars. The Jacksons had just performed a group of shows at the **Circle Star Theatre (2 Circle Star Way, San Carlos).**

JIMI HENDRIX HOUSE
1524-A Haight St.
Dubbed the Red House after being painted in tribute by a fan, Hendrix counted among his many crash pads around the world this place right in the thick of the Haight.

Mike Katz

THE PSYCHEDELIC SHOP
1535 Haight St.
Brothers Ron and Jay Thelin opened this pioneering store on January 3, 1966, in order to sell an eclectic assortment of wares, including posters, drug accoutrements, incense, and books that appealed to the burgeoning youthful Haight-Ashbury community. It evolved into a de facto hippie community center and soon inspired other similarly themed shops in the area. Not everyone was enamored with the shop, however, and it

was raided by police on November 15 for selling a book of poetry regarded as "obscene material." By the following year, the throngs of tourists and some questionable management practices had soured the Thelins on the business and the shop closed on October 6, 1967.

THE PRINT MINT
1542 Haight St.

This offshoot of the Berkeley institution established by Don and Alice Schencker opened in 1966, specializing in poster art by the major local artists including Rick Griffin, Victor Moscoso, and Stanley Mouse. It was also a publisher and outlet for underground comix featuring the works of Gilbert Shelton, Robert Crumb, S. Clay Wilson, and many others. The original offices of *The Oracle*, San Francisco's influential countercultural newspaper, were located in a back room here. The store lasted until December 1967.

STRAIGHT THEATER
1702 Haight St. ⊘

Former location of the Straight Theater, an old movie house turned into a hippie hangout and venue in 1967. The Grateful Dead used it as a rehearsal space before its July 1967 opening, and they played gigs there too. Big Brother and the Holding Company, Country Joe and the Fish, the Charlatans, and Quicksilver Messenger

Poster by Terre

THE ART OF THE POSTER

Throughout the intensely creative period of San Francisco's thriving '60s counterculture, graphic artists contributed by providing a visual representation of the unique vibe then emanating from the clubs and music halls. Traditionally, concert posters were often bland broadsheets with thick type and little to discern them from prizefight announcements. In the hands of a bevy of young Bay Area artists, however, the concert poster became an explosion of color, lettering, and design that matched the energy of the musicians and audience they represented.

Former studio of Alton Kelley and Stanley Mouse, 74 Henry Street

Inspired partly by the classic graphics of the art nouveau period and most likely by the consciousness expanding pharmaceuticals of the time, posters and handbills for shows at the **Avalon Ballroom (1244 Sutter St., San Francisco)**, **Fillmore Auditorium (1805 Geary Blvd., San Francisco)** and many other venues became ubiquitous in the Bay Area. Awash in psychedelic colors with (in some cases) nigh unreadable text, they have come to immortalize the performances they were created for, as evidenced by the several posters reproduced throughout this book.

The most prominent of the poster artists were the so-called Big Five, consisting of Rick Griffin, Alton Kelley, Victor Moscoso, Stanley Mouse, and Wes Wilson, who often collaborated

Poster by Wes Wilson, 1966

with one another and also established a distribution company, **Berkeley Bonaparte (1940A Bonita St., Berkeley)**, to manage the eventual nationwide demand for their work.

In addition to a printed mail order catalog, the works were also often available at local record stores and head shops throughout the Bay Area, as well as specialty locations like **The Print Mint (2494 Telegraph Ave., Berkeley & 1542 Haight St. San Francisco)**. Many of the artists ultimately branched out into other creative endeavors, including album covers, underground comix, and various other original graphics, including Rick Griffin's logo design for *Rolling Stone* magazine.

Today, the original posters and early reproductions command high prices on the collector market, befitting their status as highly sought-after works of art. More than concert announcements, they represent a unique blossoming of American creativity that conveys the spirit and the times in which they were produced.

Poster by Victor Moscoso and Rick Griffin, 1968

Service all played there on its opening weekend. Mickey Hart sat in with the Dead as a second drummer in September of that year, soon joining full time. It closed sometime in late 1968/early 1969, and was flattened by a wrecking ball a decade later.

NIGHTBREAK
1821 Haight St.
Nightbreak was a formative club for Chris Isaak, who would try out new material here ahead of his first and second album. Members of bands like Primus, Metallica and Faith No More would jam here, and '90s alt-rockers 4 Non Blondes also formed here.

THE I-BEAM
1748 Haight St.
Former location of the I-Beam, a massively important club in the old Masonic Temple. The club was originally a gay disco in the late '70s; its upstairs hall began hosting live music in 1980. Duran Duran, New Order, REM, the Cure,

Ramones, Jane's Addiction, the Replacements, Buzzcocks, Siouxsie and the Banshees, Living Colour, and Red Hot Chili Peppers were among the many, many groups that gigged here. Counting Crows played one of their earliest gigs at the club in 1991, one attended by several record company execs in town for a radio convention.

HAIGHT ASHBURY FREE CLINIC
558 Clayton St.
In operation from the mid-'60s through August 2019, the Haight Ashbury Free Clinic has likely seen to the medical needs of countless musicians and music fans. In 1974, former Beatle George Harrison visited the clinic and donated $66,000, his proceeds from his concert with Ravi Shankar the previous night at the Cow Palace. In 1989, members of Nirvana were reportedly treated here for the flu. The group supposedly named their debut album *Bleach* after the clinic's citywide campaign to get intravenous drug users to "bleach your works."

Mike Katz

AMOEBA MUSIC
1855 Haight St.
Founded in Berkeley in 1990, Amoeba Music has long since stretched its pseudopods across the bay into San Francisco, and much further south along the coast to Los Angeles. The Haight Street location opened in 1997 in the former Park Bowl bowling alley, retaining some of its cavernous character in the sunken sales floor, with rows of records and compact discs replacing the lanes.

In addition to boasting a colossal amount of music for sale, Amoeba also stocks everything from T-shirts, to gig-posters, books to movies, the latter of which can be found in a separate room. The Haight Street location has also hosted free live performances by Faith No More, Sleater-Kinney, Elvis Costello, Elliott Smith, Joe Strummer and the Mescaleros, and Flipper.

San Francisco's Amoeba Music is open seven days a week, including its popular trade counter, where a stack of records can net you a tidy sum in cash or store credit.

SID VICIOUS OD'S
32 Delmar St.
Though often erroneously cited as a residence of the Sex Pistols' bass guitarist, this was actually the home of Lamar St. John, one of the original San Francisco punks who'd traveled with friends to see the band at prior tour stops through the deep south. After the Sex Pistols' final show at **Winterland (2000 Post St., San Francisco ⊘)** on January 14, 1978, Sid Vicious stayed in town to party. The following day, Vicious was hanging around at St. John's apartment when he and a few others decided to get high. In an expanded 2006 edition of James Stark's 1992 book for RE/Search, *Punk '77: An Inside Look at the San Francisco Rock N' Roll Scene 1977*, St. John said that after the connection left the apartment, Vicious turned blue. Because of her close proximity to the **Haight Ashbury Free Clinic (558 Clayton St., San Francisco)**, St. John ran there for help.

"It was really sad," said St. John. "Like I just wanted to be his friend and everybody just wanted to fuck his brains out. This guy is just this young boy that doesn't know shit about shit and he is fuckin' blasted, you know, and stayed blasted the whole time."

Vicious survived a nonfatal overdose on Delmar Street, but would die from another OD in New York City a little over a year later.

TOM DONAHUE

The musical explosion that took place in San Francisco in the '60s was, like many seismic cultural events, dependent upon a confluence of several factors. The talent, of course, places to play and develop, sympathetic promoters, and most importantly, an audience that was on the same wavelength as the performers. Another element that was critical to embracing and disseminating the uniqueness of the San Francisco sound was the rise of FM radio, and Tom "Big Daddy" Donahue was its prime exponent.

Donahue arrived in San Francisco in 1961 after a successful 10-year run as a DJ at WIBG in Philadelphia. The recent spate of payola investigations in the northeast made job security somewhat tenuous, and his former colleague Bobby Mitchell encouraged the move westward to join him at KYA. In addition to being a popular top-40 AM DJ, Donahue partnered with Mitchell to promote local concerts, and opened a club, **Mother's Blues Club (430 Broadway, San Francisco)** in North Beach to feature local acts. The duo also launched a record label, **Autumn Records (70 Dorman St., San Francisco)** which released discs by Bay Area native Bobby Freeman ("C'mon and Swim") and the Beau Brummels, generally considered San Francisco's first nationally successful rock act, who released "Laugh, Laugh" and "Just a Little." Autumn's house producer was a young Sylvester Stewart, later known as Sly Stone. Another local group recorded by Autumn was the Great Society, featuring Grace Slick prior to her move to Jefferson Airplane, who released "Someone to Love" on Autumn's North Beach subsidiary label in 1966. The tune was

"BIG DADDY" TOM DONAHUE

later retitled "Somebody to Love" and became Jefferson Airplane's breakout hit the following year. Autumn Records, by that time, had shuttered with its assets sold to Warner Brothers. Also in 1966, Donahue produced the last ticketed Beatles concert on August 29 at **Candlestick Park**.

In November 1967, Donahue declared "AM Radio Is Dead and Its Rotting Corpse Is Stinking Up the Airwaves" in an article for the freshly launched *Rolling Stone* magazine. Shortly thereafter, he went to work for **KMPX 106.9 FM (50 Green St.)**, known primarily as a foreign language station, and introduced what came to be known as "free-form" or "underground" radio. He tended to ignore AM-friendly singles and instead featured album cuts and less commercial material. Donahue worked the 8 p.m. to midnight shift, which led into Larry Miller's program in the wee hours. Miller, who predated Donahue at the station, was already employing a similar philosophy to his on-air selections. When the Beatles' *Sgt. Pepper's* album was released it was played uninterrupted in its entirety. Significantly, Donahue also featured local area bands, such as Jefferson Airplane, the Grateful Dead, and Creedence Clearwater Revival well before they were embraced by the national audience. So successful was the new format that Donahue

and his wife Raechel were given the opportunity to reproduce the programming for KMPX's sister station in Pasadena, KPPC. For both stations, Donahue hired like-minded engineers and DJ's who would continue to refine the progressive format, including Edward Bear, Bob McClay, Abe "Voco" Keshishian, Sue Henderson, and Dusty Street.

As the station became more successful, its owners attempted to clamp down on some of the music choices to sell more lucrative commercial time, as well as curtailing the noncorporate culture of the station's personnel, leading to a strike on March 18, 1968. Local musicians, including the Grateful Dead, Blue Cheer, and Creedence, performed outside on a flatbed truck in support of the staff. Ultimately, Donahue and his team left the station and moved to classical station KSFR 94.9 FM, which was transformed to KSAN and continued the successful formatting pioneered at KMPX. The staff of KPPC in Pasadena also jumped ship—to KSAN's partner station KMET in Los Angeles. KSAN pushed and refined the progressive aspects of FM radio even further, extending the concept to news reporting and community involvement as well. Donahue became program manager in 1972, but was felled at the age of 46 by a heart attack in 1975.

By the late '70s KSAN was on the decline, and in 1980 it became a country music station. It later changed frequencies as KYLD, before reverting to its original frequency and the KSAN call letters in 1997, when it became a Classic Rock station.

Donahue as depicted in a Family Dog postcard by George Hunter and Jerry Wainwright, 1968

JEFFERSON AIRPLANE

Pictorial Press Ltd./Alamy

"The '60s were a time when people with electric guitars naively but nobly thought they could change the whole genetic code of aggression by writing a few good songs, and using volume to drown out the ever-present whistling arsenal."
—GRACE SLICK, *SOMEBODY TO LOVE*, 1998

Some artists have conflict thrust upon them, but Jefferson Airplane reveled in their role as subversives, and embraced their position as musical standard-bearers for San Francisco's psychedelic culture. As the first band from the new scene to achieve national recognition, Jefferson Airplane took its place at the point of the spear, singing and speaking openly about drugs, unromantic love, and sociopolitical engagement. Through a succession of landmark performances and groundbreaking albums, they made a lasting impact on both San Francisco and rock and roll history.

Folkies Marty Balin and Paul Kantner first conceived the new group when they met at **The Drinking Gourd (1898 Union St., San Francisco)** in 1965, a popular venue and meeting place for the folk community. Balin, then singing solo and with the popular Town Criers, already had considerable experience

under his belt, and knew an electric group would be a tough sell for North Beach establishments. With a group of investors he took over a defunct pizza parlor and created his own club, **The Matrix (3138 Fillmore St., San Francisco)** in the Marina. The club was aimed

JEFFERSON AIRPLANE LOVES YOU

squarely at the emerging folk-rock phenomenon, and the new Jefferson Airplane premiered there on August 13, 1965, quickly becoming San Francisco's premier electric folk-rock group when such a thing was still a fairly radical concept.

By the time they recorded their first album in 1966, *Jefferson Airplane Takes Off*, the group consisted of Balin (vocals), Kantner (guitar), Jorma Kaukonen (lead guitar), Jack Casady (bass), Skip Spence (drums), and Signe Anderson (vocals). Spence (later of Moby Grape) exited before its release and was replaced by Spencer Dryden. Balin and Anderson shared vocal duties, providing a soulful one-two combination that was relatively unique for a rock-oriented group. When Signe chose to devote time to her family and leave the group, Grace Slick, vocalist with the rival Great Society was brought on board. Importantly, Slick also added, via her songwriting, live performances, and often daring media appearances an element of confrontation that cemented the band's position as cultural provocateurs. Along with

Millions read about it in "LOOK"...
Their "Surrealistic Pillow" album is now Top 10...
"Pillow" features their current Top 10 single "Somebody to Love"...
Now, a second great single from the same sensational album:
"WHITE RABBIT"
b/w "Plastic Fantastic Lover" #9248
RCA VICTOR
The most trusted name in sound

her magnetic presence and searing vocals, Slick brought a couple of songs from her disintegrated former band that would prove fruitful for the now "classic" Jefferson Airplane lineup, "Somebody to Love" (written by brother-in-law Darby Slick) and her own composition, "White Rabbit." Both tunes would become big hits and propel the band's second album *Surrealistic Pillow* to international prominence in 1967, sounding the clarion for psychedelic rock and the San Francisco sound.

Even before the group became nationally successful, Jefferson Airplane was directly involved in the development of the Bay Area music scene, working with emerging promoters and making pioneering appearances at venues not previously welcoming to rock bands. On October 16, 1965, they played the first show promoted by Family Dog at **Longshoremen's Hall (400 North Point St., San Francisco)** along with the Great Society and the Charlatans in what was billed as a 'tribute to Dr. Strange,' the Marvel Comics character. A few weeks later on November 6, they played the first show promoted by Bill Graham, a benefit for the San Francisco Mime Troupe at the **Calliope Warehouse Ballroom (924 Howard St., San Francisco ⊘)** which included the Fugs, Lawrence Ferlinghetti, and Allen Ginsberg. The second benefit followed on December 6 at the **Fillmore Auditorium (1805 Geary Blvd., San Francisco),** Graham's first production at that legendary venue. From February 4–6, the Airplane performed along with Quicksilver Messenger Service at Graham's first commercial shows there. In the ensuing years, the Fillmore became a hugely critical live venue not only for Airplane, but for the entire San Francisco scene.

Jefferson Airplane became the first electric group to play the **Berkeley Folk Festival** on July 3–4, 1966 **(Pauley Ballroom, 2495 Bancroft Way & Greek Theatre, 2001 Gayley Rd, Berkeley).** The gig was arranged by Marty

Balin, much to the ire of then-manager Matthew Katz. Katz was trying to direct the group toward the teenage pop market, which the band strongly resisted, demanding to be regarded as serious musicians. On September 17 they appeared at the **Monterey Jazz Festival**

(Monterey County Fairgrounds, 2004 Fairground Rd, Monterey), which traditionally featured an afternoon blues set, but this year included both the Airplane and the Paul Butterfield Blues Band.

As champions of the consciousness-expanding properties of LSD, the group frequently tossed fistfuls of the drug to their audiences as though they were jelly beans. When California declared LSD illegal in October 1966, the countercultural Haight-Ashbury community responded with **A Gathering of Tribes—A Human Be-In (Polo Grounds, Golden Gate Park)** on January 14, 1967, a wide-ranging celebration of community, higher consciousness, and music. Jefferson Airplane, the Grateful Dead, Blue Cheer, Big Brother and

HOT TUNA

Jorma Kaukonen and Jack Casady were making music together long before their involvement with Jefferson Airplane, when both were high school students in Washington, DC. Formed during a 1969 break for Airplane, Hot Tuna was an opportunity to reexplore their acoustic country and blues roots. They played a few clubs in the Bay Area, particularly **The Matrix (3138 Fillmore St., San Francisco)** before opening some dates for the reactivated Jefferson Airplane. In 1970 they released their first album, *Hot Tuna*, recorded live during a residency at **New Orleans House (1505 San Pablo Ave, Berkeley)**. In succeeding years they toured in both electric and acoustic forms, usually

playing more intimate spaces and releasing several acclaimed albums. In 2019 the duo celebrated their 50th year together.

Album cover by Grace Slick

the Holding Company, and others provided the soundtrack while Timothy Leary, Allen Ginsberg, and other luminaries addressed the assembled masses. Media coverage of the event would inspire hippies and other disaffected young people from around the country to converge on San Francisco for the vaunted Summer of Love shortly thereafter.

By June 1967, Jefferson Airplane had a hit single ("Somebody to Love" reached #5 on the *Billboard Hot 100*) and a hit album. At the outset of what became the Summer of Love, the group appeared on June 11 at the **KFRC Fantasy Fair and Magic Mountain Festival (Cushing Memorial Amphitheater, Mt Tamalpais State Park)**, a two-day event cited as the first multiday outdoor rock festival in America. Other participating artists included the Doors, Canned Heat, the Charlatans, the Byrds, Tim Buckley, Captain Beefheart, and Country Joe and the Fish. The festival had been scheduled for the previous week, but was

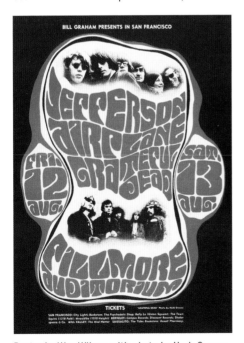

Poster by Wes Wilson with photo by Herb Greene, 1967

delayed due to rain. The following week found the group in Monterey again for the one and only **Monterey Pop Festival (Monterey County Fairgrounds, 2004 Fairground Rd, Monterey)**. The now-mythic three-day event (June 16–18) and the film compiled from it only enhanced the already growing national reputation of Jefferson Airplane and helped propel the careers of Janis Joplin, Jimi Hendrix, and the Who, among many others. As Grace Slick recalled in *Somebody to Love*, "it's the only festival I can think of that was excellent in every way. . . . I felt lucky to be there, observing one of the great examples of human celebration."

Only a week later on June 21, with the Summer of Love in full swing, Jefferson Airplane appeared at the **Summer Solstice Festival (Speedway Meadows;** now **Old Hellman Hollow, Golden Gate Park)**, an event organized by the Diggers that also featured the Grateful Dead, Big Brother and the Holding Company, and others.

In an attempt to create a new alternative concert venue, the band partnered with Quicksilver Messenger Service and the Grateful Dead in January 1968 to take over the **Carousel Ballroom (10 South Van Ness Ave., San Francisco)**. Virtually every important San Francisco band performed there, including the three partners, but the enterprise proved to be a financial quagmire and after six months it was taken over by Bill Graham and renamed the **Fillmore West**. As Paul Kantner stated to *Rolling Stone* in 1970, "It wasn't a business trip as much as setting up a place where we could have fun."

In May 1968 the group paid $73,000 for the distinctive three-story mansion with Corinthian columns at **2400 Fulton Street** at the northeastern corner of Golden Gate Park. Originally built in 1904 for a lumber magnate, it had survived the 1906 earthquake and most of the 20th century before Jefferson Airplane

Poster by Alton Kelley, 1968

made it their headquarters. They built a recording studio and rehearsal space in the basement, business offices on the second floor, and living quarters for each member of the

group on the top, though in truth the entire band never lived there all at the same time. It was even painted black for a while. Paul Kantner reportedly kept the largest bedroom and stayed the longest. The house was also home to several cats, a pool table, electric chair, and a torture rack that held, at various times, a stuffed walrus and David Crosby. From here the band presided over San Francisco in decadent style, hosting countless parties with friends and fellow musicians. Spencer Dryden even had his wedding here, officiated by manager Bill Thompson. The rehearsal space in their new home proved useful for the making of *Volunteers*, their first album recorded in San Francisco at the new **Wally Heider Studios (245 Hyde St., San Francisco)**. In 1987, the address became the title of a Jefferson Airplane compilation album.

On December 6, 1969, Jefferson Airplane appeared at the **Altamont Free Concert (Altamont Raceway, 17001 North Midway Rd, Tracy)** with the Rolling Stones, Santana, Flying Burrito Brothers, and Crosby, Stills, Nash &

2400 Fulton Street

JEFFERSON STARSHIP

Jefferson Starship has its origins in Paul Kantner's 1970 *Blows Against the Empire* science fiction concept album, credited to "Paul Kantner and Jefferson Starship," recorded at **Pacific High Studios (60 Brady St., San Francisco)** and **Wally Heider Studios (245 Hyde St., San Francisco)**. Members of the Airplane, the Grateful Dead, Quicksilver Messenger Service, and Crosby, Stills & Nash appear on the album, along with several others.

The actual Jefferson Starship group formed four years later for *Dragon Fly*, consisting of Kantner, Grace Slick, Papa John Creach, Quicksilver veteran David Freiberg, Pete Sears, Craig Chaquico, and drummer John Barbata, who also played on the final Airplane album in 1972. Marty Balin contributed a single tune, the extended ballad "Caroline." He returned as a full-fledged member on the succeeding album *Red Octopus*, and produced one of the biggest hits in Airplane/Starship history, "Miracles."

Jefferson Starship in various forms released several more hit albums well into the '80s with both Balin and Slick in and out of the lineup, eventually eclipsing Airplane in sales and producing several hit singles, something that eluded the original group. When Kantner left in 1984, he took the "Jefferson" with him, leaving the remaining group as Starship. Their hitmaking continued unabated, including the notorious "We Built This City." When Paul Kantner relaunched Jefferson Starship in the '90s he brought along some of his former Airplane cohorts, including Marty Balin, Jack Casady, and Grace Slick for guest appearances. Kantner continued to perform and tour well into the 21st century until his death in 2016. Jefferson Starship continues today under the stewardship of David Freiberg.

days before the scheduled event. The concert proved to be a disaster, marked by four deaths, including a stabbing during the Stones's performance by Hells Angels hired as security. Jefferson Airplane didn't emerge unscathed either, as Marty Balin was knocked unconscious during a scuffle with the Angels during their set. What had been conceived as a West Coast Woodstock has instead come to be regarded as one of rock's darkest days. Spencer Dryden left the group shortly thereafter, with Marty Balin departing in the fall of 1970. A reconfigured Jefferson Airplane soldiered on, adding drummer Joey Covington and fiddler Papa John Creach.

Young. The Grateful Dead were slated to appear as well, but sensed the bad vibes and split. The concert was originally slated for Golden Gate Park, but the political landscape had changed by late 1969 and the city was uncooperative. As shown in the documentary film *Gimme Shelter*, what followed was a series of desperate negotiations that settled on a venue only

Like many great bands, Jefferson Airplane was composed of disparate creative personalities that ultimately splintered, broke apart, and regrouped in new forms, producing notable offspring, including Jefferson Starship, Hot Tuna, KBC Band, and a slew of solo projects. There was even a reunion of sorts with the classic Jefferson Airplane in 1989.

MORE JEFFERSON AIRPLANE

NOTEWORTHY LIVE PERFORMANCES

Coffee and Confusion (1339 Grant Ave., San Francisco): Originally known as the Fox & Hound, Marty Balin, Paul Kantner, and Jorma Kaukonen all played this North Beach folk music venue in the early '60s.

Coffee Gallery (1353 Grant Ave., San Francisco): Another focal point for the Bay Area folk community played and frequented by Jefferson Airplane personnel before the formation of the group. Additionally, the Great Society with Grace Slick made its debut here on October 16, 1965.

Palace Hotel (2 New Montgomery St., San Francisco): On June 6, 1966, Jefferson Airplane was booked to play a fundraiser for the California Republican Party, which they deeply

Poster by Stanley Mouse and Alton Kelley, 1966

resented, and manager Matthew Katz was dumped shortly thereafter. Significantly, it was Spencer Dryden's first gig with the band.

Avalon Ballroom (1244 Sutter St., San Francisco): On July 22 and 23, 1966, Jefferson Airplane (with Signe Anderson) played two dates with the Great Society (with Grace Slick) here, the Family Dog's showcase venue and main competitor to Bill Graham's Fillmore. Graham had been an early supporter of the Airplane and was irate, accusing them of disloyalty. The group made him their manager for a time afterward.

Fillmore Auditorium (1805 Geary Blvd., San Francisco): The Airplane played three weekend gigs on October 14, 15, and 16, 1966. By then Signe had agreed to leave the group, and Grace Slick had accepted the job as her replacement, carefully learning the songs and watching from the wings. Signe didn't turn up for the Sunday show, so Grace made her impromptu debut with the band. As she explains in her memoir, *Somebody to Love*: ". . . I was scared shitless. . . . What terrified me was not the fear that I lacked the talent, or even that I lacked knowledge of the material. . . . My problem was that I detested performing without lots of rehearsals, without meticulous preparation. I'm still that way."

San Francisco Civic Auditorium (99 Grove St., San Francisco): Grace Slick made her officially scheduled debut with the band on October 19, 1966, at Fol de Rol Goes Pop!!, presented by the San Francisco Opera Guild.

Basin Street West (401 Broadway, San Francisco): The band played a two-week residency at what was ostensibly a jazz and R&B club from January 11–12, 1967, just prior to the release of *Surrealistic Pillow*. They shared a bill with jazz great Dizzy Gillespie.

Winterland Ballroom (2000 Post St., San Francisco ⊘): Jack Casady made a guest appearance on October 10, 1968, with the Jimi Hendrix Experience, playing bass on "Killing Floor." The material appeared many years later on Hendrix's *Live at Winterland* in 1987. He appeared again with Jimi on April 27, 1969, at the **Oakland-Alameda County Arena (7000 Coliseum Way, Oakland)** for a rendition of "Voodoo Child (Slight Return)" which appears on the 1998 Hendrix album *Live at the Oakland Coliseum.*

Family Dog on the Great Highway (660 Great Highway, San Francisco ⊘): Jefferson Airplane played the premier performance at this venue along the beach on June 13, 1969, after The Family Dog lost its lease at the Avalon Ballroom. The show was recorded for KSAN and has been heavily bootlegged. On February 4, 1970, the group filmed a TV special *A Night at the Family Dog* with the Grateful Dead and Santana for Ralph Gleason and KQED that aired April 27.

Jefferson Airplane's Farewell Performance: Until their 1989 reunion tour, the final show took place on September 22, 1972, at the **Winterland Ballroom (2000 Post St., San Francisco ⊘).** By this time, nearly all the individual members had solo projects or new groups in the works and were relieved to close the book on Airplane. Marty Balin, who had left the band two years prior, made a surprise encore performance of "You Wear Your Dresses Too Short." It appears as the last track of the *Jefferson Airplane Loves You* boxed set.

KBC Band: After Paul Kantner left Jefferson Starship he joined forces with Marty Balin and Jack Casady, along with Slick Aguilar (guitar), Tim Gorman (keyboards), Keith Crossan (guitar, sax), and Darrell Verdusco (drums) for this well-received but short-lived group, which released one self-titled album in 1985. For their November 27, 1985, gig at the **Fillmore Auditorium (1805 Geary Blvd., San Francisco)** they were joined by Signe Anderson and Spencer Dryden for renditions of "It's No Secret" and "Plastic Fantastic Lover."

The Cabale (2504 San Pablo Ave., Berkeley): Both Marty Balin and Paul Kantner played this popular early '60s folk music coffee house establishment on multiple occasions.

Cow Palace (2600 Geneva Ave., Daly City): Jefferson Airplane appeared on June 24, 1966, at a KFRC Summer Spectacular which featured the Beach Boys, the Lovin' Spoonful, the Byrds, Neil Diamond, and Sir Douglas Quintet, among others. They returned here on July 26 with Sopwith Camel, the Standells, and the McCoys in support of the Rolling Stones. The Airplane reportedly snuck Jerry Garcia in as a member of their crew so he could see the Stones.

Harmon Gymnasium (115 Haas Pavilion, Berkeley): As the Airplane continued to evolve as an electric folk-rock band, the decision was made to replace bassist Bob Harvey, who was more in tune with folk than rock. Jorma Kaukonen recruited Jack Casady, his high school buddy from Washington, DC, to replace him. Casady gave up a fairly lucrative trade as a music teacher, but did indeed make the trip. He played his first gig with the band here on October 30, 1965.

The Greek Theatre (2001 Gayley Rd, Berkeley): On September 22, 1989, Jefferson Airplane landed in the Bay Area here for the first time since September 22, 1972, as part of their

reunion tour. This was followed by a show the following night at the **Concord Pavilion (2000 Kirker Pass Rd, Concord)** plus three shows at the **Fillmore** (Sept. 26–28) and an appearance on Sept. 30 at **Golden Gate Park's Polo Field (1232 John F. Kennedy Dr, San Francisco).**

Top of the Tangent (117 University Ave., Palo Alto): This performance space above a deli was an important venue in the peninsula folk music circuit of the early '60s. Jorma Kaukonen and Paul Kantner both played here, as did Janis Joplin.

Stanford Basketball Pavilion (615 Serra St., Stanford): Jefferson Airplane and the Paul Butterfield Blues Band played here on October 6, 1966. This was the day that California declared LSD illegal. The facility is now known as Burnham Pavilion.

The Folk Theater/Offstage (970 South 1st St., San Jose): Paul Kantner and Jorma Kaukonen were regular performers here, as were some of the personnel who would ultimately comprise the Grateful Dead at what was arguably the most important folk music venue in the South Bay area of the early '60s.

The Shelter (438 East William St., San Jose): Jorma (as Jerry) Kaukonen often played here in his student years at Santa Clara University.

Losers North & Losers South (1500 Almaden Expressway, San Jose): In the early days Jefferson Airplane bounced back and forth between playing gigs for teenagers and the more dedicated folk-rock audience. This pair of companion clubs neatly catered to both, with North for the over-21's, and South for the younger crowd. Airplane, at various times, played both. On July 1–2, 1966, they played Losers North with Jackie DeShannon, and August 2–5 they played Losers South with Big Brother and the Holding Company. The joint venues did not last much longer.

NOTEWORTHY RECORDING SESSIONS

Wally Heider Studios (245 Hyde St., San Francisco): *Bark*, the Airplane's first album without Marty Balin, was recorded over a period of several months from late 1970 to the summer of 1971. Balin did record some tunes prior to his departure, but they were not included on the album. It was also the first album to feature drummer Joey Covington and fiddler Papa John Creach. Grace was not a fan of the facilities. As she states in *Somebody to Love*, "It was a dark time for us; even the studio that we used for *Bark* and *Long John Silver* was depressing. Located in a San Francisco slum, there were bars on three corners and a methadone clinic on the fourth."

By the time the Airplane reconvened for *Long John Silver* over three months in 1972, serious fractures were disintegrating the band, and it would, in fact, prove to be their last album until the 1989 reunion. The newly born Jefferson Starship, however, worked very well at Heider, recording several successful albums on the premises, including *Dragon Fly, Red Octopus, Spitfire,* and *Earth*. Slick also recorded her solo debut *Manhole* here in 1974, as well as her joint album with Kanter and David Freiberg, *Baron von Tollbooth and the Chrome Nun*.

Coast Recorders (665 Harrison St., San Francisco): In 1992 Paul Kantner reclaimed the Jefferson Starship name but did not record a new album until 1996–1998 at the former Golden State Recorders building. In addition to Slick Aguilar (guitar), T Lavitz (keyboards),

Prairie Prince (drums) and vocalist Diana Mangano, he enlisted his old bandmates Jack Casady, Marty Balin, and for one tune, Grace Slick to produce *Windows of Heaven*, the most highly acclaimed album with the name Jefferson Starship attached to it in many years. This incarnation of Coast Recorders closed in 2000 and the building is currently awaiting redevelopment.

Record Plant (2200 Bridgeway, Sausalito): Marty Balin formed the group Bodacious DF in 1973 and recorded their sole album *Bodacious DF* here. They split up shortly after the album's release and Balin joined Jefferson Starship.

OTHER NOTEWORTHY LOCATIONS

Buchwald Family Home (3121 & 3620 Anza St., San Francisco): Young Martyn Buchwald came to San Francisco from Cincinnati with his family in the late '40s and grew up here at 3121, moving to 3620 in 1957. In 1962 he recorded a pair of pop singles for Challenge Records in LA that didn't chart, but have the distinction of introducing his new nom de guerre: Marty Balin.

George Washington High School (600 32nd Ave, San Francisco): Marty Balin attended and graduated from this school, and took college prep classes at **San Francisco State (1600 Holloway Ave).** He passed on college for his career in music.

22 Belvedere St., San Francisco: Marty Balin and Bill Thompson shared this apartment in 1964–1965. Thompson later became press agent and then manager for Jefferson Airplane, Jefferson Starship, and Hot Tuna.

Wing Family Home (1017 Portola Dr., San Francisco): Ivan Wing moved his family here, near the foot of Mt. Davidson, from Los Angeles

22 Belvedere Street

in 1945. Young Grace attended **Miraloma Elementary School (175 Omar Way., San Francisco)**, a converted military barracks. That building was replaced in 1952, around the time the family departed for Palo Alto.

623 Hayes St., San Francisco: The home of poet and artist Kenneth Milton, a popular hangout for the beat and folk community in the early '60s. Paul Kantner spent many evenings here in the company of Neal Cassady and other colorful characters.

Grace Cathedral (1100 California St., San Francisco): Appropriately, Grace Wing and Jerry Slick were married here in 1961. The reception was held in the Gold Room at the nearby **Fairmont Hotel (950 Mason St., San Francisco).**

3228 Washington Street

I Magnin (233 Geary St., San Francisco): A newly married Grace Slick worked here as a couture model in 1961–1962. It was to be her last regular job before taking the plunge into music. This Union Square institution was later swallowed by Macy's and ultimately closed in 2018.

Herb Greene's Apartment (828 Baker St., San Francisco): Photographer Herb Greene shot the iconic black and white image of Jefferson Airplane for the cover of *Surrealistic Pillow* here in his studio on the top floor of this Victorian building in late 1966.

1145 Divisadero St., San Francisco: Jorma Kaukonen and his wife Margareta lived here in 1966–1967, just as the band was getting a taste of success.

3228 Washington St., San Francisco: Jorma and Margareta Kaukonen moved to this Pacific Heights home after the success of *Surrealistic Pillow*. Soon after, Grace Slick and Spencer Dryden moved downstairs. Grace and Spencer lent their pad out to some hippie friends while the band was on the road, who promptly set fire to it. Upon return, the two couples decamped to the newly acquired mansion at 2400 Fulton Street.

Caffe Trieste (601 Vallejo St., San Francisco): This North Beach stalwart has been a welcoming home to writers and artists since it first opened its doors in 1956. Lawrence Ferlinghetti, Jack Kerouac, Allen Ginsberg, and many others have congregated here, including Paul Kantner, who made it his living room, of sorts, in later years.

Wally Heider Studios (245 Hyde St., San Francisco): *Go Ride the Music* was a 1970 TV special produced by the omnipresent Ralph Gleason that showcased footage of the Jefferson Airplane performing on April 2nd. It aired on December 6, 1970. Gleason, a respected jazz critic, had long been an advocate of the new

generation of musical artists, even writing a book, *The Jefferson Airplane and the San Francisco Sound* in 1969.

Grace Slick's Car Crash (Doyle Drive., San Francisco): After leaving a late night recording session for *Bark* in 1971, Grace and Jorma raced their cars at high speed along what was then the Doyle Drive approach to the Golden Gate Bridge in the Presidio. She hit a concrete wall at 80 mph, totaling her Mercedes (some accounts say an Aston Martin) and spent a week in the hospital with a concussion, split lip, and assorted bumps and bruises. That stretch of road has since been completely redeveloped as Presidio Parkway.

Bammie Walk of Fame (Bill Graham Civic Auditorium, 99 Grove St., San Francisco): Jefferson Airplane was enshrined on the sidewalk with other Bay Area greats on March 10, 1999. Marty, Spencer, Jorma, and Jack attended.

St. Mary's College High School (1294 Albina Ave., Berkeley): Paul Kantner attended school here, although the once magisterial building he knew was razed in 1959. Both Tom and John Fogerty of Creedence Clearwater Revival also attended, though it's not known if their paths ever crossed with Kantner's.

Mills College (5000 MacArthur Boulevard, Oakland): On March 19, 1967, Ralph Gleason hosted a Rock and Roll Conference with special guests Jefferson Airplane and Phil Spector. Part performance, part academic forum, it came shortly after the release of *Surrealistic Pillow*. Ironically, Spector had auditioned and passed on an early edition of the group a couple of years before.

Marty Balin's Home (180 East Blithedale Ave, Mill Valley): Like many of his musical peers, Balin sought the more peaceful environs of Marin County, and resettled here in 1968. Generally speaking, he found that peace, though there was the occasional overzealous fan. "And one time I had this fan pick up my garbage can and throw it through my kitchen window. This giant crash. And the cops were very quick . . . and this guy was a big fan of mine and he just loved me so much he wanted to tell me that," recalled Balin in a 2017 interview for the Mill Valley Oral History Program. Balin remained at the house until 1996, when he moved to Florida. The home is distinguished by a pyramid-like tower.

99 Brighton Ave, Bolinas: Grace Slick and Paul Kantner resided in this large beachfront home from 1970–1973. The commute to recording sessions in the city became too laborious, however, and the couple eventually moved to Sea Cliff.

St. Joseph's Military Academy (1000 Alamedas de las Pulgas, Belmont): Paul Kantner's traveling salesman father, after his wife's death, sent his son to this Catholic boarding school. It was here that Kantner developed his love of science fiction as an escape from the rigors of both parochial and military discipline. Today the site is home to Immaculate Heart of Mary School.

Wing Family Home (1310 Greenwood Ave., Palo Alto): The family moved here in the early '50s and this was Grace's home until she left for college. The ten-year-old Grace first met Jerry Slick, a neighbor, whom she would eventually wed a decade later. She attended nearby **Jordan Junior High School (750 North California Ave., Palo Alto)** and **Palo Alto High School**

1310 Greenwood Avenue, Palo Alto

(50 Embarcadero Rd.), but transferred to and graduated from **Castilleja School (1310 Bryant St., Palo Alto)**, a private school for girls. Jordan Junior High is now known as Greene Middle School. After Grace left for college, the Wings moved to a Tudor style home at **1416 Hamilton Avenue** in the Crescent Park neighborhood. She moved back in and lived here until she married Jerry Slick in 1961.

Santa Clara University (500 El Camino Real, Santa Clara): Jorma Kaukonen transferred here from Antioch in 1962 and graduated with a degree in Sociology in 1964. His first dormitory was **Nobili Hall**, followed by **Dunne Hall (Room 329)** the following year. It was in his room at Dunne where he first learned of the assassination of President John F. Kennedy on November 22, 1963. He later attended a memorial service in the campus's **Mission Church**. As he recounts in his memoir *Been So Long: My Life and Music* in 2018, ". . . we all knew that the world was changing faster than our awareness allowed us to fully grasp. The assassination of our president impacted everyone profoundly." Paul Kantner also attended Santa Clara for a time, but later transferred to **San Jose State (1 Washington**

Square, San Jose), giving that up for his eventual life in music. Paul and Jorma knew each other from the area coffee houses, and it was Kantner that helped Jorma secure a regular job giving guitar lessons.

Benner Music Company (1884 West San Carlos St., San Jose): Established decades earlier as a piano shop, Benner by the early '60s was an important fixture for the folk music community, selling guitars, banjos, mandolins, and other tools of the trade. Paul Kantner started working here in 1961–1962 and established a Folklore Center to further appeal to the nascent scene. Later he brought Jorma Kaukonen on board to teach guitar lessons in a small basement room, a position he held well into the first year or so of his Jefferson Airplane career.

1159 & 1174 Fremont Ave., Santa Clara: Jorma and his new wife Margareta settled here in 1964, in what was then a long dingy shotgun apartment. Later that year they recruited a pair of roommates and rented the much more spacious house across the street at 1174. The acoustics of the old wooden house were superb for capturing the sound of his guitar, so Jorma picked up a Sony TC-100 mono reel-to-reel tape recorder. Janis Joplin was a budding singer on the coffee house circuit he knew, and she asked him to accompany her for an upcoming

benefit performance at the **Coffee Gallery (1353 Grant Ave., San Francisco).** Janis came down to Santa Clara to rehearse several blues standards, which Jorma recorded. Margareta was in the next room typing a letter to her family in Sweden, which was captured on the tape. Over the years the recordings made their way into the ether of bootleg distribution, where they took on mythic status as *The Typewriter Tapes.* It was also in this house that Jorma dropped acid for the first time, with roommate Steve Mann. LSD was legal then, and as he describes in *Been So Long: My Life and Music*: ". . . it didn't take long to realize this was not just some sort of supercharged version of the crappy pot we smoked," and "The walls and the air around me were kaleidoscopic and the music was like pillars of sound."

THE BRIAN JONESTOWN MASSACRE

John Bentley/Alamy

Since coming together in San Francisco in the early '90s, the Brian Jonestown Massacre (BJM) have been a loose collective of lysergic wayfarers guided by the mythic musical whims of Anton Newcombe, the group's indisputable leader. Their music is awash in psychedelia, though not necessarily of the old school San Francisco vintage, with myriad other influences that appear to have soared in from almost anywhere, including outer space. Newcombe has since moved to Berlin, but the indelible imprint of the BJM remains, especially in the Lower Haight, which in the early-to-mid-'90s was a cauldron of creativity and bonhomie.

"You would just come across houses, and the doors would open and there's a hundred people in there going nuts, and you'd say, 'Oh, cool,' and just walk in," said the BJM's Joel Gion

in 2019. "And that would happen *everywhere*. There was always something to do. That time back then seems like so much more went on compared to now. You'd get so much more done in a day as far as making memories goes."

Gion, the group's longtime tambourine player and raconteur, grew up in the suburbs of San Jose, but was forever spellbound by San Francisco, where he still lives today.

"It was just so chaotic in a way where everything that I could imagine or not imagine was just happening all around me," he said. "I was just fascinated with this place. We made a couple of trips when I was a kid. Riding the cable cars and going through Chinatown, and all the sensations that assault you in these types of environments were just mind-blowing. I was so in love with San Francisco that I turned

18 two weeks before I was going to graduate high school and I quit and moved here: 'You keep it, baby, because that's nothing to do with being in a band. I don't need it.'"

Gion's first apartment in San Francisco was at **2220 Taylor Street** in North Beach, but he soon felt too far away from where the action was.

"Everything was going on in the Lower Haight," he said. "I had to get the bus and go down to Market and get another bus, and coming back after midnight was a pain in the ass. So I finally moved my ass over there."

Shortly after moving his ass over there, Gion's first experience with the BJM unfolded at one of the group's many early gigs at **The Peacock Lounge (552 Haight St., San Francisco).**

"It was like walking into a bar from Dolemite, replete with purple and green lights," said Gion. "It was awesome."

Gion wouldn't join the group as their tambourine player and co-provocateur for a couple of years, though he did dip his toe in the group's water playing guitar with the BJM under the unlikeliest of circumstances, The Nightmare Before KISSmas, a tribute to theatrical '70s stadium rockers Kiss that was held at **Brave New World (1751 Fulton St., San Francisco)** on December 17, 1993. The BJM's reinterpretation of Kiss live staple "Rock and Roll All Nite" did not go over well.

"Looking back on it I almost had to think (Anton) had booked that just to go there and fuck with everybody," Gion said. "Because why the hell would Brian Jonestown play a Kiss cover

BLACK REBEL MOTORCYCLE CLUB

Not long after his brief stint in the BJM ended in 1998, guitarist Peter Hayes connected with Robert Levon Been, a friend from **Acalanes High School (1200 Pleasant Hill Rd., Lafayette)** in the East Bay. The fledgling outfit, with drummer Nick Jago rounding out the trio, dubbed themselves Black Rebel Motorcycle Club, a nod to Marlon Brando's motorcycle gang in the 1953 outlaw biker film *The Wild One*, their sound a heady blend of psychedelia and howling guitars not unlike dropping a transistor radio into a motorcycle engine. The band's first gig took place at **Club Cocodrie (1024 Kearny St., San Francisco)** on January 14, 1999. Other early local shows during the group's first few crucial months took place at **The Purple Onion (140 Columbus Ave., San Francisco)**, **Bottom of the Hill (1233 17th St., San Francisco)**, **Paradise Lounge (1501 Folsom St., San Francisco)**, **Club Boomerang (1840 Haight St., San Francisco)**, **Stork Club (2330 Telegraph Ave., Oakland)**, **Cat Club (1190 Folsom St., San Francisco)**, and **The Starry Plough (3101 Shattuck Ave., Berkeley)**.

Black Rebel Motorcycle Club are still active, releasing eight studio albums between 2001–2018, and touring the world many times over.

show? And the first thing he does (on stage) is say, 'Despite the fact that you all think I'm a fag, I'm getting paid to make fun of you!,' and he turns around and says, '*GO!*' And we played these two Death in June chords and freak folk flute and this guy doing the *Psychocandy* stand-up two drums, and everybody booed. (Original Kiss drummer) Peter Criss was there, and he was all pissed."

Even early on, the BJM were comfortable courting controversy. But it wasn't until a March 5, 1995, gig at **Great American Music Hall (859 O'Farrell St., San Francisco)** supporting Spectrum and Low that they were first banned from a local venue.

"At the Great American, a couple of things happened in the same night," remembered Gion. "I was pretty jacked up, and I was sitting there thinking, 'This tambourine, doing this is just not enough! I feel like I'm going to explode!' So I just chucked my tambourine into the air as high as I could, and to my great surprise it went straight up and came right back to me and I caught it."

Gion repeated the maneuver, but this time the tambourine fell to the stage just out of reach and broke.

"'*Fuck!* Now I've just got these two pieces! How am I supposed to get through the show?!?'" Gion recalled. "So I've got these two pieces, and I'm really just jacked up and I'm like, 'This fucking sucks!' And I drop-kicked one of the pieces and it goes flying."

Years later, Gion met a girl at a party who was there that night.

"She said, 'Hey, you remember the Great American Music Hall when you kicked that tambourine into the crowd? Yeah, you hit me right in the face and scratched my face. And my boyfriend tried to get onstage to kill you, but he couldn't get onstage because Anton got a mic stand and kind of held him back from getting onstage. And your other guitar player'—who was Jeff Davies—'tried to squirt some water on him.' He thought it was going to be this fire hose, like, 'Take this, man, here's a bunch of water in your face!' And it just went, '*Pfhhht*' right into the monitor, the whole bottle. Fried the monitor. So we got banned from there."

It was the first, but by no means last time the BJM would be banned.

The BJM are still going strong, touring the world and releasing sonically adventurous music.

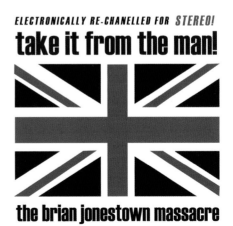

MORE BRIAN JONESTOWN MASSACRE

NOTEWORTHY LIVE PERFORMANCES

Spaghetti Western (576 Haight St., San Francisco): Early in the band's history, the BJM clambered out onto the first-floor roof of then-favored brunch spot Spaghetti Western to play an impromptu gig, stopping traffic before they were shut down. Spaghetti Western has since closed, with the space now occupied by Memphis Minnie's BBQ Joint.

Arena Interplay (701 Oak St., San Francisco): The BJM, billed on a flyer as "the brand more dentists use," played an early gig at Arena Interplay.

Club Boomerang (1840 Haight St., San Francisco): Now the Milk Bar, the BJM played this location numerous times in its former incarnation as Club Boomerang.

The Independent (628 Divisadero St., San Francisco): The BJM most recently played the Independent as the San Francisco stop on their 2016 world tour, but they also took the stage back in the mid-'90s when it was called the Crash Palace.

Slim's (333 11th St., San Francisco): Among the venues where flyers asked fans to "Take acid now and come see the Brian Jonestown Massacre" was Slim's, which was opened by musician Boz Scaggs in 1988.

"We played with Mercury Rev there once," said Gion. "We were really jamming, and Anton didn't want to stop. It was, 'Let's just go until we can't go anymore.' And the guy's at the side of the stage pointing at his watch, that typical kind of thing: 'You're done!' So finally they brought down the screen, and Anton was literally just bending down with his guitar as the screen goes down."

DNA Lounge (375 11th St., San Francisco): Another landing spot for the early BJM was this longtime all-ages nightclub.

Bottom of the Hill (1233 17th St., San Francisco): This intimate club was the location of many early BJM shows, perhaps none more memorable than the first Bay Area visit by BritPop legends Oasis in September 1994. Gion, who'd only joined the group earlier in the year, said he was rebuffed in trying to get acquainted with the Mancunian group's songwriter and guitarist Noel Gallagher with a proffer of speed—"No thanks, we only do coke"—but a female friend had an easier time with the rest of the group, including brash frontman Liam Gallagher, Noel's brother. Their overeager sniffing nearly ended Oasis, derailing their gig the next night in Los Angeles, after which Noel flew back to San Francisco to cool off for a few days.

Gion still loves Bottom of the Hill today.

"We were really good friends with the gal that ran it, Ramona (Downey), super cool and looked out for us," he said. "The room itself has

The Brian Jonestown Massacre
JASON FALKNER
RED PLANET
May 7
9:30PM 21+
BOTTOM OF THE HILL
1233 17TH ST.
SAN FRANCISCO

just got a really great vibe to it. It's a small rock club and it's not a dump, but it's not trying to be fancy either. It's kind of the perfect middle ground. It's the perfect capacity for the kind of band we were at that time. And the sound is also amazing. One of the best sounding rooms in the city. And you can smoke in the back!"

Trocadero Transfer (520 4th St.): The BJM played the Trocadero Transfer shortly after supporting Oasis at Bottom of the Hill in autumn 1994, playing with the Dandy Warhols for the first time.

"That was kind of an historic night, because they'd just signed to Capitol (Records) and they were touring with Love and Rockets," Gion said, laughing. "We'd been total buddies, the revolution all that jive. And we're backstage, and I said, 'Oh great, beer,' because we had to share the backstage. And then Eric (Hedford), who doesn't play drums with them anymore,

said, 'Oh, *great*, now they're going to drink our beer.' The whole war, which was covered in the movie (*Dig!*), that's when the war started with me. 'Okay, you're not going to share beer now? *I hate you. We're not friends anymore.*'"

Black Rose (335 Jones St., San Francisco): Not long after they formed, the BJM—possibly billed as Electric Kool Aid—played a gig at this former bar in the Tenderloin.

The Purple Onion (140 Columbus Ave., San Francisco): This since-shuttered former Beat-Era club once popular with comedians was by the early '90s hosting live music. The BJM played here, but the venue looms largest in their history as the site of a scene in the notorious documentary *Dig!,* where Newcombe arrives on Rollerblades to deliver personalized, individually wrapped shotgun shells to then-rival the Dandy Warhols.

Bimbo's 365 Club (1025 Columbus Ave., San Francisco): The BJM played a pair of sold-out dates at Bimbo's in May 2018, as part of their world tour.

Maritime Hall (450 Harrison St., San Francisco): A short-lived venue on the Sailor's Union of the Pacific, Maritime Hall hosted the BJM on November 28, 1997. Though the entire show has yet to circulate, Gion recently posted an 18-minute sampler of pro-shot video to YouTube of the group at the height of its mid-'90s powers.

Adam Grant Building (114 Sansome St., San Francisco): Topping out at six-stories when built in 1908, the Adam Grant Building had an additional eight stories added by Lewis P. Hobart in 1926. Much of the building's original Jazz Age grandeur was restored in the early part of the 21st century, including its entryway

and marble floor. In celebration of his first solo album *Apple Bonkers*, Joel Gion and the Primary Colours played a gig on the Adam Grant rooftop on August 23, 2014.

The Fillmore (1805 Geary St., San Francisco): Gion reckons the BJM received a preemptive ban from the Fillmore after being blacklisted at Great American Music Hall in 1995. It wasn't until 2009, and only then as a support act for Primal Scream, that the group took to the venerable stage.

"Everything is going great, it's sold out," said Gion. "But the monitor guy is pissed, because he was the only guy who wasn't able to go see Roger Waters at AT&T Park, because he had to work. So he was totally fucking with us, totally on purpose. Anton put down his guitar and went into this whole rant. He said, 'We're from the Lower Haight . . . and I didn't come through it all to finally headline this place just to get shit from you because you didn't get to see Roger Waters!' He started going into it, and the more he's going, I'm like, 'He's absolutely fucking right! And by the end of it I'm like, 'Yes! Testify, brother!' But in the end it got us thrown out again, because you just can't display that kind of decorum towards the staff, whether Roger Waters is playing or not."

734 Shrader Street

NOTEWORTHY RECORDING LOCATIONS

"She Made Me"/"Evergreen" (734 Shrader St., San Francisco): The first BJM single, "She Made Me" and its b-side "Evergreen" were recorded in the basement of this two-bedroom flat Newcombe shared with Travis Threlkel, one of the group's original guitarists.

The Compound (1070 Van Dyke Ave., San Francisco ⊘): The Compound was a multipurpose endeavor run by Naut Humon located in a state-owned building along a dirt road. Newcombe honed his recording skills there thanks to the generosity of Humon, who became a fan of the group's music after running into Travis Threlkel, then a guitarist in the BJM, at a My Bloody Valentine concert, in the early '90s.

"And then I started inviting Anton to come out to the Compound," said Humon in 2019. "I was just kind of opening doors for their projects. I was into them back in the days when he had audiences of 50 or, you know, small audience. I just liked their songs. Yeah, this is good music to me."

Though it's tricky to definitively trace the recording locations of specific BJM albums or tracks, it's believed much of *Their Satanic*

Majesties Second Request and *Spacegirl and Other Favorites* were recorded at Bloody Angle, the studio within the Compound. Newcombe also crashed at the Compound from time to time, though Humon said that was not unusual.

"That was a rotating thing," said Humon in 2019. "I mean, Anton and Courtney from the Dandy Warhols would be in there sometimes."

Anton Newcombe Apartment (359 Haight St., San Francisco): Newcombe lived in an apartment here in the early '90s, when the monthly rent was $250.

Horse Shoe Cafe (566 Haight St., San Francisco): Newcombe and founding member Ricky Maymi—who left the group for a decade before returning in 2003—used to hang out here playing chess.

674 Haight Street

Birthplace of the Brian Jonestown Massacre (674 Haight St., San Francisco): The BJM reportedly came together for the first time in the early '90s in the apartment of Sean Curran, who would go on to occasionally play guitar and bass with the group during their formative years.

Reckless Records (1401 Haight St., San Francisco): In the mid-'90s, Joel Gion worked in this since-shuttered record shop, an outpost of the longtime London original. He lasted around a year.

"I used to trade records in there all the time," Gion said. "You could turn a record into a pizza, so I'd bring my records in there from time to time and sell them. And this one guy I kind of got a rapport with, and they ended up needing somebody and I applied and I got it. And I made them look really bad, because that was right before I discovered speed and ecstasy. I wasn't like Mr. Jacked Up at work, I was more like 'I just got home five minutes before my shift.'"

Escape from New York Pizza (1737 Haight St., San Francisco): Original BJM bass guitarist and vocalist Matt Hollywood slung pizzas in this Upper Haight staple in the early '90s.

The Gold Cane Cocktail Lounge (1569 Haight St., San Francisco): Open since 1926, the Gold Cane was a regular hangout for the BJM; Guitarist Dean Taylor worked in the kitchen around the time of *Strung Out in Heaven* (1998)

The Mitchell Brothers O'Farrell Theater (895 O'Farrell St., San Francisco): Gion's first job was at this legendary strip club and adult emporium, where he was hired sight unseen because of a friend already working there. Gion was given his orientation by Jim Mitchell, who would soon go on to murder his brother and

business partner Artie. Though he played it cool with Mitchell, Gion's first day on the job was also his last.

"Inside I'm like, 'Holy shit, I've never even been in a strip club and now I've got to start copping people if they've got their hands on their penises and hosing semen on the seats, and I've got to stop them doing it,'" Gion said. "(Mitchell) sends me in the main room to watch the girls dance. When my friend announced the girl, I just thought, there's no way on earth I can do this: 'Nowwww, the *sultryyyy Sabrinaaaaaa*!' And I literally snuck back up to the doors, saw (Mitchell) was yelling at some other people, and I just ran for the door, tippy-toe high-stepped across the carpet, pushed the door open and ran down the street.

MOJO-NAVIGATOR HQ
2707 McAllister St.

Mojo-Navigator R&R News, published from this apartment building by teenagers David Harris and Greg Shaw in August 1966, was San Francisco's first attempt at serious rock journalism, preceding *Rolling Stone* by more than a year. In its 14-issue span it featured news, record reviews, and interviews with local groups like the Grateful Dead and Big Brother and the Holding Company. The publication was mimeographed and stapled, selling for one thin dime at outlets like City Lights Booksellers and the Psychedelic Shop.

2707 McAllister Street

OUTSIDE LANDS
Golden Gate Park

An annual three-day music and arts festival which takes place in August, Outside Lands boasts eclectic lineups of musicians, comedians, food, wine, beer, chocolate, and as of 2019, Grass Lands, a marketplace of legal cannabis products. Outside Lands makes the most of its leafy setting, stretching out to encompass much of the Polo Fields, Hellman Hollow, Marx Meadow, and Lindley Meadow, giving attendees the rare large festival experience of having room to breathe. The inaugural lineup in 2008 was headlined by Radiohead, Tom Petty and the Heartbreakers, and Jack Johnson. In the ensuing years, Pearl Jam, Phish, Arcade Fire, Metallica, Stevie Wonder, Paul McCartney, Elton John, the Who, Janet Jackson, and Paul Simon have received top billing.

KEZAR PAVILION
755 Stanyan St.

Built in 1924 and used over the years for everything from basketball to roller derby, Kezar Pavilion has periodically opened its doors to rock shows, with David Bowie, the Specials, the Clash, the Cramps, Flipper, and Dead Kennedys all playing there.

Mike Katz

WILD WEST FESTIVAL
Kezar Stadium, 670 Kezar Dr.

On the surface, the motivation behind the planned Wild West Festival seemed noble enough: Three concerts during the last weekend of August 1969, at Kezar Stadium featuring some of the premier bands of the scene, with tickets for each night $3 apiece; scattered throughout Golden Gate Park would be free performances by other artists, with the entire festival funded by ticket sales from Kezar. Remaining funds going toward the establishment of a public arts center to give the local scene an opportunity to continue to grow, and to ensure free music for the people would be supported into the future.

The San Francisco Music Council was formed to ensure musicians, artists, and activists had a voice in the proceedings, and

Poster by Wes Wilson and Victor Moscoso, 1969

the resulting Kezar lineup was stacked: Grateful Dead, Janis Joplin, and Quicksilver Messenger Service on Friday; Jefferson Airplane, Sons of Champlin, and a supergroup featuring Mike Bloomfield and Nick Gravenites on Saturday; and closing out Kezar on Sunday, Country Joe and the Fish, Sly and the Family Stone, Santana, and Youngbloods.

But Wild West never happened, with the fete succumbing to opposition raised not by the establishment, but by pockets of the counterculture, who among other things felt the festival was exploitative of the very scene it professed to represent. Tensions between the two sides continued to rise in early August, and efforts to bridge the chasm between festival organizers and protestors were for naught. A few weeks before Wild West was meant to happen, the plug was pulled.

KEZAR STADIUM
670 Kezar Dr.

Opened in 1925 at the southeastern corner of Golden Gate Park as a nearly 60,000-seat stadium, Kezar was home for decades of numerous large-scale sporting events, and was home to both the San Francisco 49ers (1946–1970) and Oakland Raiders (1960). When the 49ers moved to Candlestick Park in 1971, Kezar began booking concerts, with touring artists like Led Zeppelin, Bob Dylan, and Neil Young, along with local favorites Jefferson Starship, Grateful Dead, and Graham Central Station all playing there.

Kezar Stadium underwent a major renovation in 1989 to remove its towering bleachers. The seating around the infield and track today totals a much more modest capacity of 10,000.

GRATEFUL DEAD

Gijsbert Hanekroot/Alamy

"And the thing about Golden Gate Park is that if you go from one end of it to another, you find yourself in these different worlds."

—JERRY GARCIA

Though their name is rightly synonymous with classic San Francisco rock venues like the Fillmore—Auditorium and West—and both the Avalon and Winterland ballrooms, the Grateful Dead were truly at home in Golden Gate Park. With its meandering paths and rolling meadows, a long stroll through Golden Gate Park unfolds like the music of the Grateful Dead, its twists and turns brimming with adventure, taking in unexpected pastoral delights, communing with towering trees, and feeling the pulse of the psychedelic city streets or the distant steady thrum of rolling waves through the Gulf of the Farallones off to the west. Enter Golden Gate Park and you immerse yourself in these different worlds.

Built in the late 19th century as an urban oasis in the then-recent tradition of New York City's Central Park, Golden Gate Park serves the same purpose today, its 1,017 acres stretching west from Stanyan Street in the Haight-Ashbury to the Great Highway and Ocean Beach. It boasts museums and gardens, pathways and waterways, and it remains one of the City of San

Francisco's great utilitarian wonders, available for the amusement of anyone and everyone. This was part of its appeal for the Grateful Dead, who rarely shied away from an opportunity to take their music to the people by throwing both planned and impromptu free shows.

For the Grateful Dead, Golden Gate Park offered an expanded playground close to home, especially when much of the band was living in their celebrated '60s headquarters at **710 Ashbury Street**, six blocks away from its southwest corner. Even closer was the Panhandle, a separate narrow park that joins Golden Gate Park at its eastern end, its ¾-mile length stretching to Baker Street, with Ashbury cutting roughly through its middle. On a map, the Panhandle reveals the wisdom in its name, its expanse just a block wide, running between Fell and Oak streets to Stanyan and Golden Gate Park.

Just three blocks north of 710 Ashbury, the Panhandle would see the Dead and other groups set up shop on flatbed trucks, running in free electricity from wherever their network of

Crispin Kott

710 Ashbury Street

purloined extension cords could find purchase, to play impromptu sets for anyone who happened to be within earshot.

One crucial Panhandle show took place on October 6, 1966, with the Dead joining Big Brother and the Holding Company for the Love Pageant Rally, scheduled for the day LSD became illegal in California. Thousands of people turned up for the event, organized by Allen Cohen and Michael Bowen, publishers of underground newspaper *The Oracle*. Ken Kesey and the Merry Pranksters were also on the scene, their ubiquitous party bus topped with revelers.

Ten days later, the Dead returned to the Panhandle for the two-day Artist's Liberation Front Free Fair, playing its second day on a bill with groups like Quicksilver Messenger Service and Country Joe and the Fish. That night, the action moved to the **Avalon (1268 Sutter St., San Francisco),** for the first anniversary celebration of the Family Dog's primary hall. The Dead didn't play the show, but Garcia joined Big Brother and the Holding Company for a number.

On January 1, 1967, the Grateful Dead and Big Brother and the Holding Company played a

free show in the Panhandle after having held New Year's Eve gigs at the **Fillmore Auditorium (1805 Geary Blvd., San Francisco)** and Avalon Ballroom respectively the night before.

Rumors abound of other Panhandle shows around this time, with former Dead manager Rock Scully claiming in his memoir (*Living with the Dead: Twenty Years on the Bus with Garcia and the Grateful Dead*, coauthored by David Dalton) that on June 21, 1967, the group set up equipment stolen from the Monterey Pop Festival for a celebratory gig to entertain the throngs of kids who'd made their way north looking for adventures. Scully claims the Dead were joined by Eric Burdon and Jimi Hendrix at this Panhandle gig, though there's skepticism among the fanbase about its accuracy. Hendrix followed the Monterey Pop flow to San Francisco, playing a free show in the Panhandle with support from the Ace of Cups on June 25, 1967.

Dennis McNally's *A Long Strange Trip: The Inside History of the Grateful Dead* cites a June 21, 1967, Summer Solstice "Do-In" at the Polo Grounds in Golden Gate Park, with Scully claiming in his book that the group lugged its stolen equipment deep into the trees for the gig before setting up an incognito drop to return it all near the Ferry Building along the Embarcadero at noon the next day. The Do-In featured stages set up on opposite ends of the Polo Grounds, with the Dead joined by Quicksilver Messenger Service and Mad River on one, while the Jefferson Airplane, Big Brother and the Holding Company, and the Phoenix played the other.

The Dead played another impromptu show at nearby Lindley Meadows on August 28, 1967, in honor of Chocolate George Hendricks, a popular member of the Hells Angels. In addition to the Grateful Dead, Big Brother and the Holding Company also paid tribute.

Though most of their shows in the park happened in the '60s, the Dead did return a few times in the ensuing years, including what was unofficially dubbed "the last free show," at Lindley Meadows on September 28, 1975. The show, highlighted by performances of "Franklin's Tower" and "Truckin'," was widely circulated as a bootleg and has since seen an official release as part of the comprehensive *30 Trips Around the Sun* box set.

Perhaps the most famous of all Dead shows in Golden Gate Park, the Human Be-In, was less a Dead show than a wider countercultural event that saw the group on a music bill with many of the scene's prime movers, like the Jefferson Airplane, Quicksilver Messenger Service, Big Brother and the Holding Company, and Blue Cheer. "A Gathering of the Tribes for a Human Be-In" took place on the Polo Grounds on January 14, 1967, and in addition to the musical component also featured luminaries like Allen Ginsberg, Dick Gregory, Lawrence Ferlinghetti, Gary Snyder, Michael McClure, and in his first San Francisco appearance, Timothy Leary, who famously exhorted the crowd to "Turn on, tune in, and drop out." The Dead returned to the Polo Grounds once more that decade, playing on May 7, 1969.

The Dead's final show in Golden Gate Park also took place on the Polo Grounds on November 3, 1991, as part of Laughter, Love & Music, an all-day festival celebrating the lives of Bill Graham, Melissa Gold, and Steve "Killer" Kahn, who'd died in a helicopter crash a week earlier. Joining the Dead for their set were special guests John Fogerty, Neil Young, and Blues Traveler's John Popper. Other performers on the bill included Journey; Santana; Bobby McFerrin; Crosby, Stills, Nash & Young; Los Lobos, Tracy Chapman, Jackson Browne, and many others.

In the summer of 1967, the Dead played a rare gig in the opulence of the Golden Gate Park Bandshell, aka, the Spreckels Temple of Music, on July 6 as part of the *San Francisco*

Poster by Rick Griffin, 1967

Examiner's series of free afternoon shows. Garcia would return to the bandshell as a special guest of Zeros on July 16, 1988, performing a few numbers, including "Good Night Irene."

At the southeastern corner of Golden Gate Park sits Kezar Stadium, which until its demolition and renovation in 1989 seated just under 60,000 spectators. It was, among its many guises, the first home of the San Francisco 49ers of the National Football League. It was also nearly the site of The Wild West Festival, a three-day fete with free events throughout Golden Gate Park and paid concerts within the stadium from August 22–24, 1969, one week after the Woodstock Music & Art Fair across the country.

The Dead were scheduled for the Wild West's opening night at Kezar, alongside Janis Joplin, Quicksilver Messenger Service, and Dixieland band Turk Murphy, with the Jefferson Airplane, Santana, the Steve Miller Band, and others over the breadth of the festival. But on August 6, Wild West was abruptly canceled, with dueling factions unable to come to an agreement about whether the entire festival should be free to the public.

The Grateful Dead did finally play Kezar Stadium on May 26, 1973, a show moved from the Cow Palace and promoted by Bill Graham Presents as Dancing on the Outdoor Green. With the Dead as headliners, the day also included Charlie Daniels and New Riders of the Purple Sage.

The Dead would return to Kezar Stadium on March 23, 1975, for S.F. SNACK, a benefit for San Francisco Students Need Athletics, Culture & Kicks, after the San Francisco Unified School District canceled funding for after-school programs. Billed on ads as Jerry Garcia and Friends, this was a full Grateful Dead show, including the return of Mickey Hart on drums. Also performing at the benefit show were Bob Dylan, Neil Young, Jefferson Starship, Tower of Power, Joan Baez, the Doobie Brothers, and many others.

One corner of the park the Dead tried but ultimately failed to play was Speedway Meadows, now known as Hellman Hollow. On June 9, 1968, the Dead and Jefferson Airplane attempted to perform a free gig to an estimated 3,000 people, but were thwarted by police for lack of a permit; the Cub Scouts, who did have a permit for the site, were allowed to hold their own event. A brief story in the *Hayward Daily Review* ("Cub Scouts Beat 'The Airplane'") quoted Jefferson Airplane manager Bill Thompson as saying: "This is not a concert. It is a wake for the late Sen. Robert Kennedy, and the Cub Scouts would like the music." Kennedy was assassinated in Los Angeles three days earlier.

Further north from Hellman Hollow is Marx Meadows, and while the Dead didn't play there Jerry Garcia did, first with Merl Saunders on September 2, 1974, and later with the Diga Rhythm Band supporting Jefferson Starship.

One area of Golden Gate Park which has perhaps erroneously attracted plenty of Grateful Dead attention is Hippie Hill, a rolling spread just below John F. Kennedy Drive in the eastern part of the park. While the vibe is undeniably hippie-centric, there's nothing beyond rumors to indicate the Dead ever played there, at least in a formal way. It's certainly possible members of the group strolled into the park from Haight Street and jammed, but that's the kind of speculation best left for your own Golden Gate meanderings.

Golden Gate Park remains one of San Francisco's crown jewels, with as much adventure and music as when the Grateful Dead were playing in among the trees and fields. Have a wander around and see if you can't still hear faint traces of their sounds echoing across its great expanse.

MORE GRATEFUL DEAD

NOTEWORTHY LIVE PERFORMANCES

Magoo's Pizza Parlor (639 Santa Cruz Ave., Menlo Park): The Warlocks, the Dead as they were known before the Dead, made their live debut at this pizza-parlor-cum-hootenanny-stomp on May 5, 1965. They would return a few more times that month, still as the Warlocks, attracting curious crowds of teenagers from nearby **Menlo Atherton High School (555 Middlefield Rd., Atherton)**. The group at the time featured Jerry Garcia and Bob Weir on guitar and vocals; Ron "Pigpen" McKernan on keyboards, harmonica, and vocals; Bill Kreutzmann on drums; and Dana Morgan, Jr. on bass guitar. By the end of the month, Morgan was out and Phil Lesh was on bass guitar, forming the nucleus of the Grateful Dead.

Frenchy's (29097 Mission Blvd., Hayward): On June 18, 1965, bass guitarist Phil Lesh played his first gig with the Warlocks at this club, which has been described as an island of hipness in a sea of uncool. According to Lesh, the group was not invited back after their first of three planned gigs.

The Big Beat (998 San Antonio Rd., Palo Alto): The Grateful Dead appeared at Yvonne Modica's Big Beat club just days before it opened, a featured act during one of Ken Kesey's Acid Tests, held on December 18, 1965.

The Cinnamon Tree (900 American St., San Carlos): The Warlocks played a Battle of the Bands here in August 1965, beating the tricorn-hat-bedecked William Penn and His Pals, a group which included future Santana and Journey founding member Gregg Rolie on keyboards.

Poster by Paul Foster

The In Room (1048 Old County Rd., Belmont): The Warlocks played a six-week engagement at this bar, playing five 50-minute sets five nights a week, from mid-September through late-October 1965.

Pierre's (546 Broadway, San Francisco): The Warlocks had a brief, unsuccessful stint backing topless dancers at this club in November 1965.

Big Nig's House (43 S 5th St., San Jose/635 E. St. James St., San Jose): On December 4, 1965, the Grateful Dead played their first gig as the Grateful Dead at one of Ken Kesey's Acid Tests at Big Nig's House on S. 5th St. in San Jose. According to Bill Wyman's memoir *Stone Alone*, Keith Richards and Brian Jones came to the wild party after flyers were handed out to attendees at the Rolling Stones' gig at the **San Jose Civic Auditorium (135 W. San Carlos St., San Jose)**

earlier that evening. The entire house—and its attendant parties and musical endeavors—was moved to East St. James St. by the San Jose Redevelopment Agency during construction and renovation surrounding the San Jose City Hall.

The Folk Theater/The Offstage (970 South 1st St., San Jose): A key folk venue, the Offstage also saw many key Bay Area musicians give pre-fame lessons, including Jerry Garcia (guitar and banjo) and Paul Kantner (guitar), who would go on to form the Jefferson Airplane. Garcia, Bob Weir, and Ron "Pigpen" McKernan's pre-Dead folk act Mother McCree's Uptown Jug Champions also played there.

Fillmore Auditorium (1805 Geary Blvd., San Francisco): The Grateful Dead played the S.F. Mime Troupe's second appeal for "continued artistic freedom in the parks" at the venerable Fillmore Auditorium on December 10, 1965. The Dead were so new and relatively unknown that they weren't included in any of the ads or posters on a bill which featured the Jefferson Airplane, the Great Society, the John Handy Quintet, and the Mystery Trend. The group would play the Fillmore Auditorium over 50 times.

Muir Beach Tavern and Lodge (Muir Beach): Originally intended for Stinson Beach, the Acid Test held on December 11, 1965, was moved to Muir Beach over concerns about law enforcement. The Grateful Dead and the Fugs played for the Merry Pranksters and others.

The Matrix (3138 Fillmore St., San Francisco): A folk rock club designed with the fledgling Jefferson Airplane in mind, the Matrix was partly owned by the group's singer, Marty Balin. The Grateful Dead played the Matrix several times through 1966, returning to the club in various guises for the next few years, and with

members playing with other musicians like Merl Saunders, and New Riders of the Purple Sage. Garcia, Lesh and Hart backed David Crosby in December 1970, as David and the Dorks as the former Byrd was nearing completion of his star-studded solo debut *If I Could Only Remember My Name*.

Longshoremen's Hall (400 N. Point St., San Francisco): Site of legendary concerts promoted by the Family Dog, Longshoremen's Hall was built in 1959 as a sailor's union hall. The Grateful Dead played a few iterations of the Trips Festival there between January and April 1966.

Harmon Gymnasium (14 Frank Schlessinger Way, Berkeley): The Grateful Dead played Harmon Gym on the UC Berkeley campus as part of a Peace Rock show on May 7, 1966, sharing the bill with the Great Society, Billy Moses, the Charlatans, and M. C. Russ "The Moose"

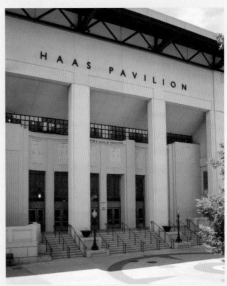

Haas Pavilion, UC Berkeley

Mike Katz

Poster by Alton Kelley and Stanley Mouse, 1966

Syracuse. The gym has since been renamed Haas Pavilion.

Veterans Memorial Hall (1931 Center St., Berkeley): The Grateful Dead performed at a dance concert here on May 14, 1966.

Avalon Ballroom (1268 Sutter St., San Francisco): The Dead played the Family Dog's crown jewel for the first time on May 19, 1966, returning numerous times through 1969. On January 29, 1967, the Avalon hosted the Mantra-Rock Dance, billed as Krishna Consciousness Comes West, with proceeds going to the founding of a new temple for the International Society for Krishna Consciousness. The Radha Krishna Temple opened at **518 Frederick Street** later that year. Playing the Mantra-Rock Dance were the Grateful Dead, Big

Brother and the Holding Company, and Moby Grape.

Rancho Olompali (8901 Redwood Blvd., Novato): The Grateful Dead played afternoon outdoor shows at Rancho Olompali numerous times in mid-1966, performing on the lawn outside of the property's Burdell Mansion. The Jefferson Airplane and Quicksilver Messenger Service were also involved in many of the loose jams which took place there. The Dead also lived at Olompali for around a month in the summer of 1966. The property was the home of the Chosen Family commune for around two years until a February 1969 electrical fire led

Poster by Harvey W. Cohen, 1966

to widespread fire damage at Burdell Mansion. The photograph on the back cover of the Dead's 1969 album *Aoxomoxoa* was taken at Rancho Olompali early that year.

California Hall (625 Polk St., San Francisco): The Grateful Dead and the Charlatans played a benefit here for the legalization of marijuana on May 29, 1966. The Dead would return that Halloween for the Dance of Death Costume Ball, playing on a bill with Quicksilver Messenger Service and Mimi Farina.

Santa Venetia Armory (153 Madison Ave., San Rafael): The Grateful Dead were one of many psychedelic-era Bay Area bands to play teen dances at this National Guard Armory on June 8 and 9, 1966. They would return to the Armory with Moby Grape on December 29 of the same year.

Poster by George Hunter, 1966

I.D.E.S. Hall (2 Stage Rd., Pescadero): The Dead joined Quicksilver Messenger Service as musical acts performing during the Tour Del Mar Bicycle Race and Folk Rock Festival held in late August 1966.

La Dolphine (1761 Manor Dr., Hillsborough): The Dead played a debutante dance for Ayn and Lyn Mattei at this plush estate on September 2, 1966. According to Frances Moffat's Who's Who column in the *San Francisco Chronicle*, the Dead's set in the estate's garden was loud enough to draw complaints from area residents, so the rest of the gig was moved inside.

Pioneer Ballroom (corner of Morgan and Kellogg Streets, Suisun City): The Dead played a two-night stint at the Pioneer Ballroom on September 23 and 24, 1966. Admission was "Only $1.99 cheap" and psychedelic lights were run by Diogenes Lantern Works.

San Francisco State University (1600 Holloway Ave., San Francisco): The Grateful Dead played the "Whatever It Is" Trips Festival at San Francisco State College (now University) from September 30–October 2, 1966. The three-day multimedia event was held in numerous campus locations across the weekend, with the Dead playing the International Room (Sept. 30), the Women's Gym (Oct. 1), and the Commons Lawn (Oct. 2) during the festival. Years later, the Jerry Garcia Band played the Barbary Coast Room on March 3, 1982.

Peninsula School (920 Peninsula Way, Menlo Park): Jerry Garcia and Robert Hunter got their first-ever paying gig as a folk duo in 1961 at this progressive school, which served kids from nursery school through 8th grade. They played that year's 8th grade graduation ceremony. Garcia would return in 1969 alongside John

Dawson, playing together at the school in New Riders of the Purple Sage the following year.

St. Michael's Alley (436 University Ave., Palo Alto): A key spot in the friendship of Jerry Garcia and Robert Hunter, who shot the breeze at this coffee shop and folk music venue late into the evening sometime in 1961. Garcia also played here at various times during the early '60s, but the Warlocks were rumored to have failed an audition as a collective.

El Camino Park (100 El Camino Real, Palo Alto): The Dead played a free Be-In in this park in early summer of 1967 alongside Big Brother and the Holding Company, and the Sons of Champlin.

Stanford Music Hall (221 University Ave., Palo Alto): The Stanford Theater opened in 1925

as a cinema and has since been restored to serve that purpose. But during a brief time in the mid-'70s, it was the Stanford Music Hall hosting live gigs. Among those who played there were Kingfish, a group featuring Bob Weir, who performed on New Year's Eve 1974 and again on September 13, 1975.

The Poppycock (135 University Ave., Palo Alto): Garcia played this fish and chips joint and live music venue in mid-November 1969 as a member of New Riders of the Purple Sage.

Top of the Tangent (117 University Ave., Palo Alto): A delicatessen with a folk club on the second floor, the Top of the Tangent was an intimate space where the Warlocks played a few hoot nights in the summer of 1965. Pre-Warlocks, Bob Weir had played the room as a member of the Uncalled Four. Weir, Jerry Garcia, and Ron "Pigpen" McKernan's pre-Dead folk act Mother McCree's Uptown Jug Champions also played here, and a recording of a July 1964 performance was officially released on Grateful Dead Records in 1999.

Homer's Warehouse (79 Homer Ln., Palo Alto): Open for just a few years in the early '70s, Homer's Warehouse was an actual semi-converted warehouse popular with local bikers. Among the acts who played there were the Garcia-Saunders Group, and Old and In the Way, Garcia's bluegrass outfit. The OITW show on July 24, 1973, was broadcast live KSZU, Stanford University's college radio station.

Stinson Beach Community Center (32 Belvedere Ave., Stinson Beach): The Grateful Dead held rehearsals in this rustic hall in March 1972. Jerry Garcia would return here on September 30, 1973, to perform with OITW, a

Crispin Kott

Stanford Theater

bluegrass group he formed with David Grisman, Peter Rowan, Vassar Clements, and John Kahn.

Menlo College (1000 El Camino Real, Atherton): The Warlocks played a dance in the dining hall at this college in autumn 1965.

The Underground (1029 El Camino Real, Atherton): Shortly before they became New Riders of the Purple Sage, a group featuring Jerry Garcia and friends David Nelson and John Dawson, played a run of shows at this beer hall in mid-1969.

Mt. Tamalpais Outdoor Theater (Mount Tamalpais State Park, Mill Valley): The Dead played a Peace rally and write-in initiative for California congressional candidate Phil Drath on October 8, 1966. Also on the bill were Bola Sete and Quicksilver Messenger Service, with Joan Baez and Mimi Farina also appearing. The theater has since been renamed the Sidney B. Cushing Memorial Amphitheatre.

Tressider Memorial Union (459 Lagunita Dr., Stanford): The Dead played Stanford's Student Union on October 14, 1966, for the first and only time. They were banned from campus following the raucous show.

Sausalito Heliport (Bolinas St., Sausalito): The Dead played a show at this active heliport on October 15, 1966, returning in mid-1967 to set up shop in the Gate 6 warehouse when they needed a rehearsal space outside of San Francisco.

Las Lomas High School (1460 S. Main St., Walnut Creek): The Dead played an afternoon show at Las Lomas High School on October 23, 1966, an event so wholesome even Phil Lesh's parents were there. The gig was originally scheduled to take place at the Walnut Creek Library as part of a Sunday afternoon series,

but it was moved to Las Lomas for logistical reasons.

North Face Ski Shop (308 Columbus Ave., San Francisco): The Grateful Dead played the grand opening fashion show of the North Face Ski Shop on October 26, 1966.

The Old Cheese Factory (517 Washington St., San Francisco): The Dead played what's been reported as the only-ever rock show at the Old Cheese Factory on November 12, 1966.

Pauley Ballroom (2485 Bancroft Way, Berkeley): A "Danse Macabre" took place at U.C. Berkeley's Pauley Ballroom on December 2, 1966. The Grateful Dead and Country Joe and the Fish played the show, which according to the poster was produced for the junior class by Bill "Jolly Blue" Ehlert, then-owner of Berkeley

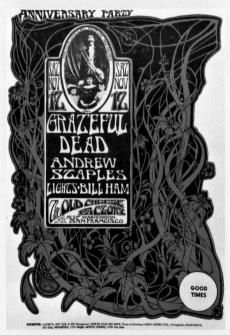

Poster by Stanley Mouse and Alton Kelley, 1966

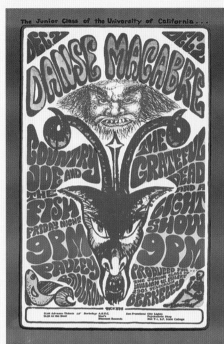

Poster by Ruth Garbell, 1966

club the **Jabberwock (2901 Telegraph Ave., Berkeley)**.

College of Marin (835 College Ave., Kentfield): The Dead played the Irwin P. Diamond Physical Educational Center gym at the College of Marin in mid-December 1966.

Ladera School (360 La Cuesta Dr., Menlo Park): The Grateful Dead played the Ladera Christmas Dance in the multipurpose room at this school on December 17, 1966, after teenagers raised the band's appearance fee.

The Continental Roller Bowl (1600 Martin Ave., Santa Clara): On December 21, 1966, the Grateful Dead played the Continental Roller Bowl. The venue's name was changed to the comparatively upmarket Continental Ballroom by the time the Dead returned the following July.

Berkeley Community Theater (1930 Allston Way, Berkeley): When Jose Feliciano's flight was delayed, the Grateful Dead filled in as support act to the Mamas and the Papas at the Berkeley Community Theater for the early show on January 13, 1967. They headed back into San Francisco to play Fillmore Auditorium that evening.

Winterland Ballroom (2000 Post St., San Francisco ⊘): The Grateful Dead's first of many appearances at Winterland was the First Annual Love Circus, presented by the Love Conspiracy Commune, on March 3, 1967. The group shared the bill with several bands, including Love and Moby Grape. The Dead played the final ever concert at Winterland on December 31, 1978, with the audience receiving a free breakfast early the next morning.

Whisky a Go Go (568 Sacramento St., San Francisco): The Dead played this San Francisco branch of the popular Los Angeles club from March 10–16, 1967. By the following month, the club was gone.

Fugazi Hall (678 Green St., San Francisco): As a celebration of the release of their eponymous debut, the Grateful Dead played a set for friends and label reps on March 20, 1967, that according to *San Francisco Chronicle* columnist Ralph Gleason was cut short by a power outage.

The Rock Garden (4742 Mission St., San Francisco): "A new concept in nightclubs," the Rock Garden hosted the Grateful Dead from March 28–April 2, 1967. The club opened a week earlier with Big Brother and the Holding Company.

San Quentin State Prison (Main St., San Quentin): Members of the Grateful Dead jammed with other musicians during protests

held on a flatbed truck outside the entrance to San Quentin sometime in mid-April 1967 and again on February 15, 1968.

The Rendezvous Inn (567 Sutter St., San Francisco): The Dead played a residency at this longtime gay bar in May 1967, likely on the first four Mondays of the month.

Chester F. Awalt High School (Truman Ave., Mountain View): At the request of one of Jerry Garcia's's former banjo students, the Dead played an afternoon dance concert in this school's Awalt Pavilion on May 18, 1967.

Napa Fairgrounds (900 Fairgrounds Dr., Vallejo): The Dead played with Project Hope at the Napa Fairgrounds on May 29, 1967, thanks to the efforts of local high school kids who helped make the arrangements.

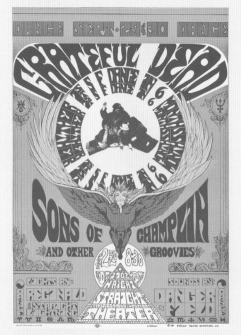

Poster by Chris Braga, 1967

Straight Theater (1702 Haight St., San Francisco ⊘): A short walk from their Ashbury Street HQ, the Straight played a briefly significant role for the Grateful Dead in 1967, with the former movie house serving as both a rehearsal space and occasional live venue. The Dead played a private party in anticipation of that weekend's Monterey Pop Festival at the Straight on June 15, 1967, ahead of the theater's official opening as a music venue in early July. During a late-September 1967 show at the Straight, Mickey Hart sat in as a second drummer with the Dead for the first time. On March 3, 1968, the Dead walked down from their 710 Ashbury Street headquarters, ran power from the Straight Theater into their amps and set up a stage right across Haight Street, playing as part of the first annual Haight Street Fair.

Monterey Pop Festival (2004 Fairground Rd., Monterey): The Grateful Dead played a mostly unmemorable set on the final day of the Monterey Pop Festival on June 18, 1967, their slot sandwiched between legendary performances by the Who and the Jimi Hendrix Experience. The group's set was interrupted by Peter Tork of the Monkees, who addressed the crowd between songs to dispel a rumor that the Beatles were going to perform.

Monterey Peninsula College (980 Fremont St., Monterey): At some point during the mid-June 1967 Monterey Pop Festival, the Grateful Dead played an impromptu set on the athletic field at this college. The group would return here almost two years to the day later for a more official gig on June 14, 1969, when they played in the school's gymnasium with Aum and the Bitter Seeds.

Oakland Auditorium/Henry J. Kaiser Convention Center (10 10th St., Oakland): After the closure of Winterland Ballroom following their New Year's Eve 1978 show, the Grateful Dead found a New Year's home at Oakland Auditorium, which changed its name to the Henry J. Kaiser Convention Center following a 1984 renovation. The Dead played Oakland Auditorium for the first time on June 28, 1967, filling in for recently defunct band the Sparrow on a bill headlined by the Young Rascals. Over the years, the Dead would revisit the auditorium on multi-night stands, playing nearly 60 shows there over two decades.

The Greek Theatre (2001 Gayley Rd., Berkeley): The Dead first played the Greek Theatre in Berkeley on October 1, 1967, sharing the bill with Charles Lloyd and Bola Sete. The show took place one day before the infamous bust at the group's home base at **710 Ashbury in San Francisco**. They would not return again until 1981.

Carousel Ballroom/Fillmore West (10 South Van Ness Ave., San Francisco): For the first half of 1968, the Carousel Ballroom served as a de facto artist-run venue, a doomed partnership between the Grateful Dead, the Jefferson Airplane, and Quicksilver Messenger Service, with Big Brother and the Holding Company also an active participant. The Dead and Quicksilver Messenger Service played the Carousel on January 17, 1968, and all three principles would play sporadic gigs there into June of that year. By July, the venue was taken over by promoter Bill Graham, who moved his base of operations here from the smaller **Fillmore Auditorium (1805 Geary Blvd., San Francisco)**. The Dead would go on to play here numerous times, the last on July 2, 1971, just two days before it closed for good.

Clifford's Catering (1300 Boulevard Way, Walnut Creek): The Dead played a pair of dates in the upstairs hall of this catering business and restaurant on March 1 and 2, 1968.

KMPX (50 Green St., San Francisco): Local rock groups joined a strike by the staff at KMPX-FM, with Creedence Clearwater Revival opening the proceedings on a flatbed truck on the afternoon of March 18, 1968. The Grateful Dead also hit the stage, though accounts vary as to whether they managed to play any songs before police shut the rally down. Two days later, the Dead performed as part of an all-star benefit fundraiser for KMPX staff at the **Avalon Ballroom (1268 Sutter St., San Francisco)**.

Northern California Folk-Rock Festival (Santa Clara County Fairgrounds, 344 Tully Rd., San Jose): Though not on the poster, the Grateful Dead were a late addition to the first annual Northern California Folk-Rock Festival, held on May 18 and 19, 1968. Also on the bill were the Jefferson Airplane, the Doors, Big Brother and the Holding Company, and many other popular groups of the era. The Dead's afternoon appearance on the 18th was sandwiched between a pair of shows at Shrine Exhibition Hall in Los Angeles on May 17 and 18, meaning they finished up their first night in L.A., flew up to play in San Jose the following afternoon, then flew back to L.A. for that evening's show.

St. Francis Yacht Club (99 Yacht Rd., San Francisco): On July 14, 1968, the Dead played "A Day on the Green," a benefit for the Action Jazz Movement, at the St. Francis Yacht Club. Also on the bill were the Ornette Coleman

Quintet, the John Handy Quintet, and the Youngbloods.

Palace of Fine Arts Theatre (3301 Lyon St., San Francisco): The Grateful Dead played an afternoon set as part of the Palace of Fine Arts Festival on September 2, 1968. Also on the bill were the Sons of Champlin, Country Weather, and the San Francisco Mime Troupe.

The Dream Bowl (intersection of Hwy. 29 & N. Kelly Rd., Vallejo): The Dead played this venue on February 21 and 22, 1969, with audio of the latter show seeing an official release in 2015 as part of the expansive 30 Trips Around the Sun set.

The Hilton Hotel (333 O'Farrell St., San Francisco): The Black and White Symphony Ball, a benefit for the San Francisco Symphony Orchestra, was held at the Hilton on March 15, 1969. The Grateful Dead were the featured performers, and according to a review by Virginia Westover in the *San Francisco Chronicle*, Bob Weir's parents hosted a pre-gala party in their suite.

Hall of Flowers/Fiesta Hall, San Mateo County Fairgrounds (1346 Saratoga Ave., San Mateo): On May 9, 1969, the Dead played a five-song set at the Hall of Flowers, originally founded in 1926 as the Little Flower Show by the Burlingame Garden and Flower Club. On December 12, 1981, the Dead returned to the fairgrounds, this time in Fiesta Hall for a Dance for Nuclear Disarmament, where they followed a set as Joan Baez's backing band with electric and acoustic sets of their own.

Campilindo High School (300 Moraga Rd., Moraga): The Dead played Campilindo High School on May 16, 1969, sharing the bill with Frumious Bandersnatch and Velvet Hammer.

Veterans Memorial Auditorium (1351 Maple Ave., Santa Rosa): Shortly before they were officially known as Hot Tuna, Jefferson Airplane members Jack Casady and Jorma Kaukonen played a pair of dates alongside the Grateful Dead in this auditorium on June 27 and 28, 1969. On the first night, Tom Ralston, drummer with opening act Cleanliness and Godliness Skiffle Band, sat in with the Dead on drums until a tardy Mickey Hart arrived.

Family Dog on the Great Highway (660 Great Highway, San Francisco): After losing their lease at the **Avalon Ballroom (1268 Sutter St., San Francisco),** the commune/promotions outfit the Family Dog set up shop in the former Edgewater Ballroom on the site of the old Playland at the Beach in June 1969. The Dead first played the new enterprise on August 2 and 3, 1969, sharing the bill with the Ballet Afro-Haiti and Albert Collins.

San Jose State University (211 S. 9th St., San Jose): The Dead played a Halloween Dance in the Loma Prieta Room in the Student Union at San Jose State on October 31, 1969. The venue had only been open for two weeks, with Garcia playing with New Riders of the Purple Sage as its debut act on October 17, 1969.

Spartan Stadium (1251 S. 10th St., San Jose): Keyboardist Brett Mydland made his debut with the Dead in San Jose State's 30,000-seat football stadium on April 22, 1979.

San Jose Civic Auditorium (135 W. San Carlos Ave., San Jose): The Dead played this 3,000-capacity venue just once, on August 20, 1972.

Chateau Liberté (22700 Old Santa Cruz Hwy., Los Gatos): Both Bob Weir (with Kingfish) and

Jerry Garcia (with Merl Saunders) played this former resort in the mid-'70s.

Shoreline Amphitheatre (1 Amphitheatre Pkwy., Mountain View): Opened in 1986 by Bill Graham Presents, Shoreline Amphitheatre played host to the Grateful Dead a total of 39 times, starting on October 2, 1987. The Dead's final Bay Area gigs took place at Shoreline between June 2–4, 1995; Jerry Garcia passed away that August 9.

Santa Cruz County Fairgrounds (2601 East Lake Ave., Watsonville, CA): The Dead played this fairgrounds on September 24, 1983.

Boarding House (960 Bush St., San Francisco): As well-known for comedy as music, the Boarding House was where Jerry Garcia's bluegrass band OITW recorded their debut album on October 8, 1973. The album wasn't released until February 1975.

Lanai Theater (520 2nd Ave., Crockett): The Dead played a Moratorium Day Gathering at this former single-screen cinema on November 15, 1969.

Euphoria Ballroom (737 E. Francisco Blvd., San Rafael): The ballroom of a former luxury hotel, by the time it was known as the Euphoria and began hosting rock concerts it was on the verge of crumbling. The Grateful Dead played here on July 14 and 16, 1970.

KQED (2601 Mariposa St., San Francisco): The Dead played in studio at KQED on August 30, 1970, a 30-minute video and radio simulcast that has since found its way online.

Santa Rosa Fairgrounds (1350 Bennett Valley Rd., Santa Rosa): The Grateful Dead and New Riders of the Purple Sage played these fairgrounds on December 12, 1970.

The Harding Theater (616 Divisadero St., San Francisco): The Grateful Dead played in this 500-seat historic theater on November 6 and 7, 1971.

Maples Pavilion (655 Campus Dr., Stanford): The Dead played Stanford University's basketball arena on February 9, 1973.

Cow Palace (2600 Geneva Ave., Daly City): Though the Dead initially had plans to play the Cow Palace for the first time in May 1973, the pair of scheduled shows were moved to Kezar Stadium in Golden Gate Park. The group finally made it to the Cow Palace on March 23, 1974, a show that has since been released as vol. 13 of the official Dick's Picks audio archive series. On New Year's Eve 1976, the Grateful

Ad for a Black Panthers benefit, 1971

Dead were joined at the Cow Palace by Santana and the Sons of Champlin. Audio of the Dead's performance that night was released by Rhino Records in 2006.

Oakland-Alameda County Coliseum (7000 Coliseum Way, Oakland): Bill Graham's Day on the Green was in its second year the first time the Grateful Dead played the cavernous outdoor Oakland Coliseum, headlining a bill that included the Beach Boys, New Riders of the Purple Sage, and Commander Cody and His Lost Planet Airmen on June 8, 1974. They would return with Day on the Green on October 8 and 9, 1976, playing with the Who. The Dead's tour with Bob Dylan also took place in the stadium on July 24, 1987.

Oakland-Alameda County Arena (7000 Coliseum Way, Oakland): This indoor venue was the permanent home of the Golden State Warriors basketball team from the 1971–1972 season through the 2018–2019 season, after which they moved to the newly built Chase Center in Mission Bay, San Francisco. The Dead first played the arena as part of a benefit for the Campaign for Economic Democracies Task Force on Environmental Cancer on February 17, 1979. It was Keith and Donna Godchaux's final gig as members of the Grateful Dead. The venue became a favorite for the Dead in their latter years.

Great American Music Hall (859 O'Farrell St., San Francisco): By 1975, the notion of seeing the Grateful Dead in a small venue was almost a fantasy. Which is what it must have felt like to catch the band play at Great American Music Hall on August 13 of that year, a concert organized for broadcast over FM radio. In 1991, the Dead released the audio of the concert as *One from the Vault*, with the audio quality far surpassing the bootlegs which had circulated for years.

Orpheum Theatre (1192 Market St., San Francisco): The Dead played a six-show residency at the fabled Orpheum in mid-July, 1976, the 50th anniversary of the theater, which opened in 1926 as the Pantages Theatre.

The Warfield Theatre (982 Market St., San Francisco): Between September 25–October 14, 1980, the Grateful Dead played 15 sold-out shows at the Warfield, performing an acoustic and an electric set each night. Songs recorded during the run were combined with others from Radio City Music Hall for a pair of double albums released the following year: *Reckoning* (acoustic) and *Dead Set* (electric). Jerry Garcia was quite fond of the Warfield, playing there with a variety of musicians nearly 90 times over the years.

Mill Valley Recreation Center (180 Camino Alto, Mill Valley): The Dead played a special acoustic show for disabled children and their families in this small rec center on December 8, 1980.

Moscone Center (747 Howard St., San Francisco): The Dead played A Night of Peace and Healing, a benefit for the Vietnam Veterans Project, at the Moscone Center on May 28, 1982. Also on the bill were Jefferson Starship, Boz Scaggs, and Country Joe McDonald.

Frost Amphitheater (365 Lasuen St., Stanford): The Grateful Dead played a two-night stand at Stanford University's Frost Amphitheater on October 9 and 10, 1982, with the latter sometimes cited as among the band's best shows of the '80s. They would return another 11 times between 1983–1989.

Marin Veterans' Memorial Auditorium (10 Ave. of the Flags, San Rafael): The Dead played a pair of Halloween shows at this 2,000-seat auditorium on October 30 and 31, 1983, returning the following spring for four more nights. The group liked the room enough that when it came time to cut the basic tracks for *In the Dark*, their 1987 album, they recorded from the stage, playing to an empty hall as though otherwise performing live.

San Francisco Civic Auditorium (99 Grove St., San Francisco): The Dead closed out 1983 with four shows at what's now known as the Bill Graham Civic Auditorium.

Laguna Seca Recreation Area (1025 Monterey-Salinas Hwy., Monterey): A Weekend in Monterey, headlined by the Grateful Dead with support from Bruce Hornsby and the Range and Ry Cooder, happened here on May 9 and 10, 1987. They would return the following July for three shows, with support from Los Lobos for the last two.

NOTEWORTHY RECORDING SESSIONS

Golden State Recorders (665 Harrison St., San Francisco): The Grateful Dead had their first group experience in a recording studio at Golden State Recorders in November 1965, booking time incognito as the Emergency Crew. Several tracks from the session were released in 2003 as part of the *Birth of the Dead* compilation, including an early version of "Caution (Do Not Stop on Tracks)," and rare originals like "Mindbender (Confusion's Prince)" and "The Only Time Is Now," neither of which stayed in the group's repertoire for very long.

Sound City (363 6th St., San Francisco): In early 1966, the Grateful Dead took part in a studio recording project designed to replicate the sound of the Acid Tests. The Dead were involved with a session at Sound City on January 29, 1966.

Scorpio Studios (737 Buena Vista West, San Francisco): The Dead laid down numerous tracks in a studio located in the home of Gene Estribou in various sessions during June and July of 1966. Scorpio Records released the first Dead single from these sessions, "Stealin'" b/w, "Don't Ease Me In" in July 1966. Those two tracks plus several others from the sessions were included on the official *Birth of the Dead* compilation in 2003. Quicksilver Messenger Service and the Steve Miller Band recorded material for the film *Revolution* in Estribou's studio. The house was built in 1897, and former residents include journalist Ambrose Bierce and author Jack London, who wrote *White Fang* here. The house was later owned by actor and activist Danny Glover.

Coast Recorders (960 Bush St., San Francisco): Located in the building that would eventually become legendary comedy and music club the Boarding House, Coast Recorders was as close as San Francisco got to a professional recording studio in the early '60s. Still, by the time local bands began making a name for themselves, they mostly decamped to higher-end studios in Los Angeles or New York. That was the case with the Grateful Dead, who recorded the bulk of their eponymous debut in sunny L.A., save for "The Golden Road (To Unlimited Devotion)," cut at Coast in January 1967. The group returned to 960 Bush to record some material for their sophomore album, *Anthem of the Sun*, an ambitious psychedelic collage assembled from live and studio tracks.

Pacific Recording Studios (1737 S. El Camino Real, San Mateo): The first 16-track recording studio in the Bay Area, the Grateful Dead recorded much of their third album, *Aoxomoxoa*, here.

Pacific High Recording (60 Brady St., San Francisco): With Richard Olsen of the Charlatans serving as the studio's manager, many San Francisco bands came through Pacific High Studios in the late '60s and early '70s. The Grateful Dead spent nine days here in 1969 recording their fourth studio *Workingman's Dead*.

Wally Heider Studios (245 Hyde St., San Francisco): Opened in October 1969, Wally Heider Studios quickly became the city's premier recording studio, with local bands able to stick close to home to get the sound they wanted. The Dead recorded *American Beauty* there in the late summer of 1970. Heider retired in the '70s, but

the since-renamed Hyde Street Studios is still active and still pushing out great music.

Record Plant (2200 Bridgeway, Sausalito): Opened in 1972, the Record Plant served as the Northern Californian outpost for a pair of studios already in operation in New York and Los Angeles. Among the historic recordings produced here were the Grateful Dead's *Wake of the Flood*, cut in 1973.

CBS Studios (827 Folsom St., San Francisco): Previously the second home of Coast Recorders and soon to become the Automatt, this Folsom St. studio was at the time owned and operated by CBS Records. Most artists tended to prefer the laid back atmosphere at Wally Heider Studios at this time, but the Grateful Dead came here in 1974 to record *From the Mars Hotel*.

Le Club Front (20 Front St., San Rafael): Rehearsal space and recording studio of Jerry Garcia's. Many Garcia-related bands jammed and recorded here, including the Grateful Dead, who cut much of *Shakedown Street* (1978) and *Go to Heaven* (1980) in the studio, as well as material for *Built to Last* (1989). The group also rehearsed here with Bob Dylan ahead of their joint 1987 tour.

Skywalker Studio (5858 Lucas Valley Rd., Nicasio): After a return to the Marin Veterans' Memorial Auditorium failed to yield similar results to the recording of *In the Dark* two years earlier, the Dead moved on to George Lucas's fabled Skywalker Ranch, where some of *Built to Last* was recorded in 1989. In the end, the album was recorded piecemeal, with the individual parts being assembled by Jerry Garcia.

American Beauty: the Grateful Dead
New on Warner Bros. Records and Tapes

OTHER NOTEWORTHY LOCATIONS

Ed's Superette (101 Calle Del Mar, Stinson Beach): The lone grocery store in Stinson Beach, Ed's Superette has a long connection to rock and roll, with Jerry Garcia renewing his lifetime love of bluegrass and the banjo following a chance meeting there with mandolin player David Grisman. For a period in the '70s, Garcia maintained an office above Ed's Superette.

Sans Souci (18 Ave. Farralone, Stinson Beach): In 1971, Jerry Garcia and Mountain Girl bought the home at 18 Ave. Farralone, which Garcia nicknamed "Sans Souci" ("No Worries") for $20,000. It has been sold numerous times since, recently hitting the market in February 2017 for an asking price of $4.35 million.

The Bridge House (68 Bridge Road, Ross): Phil Lesh bought this 7,900-square foot house designed in the early 20th century by Conrad Meussdorffer in 2002, selling it in 2016 for $9,925,000.

Owsley Stanley's House (6024 Ascot Dr., Oakland): The Dead frequently partied at this Piedmont Pines home during the late '60s, a period when it was rented by Owsley Stanley, the group's sound engineer and a chemist who produced some of the era's most sought after LSD.

Birth of the Dead (1012 High St., Palo Alto): Former residence of Phil Lesh, where as legend goes, on November 12, 1965, local band the Warlocks learned of a New York City band with the same name and set forth to devise a new moniker. Jerry Garcia suggested the Grateful Dead, thus giving the young band its new name and giving sole ownership of the name "the Warlocks" to a group on the opposite side of the

1012 High Street, Palo Alto

country. That band would soon go on to rename themselves the Velvet Underground.

Jose's Bar/The 400 Club (400 1st St., San Francisco ⊘): Former bar owned by Jerry Garcia's parents, Jose, known as "Joe" and Ruth, known as "Bobbie." After Jose's death when Garcia was five, Bobbie took over the bar.

87 Harrington Street

121 Amazon Avenue

Years later, Jerry, his brother Tiff, and his mother lived in an apartment above the newly rebuilt building, with Bobbie the proprietor of the 400 Club. Garcia was a teenager at the time.

Childhood Home of Jerry Garcia (87 Harrington St., San Francisco): Garcia and his brother Tiff lived in this Excelsior District home with his maternal grandparents, William and Tillie Clifford, following the death of his father in 1947. Garcia lived here for the next five years.

Childhood Home of Jerry Garcia (121 Amazon Ave., San Francisco): Garcia lived here with his parents, Joe and Bobbie Garcia for the first five years of his life. Garcia briefly returned to this home in 1953 after his mother remarried before the family moved to Menlo Park.

Monroe Elementary School (260 Madrid St., San Francisco): Jerry Garcia attended elementary school at Monroe.

Teenage Home of Jerry Garcia (1339 Willow Rd., Menlo Park): Garcia lived in a home at this address with his brother, mother and stepfather.

When he was 14, his mother moved the family back to San Francisco.

James Denman Middle School (241 Oneida Ave., San Francisco): Jerry Garcia attended middle school here.

Balboa High School (1000 Cayuga Ave., San Francisco): Until his penchant for trouble led his mother to move the family to rural Cazadero after his sophomore year, Garcia went to high school at Balboa.

Fort Ord (Reservation Rd., Marina): In 1960, Jerry Garcia received basic training at this since shuttered Army base. He enlisted as punishment for stealing his mother's car.

Presidio of San Francisco: During his brief time in the United States Army, Jerry Garcia was stationed here. He received a general discharge in December 1960, after going AWOL and missing roll call on numerous occasions. Phil Lesh had a successful audition for the Sixth Army Band in the late '50s, then stationed at the Presidio, but he was deemed unfit for military service.

Kepler's Books (935 El Camino Real/1010 El Camino Real, Menlo Park): Founded at 935 El Camino Real in 1955 by Roy Kepler, Kepler's was instrumental in nurturing the burgeoning bohemian scene by letting patrons drink coffee, play guitars, wax philosophical, and just hang out. Jerry Garcia was a frequent visitor in the first half of the '60s. Kepler's moved across the street to **1010 El Camino Real** in 1989, and it's still there today.

The Chateau (2100 Santa Cruz Ave., Menlo Park ⊘): Residence of Jerry Garcia, Robert Hunter, David Nelson, and a revolving cast of other South Bay bohemians in the early years of the '60s. The house has since been demolished.

Crispin Kott

The Hamilton Street House (436 Hamilton Ave., Palo Alto ⊘): After decamping from the Chateau, Hunter, Nelson, and others moved into a ramshackle Victorian home curiously dubbed—given its actual address—the Hamilton Street House. Garcia was a frequent visitor and would often play music with his friends there. The house has since been knocked down.

Gilman Street House (Gilman St., Palo Alto ⊘) : Nelson and banjo player Rick Shubb lived in a house behind the Palo Alto Post Office in 1965, and though Garcia didn't live here, it was the first place he and others from his group of musical friends first dropped acid. The house is long gone, and with it the specific address.

The Purple House (661 Waverley St., Palo Alto): Jerry Garcia lived in this purple Palo Alto house for around five months, bridging the end of 1965 and the beginning of 1966, the period when the Warlocks morphed into the Grateful Dead. Garcia and other members of the Dead moved to their infamous house on San Francisco's Ashbury Street soon after.

Ken Kesey's House (9 Perry Lane, Menlo Park ⊘): Members of the then-Warlocks attended parties at Kesey's cottage in the mid-'60s, ingratiating themselves with the Merry Pranksters prior to becoming a house band for the Acid Tests. Kesey's cottage is long gone, and Perry Lane has since been renamed Perry Avenue. Jerry Garcia and Phil Lesh supposedly met at a party here in 1962.

Menlo-Atherton High School (555 Middlefield Rd., Atherton): Bob Weir went to high school here, a school which counts among its graduates Stevie Nicks and Lindsey Buckingham of Fleetwood Mac.

Berkeley High School (1980 Allston Way, Berkeley): Phil Lesh attended high school at Berkeley High, graduating in 1957.

College of San Mateo (1700 W. Hillsdale Blvd., San Mateo): Grateful Dead bass guitarist Phil Lesh briefly attended college here, studying in the school's music department. One of the many found sounds that made their way onto the Dead's collage-assembled second album *Anthem of the Sun* was a brief snippet of Lesh playing trumpet at the College of San Mateo.

Hart Music Company (894 Laurel Ave., San Carlos): Dead drummer Mickey Hart and his father Lenny owned a drum shop on Laurel Avenue, which Mickey managed between 1965–1967.

Swain's House of Music (451 University Ave., Palo Alto): The Warlocks rented music gear from this shop in their earliest days.

Dana Morgan Music (534 Bryant St., Palo Alto): Jerry Garcia taught banjo and Bob Weir guitar at this shop owner by Dana Morgan, Sr., until they fired his son as the bass guitarist in the Warlocks and replaced him with Phil Lesh in late-May 1965. Garcia and Weir then took their teaching talents to Guitars Unlimited in Menlo Park. Fifteen-year-old Weir first met Garcia at Dana Morgan Music on New Year's Eve 1963 when he and Bob Matthews heard banjo coming from the back of the shop and discovered a perturbed Garcia, picking away while awaiting students who would never come. Weir had his guitar, a jam broke out, leading to the formation of Mother McCree's Uptown Jug Champions.

Guitars Unlimited (1035 El Camino Real, Menlo Park): Both Jerry Garcia (banjo) and Bob Weir (guitar) worked as instructors in this shop from the Warlocks era through the beginnings of the

group's time as the Grateful Dead, borrowing equipment for rehearsals and gigs. Rumor has it that much of the equipment the Dead took with them for their early-'66 run of Acid Test shows in Southern California were unofficially borrowed from—and possibly never returned to—Guitars Unlimited.

Veterans Administration Hospital (795 Willow Rd., Menlo Park): The building where Ken Kesey was an intern and was inspired to write *One Flew Over the Cuckoo's Nest* is still there, but there's no indication the LSD experiments both Kesey and Grateful Dead lyricist Robert Hunter participated in are still underway.

The Spread (Soquel Dr. and Dover Dr., Santa Cruz ⊘**):** The first of Ken Kesey's Acid Tests was held in Ken Babbs's house, known as "The Spread," on November 27, 1965. Contrary to rumors, the Grateful Dead did not perform, but Jerry Garcia, Bob Weir, and Phil Lesh were there and picked up random instruments to jam during the revelry. The Spread is long gone, but a memorial plaque is at its former site, now a stop on the 71 bus line.

The Grateful Dead House (710 Ashbury St., San Francisco): Though they only lived here for around two years, various members of the group had formative and psychedelic experiences within the walls of the unofficial City Hall of Haight-Ashbury. They were busted here—Garcia and his girlfriend Mountain Girl were out shopping—on October 2, 1967, a move which set the wheels in motion for the group's eventual decision five months later to leave the city for the relative wilds of Marin. They played one final free show on Haight in March 1968, walking there from 710 Ashbury and setting up on a flatbed truck. It remains one of the primary

sightseeing destinations for Deadheads visiting San Francisco.

Hotel Triton (342 Grant Ave., San Francisco): This boutique hotel not far from Chinatown and Union Square boasts among its rooms the Jerry Garcia Suite, designed by the late cofounder of the Grateful Dead and includes some of his watercolor paintings and drawings.

Terrapin Crossroads (100 Yacht Club Dr., San Rafael): This live music venue and restaurant founded by Dead bass guitarist Phil Lesh has been a popular local spot since opening in 2012. The first concerts were a run of 12 shows by Phil Lesh and Friends between March 17– April 1 of that year.

The Mars Hotel (192 4th St., San Francisco ⊘**):** Former derelict hotel that was for a time the home of Jack Kerouac. The hotel served as partial inspiration for the Grateful Dead's 1974 album, *From the Mars Hotel*, and can be seen on its cover. The exterior of the since-demolished hotel can be seen in the video for David Bowie's "The Jean Genie."

Mickey Hart's Ranch (2495 Novato Blvd./2200 Novato Blvd., Novato ⊘**):** Though the buildings are long gone and the land now public, Grateful Dead drummer Mickey Hart rented a ranch for over a decade that served as a de facto headquarters and rehearsal space for the Dead for a few years beginning in 1969.

Jerry Garcia Amphitheater (McLaren Park, 116 John F. Shelley Dr., San Francisco): Though the Grateful Dead's connection to Golden Gate Park may seem more tangible, the renaming of the McLaren Park Amphitheater in July 2005 makes perfect sense. It wasn't just the site of the annual Jerry Day celebrations, which began two years earlier; the 318-acre park in which the

Crispin Kott

Jerry Garcia Ampitheater, McClaren Park

amphitheater sits was also quite close to where Garcia grew up.

The Western Front (9895 O'Farrell St., San Francisco): The Western Front was a short-lived psychedelic club in 1967, but before that the Dead are rumored to have rehearsed here for around two months in mid-1966. The address is perhaps best known as the Mitchell Brothers O'Farrell Theatre, a strip club which opened in 1969.

Questing Beast (2504 San Pablo Ave., Berkeley): A short-lived folk coffeehouse, the Questing Beast is rumored to have also been home to Grateful Dead rehearsals in early 1966.

The Green Factory (1647 Virginia St., Berkeley): In the mid-'60s, this was the residence and laboratory for Dead sound engineer and LSD manufacturer Owsley "Bear" Stanley. Before neighbors complained about the noise and forced the group into the Questing Beast, they held a handful of rehearsals here.

The New Portrero Theatre (312 Connecticut St., San Francisco): The Dead rehearsed in this small, disused movie house in early 1968.

Next Door to the Fillmore (1839 Geary Blvd., San Francisco): In his memoir *Deal: Three Decades of Drumming, Dreams and Drugs with the Grateful Dead*, Bill Kreutzmann recalled the Dead rehearsing in a former synagogue in the shadow of Fillmore Auditorium. Other bands of the era used the space to prepare for gigs at the Fillmore as well. It would later serve as a punk venue.

Grateful Dead Office (2196 Union St., San Francisco): Though the Dead split the city in the first half of 1968, the group's comanagers Rock Scully and Danny Rifkin set up an office less than three miles from their former Ashbury St. HQ.

Contratti Park Baseball Field (4 School St., Fairfax): Back in the early '70s when the Grateful Dead and Jefferson Airplane used to play softball here it was called Central Field.

CASTRO—THE MISSION—CANDLESTICK PARK

CRUCIBLE OF LATIN ROCK
Mission YMCA (4080 Mission Street, San Francisco) In the late '60s, much of the Mission's social culture was defined by a wide assortment of gangs, but one unifying factor to emerge was the Malibus, a Latin-tinged R&B group led by vocalists Arcelio Garcia and Richard Bean. Their weekend dances at the YMCA got so big that by 1969 they graduated to larger venues like the **Glide Memorial United Methodist Church (330 Ellis Street, San Francisco)**, and eventually landed a six-month residency at the **Nite-Life (2470 San Bruno Avenue, San Francisco)**, where they ultimately evolved into the more overtly Latin Malo, which included guitarist Jorge Santana, younger brother of Carlos. Known nationally for their Bean-penned 1971 hit "Suavecito" (often referred to as the Chicano National Anthem), Malo emerged as the most influential Latin rock band after Santana and a Bay Area institution. Bean left in 1972 and eventually formed his own group Sapo, which continues to perform to this

day. Arcelio Garcia continued to lead Malo in its various forms until his death in August 2020.

THE ROCK GARDEN/THE GHETTO CLUB
4742 Mission St.
One of many short-lived clubs hitting San Francisco and the surrounding Bay Area in the '60s, the Rock Garden featured week-long engagements with groups like Big Brother and the Holding Company, Love, and the Grateful Dead in the spring of 1967. By 1969, it had become the Ghetto Club, a key venue in the rising fusion of Latin, soul, and rock music, with Abel and the Prophets,something of a house band.

DIFFERENT FUR STUDIOS
3470 19th St.
Founded in 1968 by fellow synthesizer enthusiasts Patrick Gleeson and John Viera, Different Fur was dubbed thus by poet Michael McClure, who initially offered "Really Different Fur Trading Company" before brevity won out. Operating in the early '70s as both a music workspace and arts commune, Different Fur's reputation as a forward-thinking studio enticed artists like Herbie Hancock, Neil Young, Devo, Taj Mahal, Van Morrison, and David Byrne and Brian Eno, who came there to work on their fabled collaboration, *My Life in the Bush of Ghosts*.

Different Fur remains active as a recording studio in its original location, and under the ownership of former intern Patrick Brown, who has expanded its use to include live performance videos.

SUAVECITO/NENA

WB 16155

Malo

WB

Andi Sumpter

Different Fur Studios

THE CHAPEL
777 Valencia St.
Breathing life into the former Gantner-Maison-Domergue Funeral Home, the Chapel was opened in 2013 by restauranteur and developer Jack Knowles, quickly establishing itself as a key live music venue in a setting that retained much of its century-old character, from its wrought iron gates to its mock Tudor interior. Since opening its doors, the Chapel has hosted Yo La Tengo, Oh Sees, Laurie Anderson, Cate Le Bon, and Peter Murphy, who performed an extended career-spanning residency there in March 2019.

STRANDED RECORDS/AQUARIUS RECORDS
1055 Valencia St., San Francisco/14 Glen Ave., Oakland
The brick and mortar arm of archival record label Superior Viaduct, Stranded has shops in San Francisco, Oakland, and across the

country in New York City. Stranded first opened in Oakland in 2012, branching out across the Bay to San Francisco four years later. The San Francisco shop is in the former location of the city's iconic Aquarius Records, which moved to Valencia Street from 3961 24th Street in 1996. It was previously located in two different storefronts in the Castro. Aquarius shut its doors for good in 2016 after nearly four decades in operation.

THE KILOWATT
3160 16th St.
For over 25 years, The Kilowatt has served the Mission as a punk rock-sports-motorcycle dive bar, with pool tables and dart boards and a fully stocked jukebox. For a few years in the mid-'90s, The Kilowatt was also a live venue, with Pavement, Fuck, Creeper Lagoon, Neutral Milk Hotel, Turbonegro, and the Apples in Stereo all playing there.

CANDLESTICK PARK
602 Jamestown Ave. ⊘
Opened in 1960 as the home stadium for the San Francisco Giants, Candlestick Park was for nearly three decades shared by the baseball club with the city's NFL franchise, the San Francisco 49ers. The Giants were the first to leave, setting up shop around seven miles north along the San Francisco Bay at **Pac Bell Park (24 Willie Mays Plaza, San Francisco)**, which as of 2020 is known as Oracle Park. The 49ers held on until 2014 when they moved out of the city altogether for newly built **Levi's Stadium (4900 Marie P. DeBartolo Way, Santa Clara)**, and Candlestick has since been demolished.

In addition to serving as the home to local sports teams, Candlestick Park also hosted live music, most famously the Beatles' final concert on August 29, 1966. Though the Fab Four made no public announcement to that effect, they were burned out by touring and wanted to

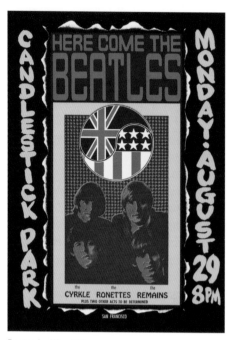

Poster by Wes Wilson

spend more time in the studio working on their increasingly complex music. Though they did play an impromptu set on the rooftop of their own Apple Corps headquarters in January 1969, the Candlestick concert is still often regarded as the band's last.

In October 1981, the Rolling Stones sold out two nights at Candlestick, with support from George Thorogood and the Destroyers, and the J. Geils Band. Van Halen, Metallica, Jimmy Buffett, Justin Timberlake, and Jay-Z also played Candlestick, but fittingly it was former Beatle Paul McCartney who played the last ever concert there on August 14, 2014.

SANTANA

Gijsbert Hanekroot/Alamy

"San Francisco became the epicenter of multidimensional consciousness—it was the place where you could dive into all this multiplicity. It wasn't just music or clothes or politics or drugs or sex or colors—it was everything together. . . . Instead of the world dragging its feet to catch up with the way people were thinking and feeling, a whole new generation was in sync."

—CARLOS SANTANA, *THE UNIVERSAL TONE*, 2014

The conventional wisdom regarding Carlos Santana, that he combined Latin music with rock, is at best facile and incomplete. The reality is that the classic Santana band, the group and sound that came together in the late '60s, was a representation of the cultural uniqueness and complexity of the Mission, the ethnically diverse San Francisco district in which he lived, and its people.

Carlos was born in Jalisco, Mexico, but grew up in Tijuana, that legendary crossroads of cultures. His father was an experienced mariachi bandleader, and encouraged him musically, first on clarinet, then violin, and

ultimately guitar by age eight. When he reached his early teens Carlos was thoroughly enthralled by the African American bluesmen of the '50s. "For me, the blues were what punk music is today," he recalled in *Voices of Latin Rock*. For us the epitome of being a rebel was to listen to John Lee Hooker or Muddy Waters. . . ." He was decidedly averse to the costumed professionalism of traditional Mexican music or the jazz he knew. When the family moved north to San Francisco in 1962, he stayed behind and continued to hone his chops playing in various Tijuana clubs. Eventually he did follow suit, but the transition was not an easy one. Initially the

2368 3rd Street

Santanas lived in a small flat above the Latin American Club where his father worked (**2368 3rd St., San Francisco**), but by the following year they had a more spacious apartment at **1A Juri Street**. Significantly, this new place also had a small storage room that gave Carlos some privacy to practice guitar. He attended **James Lick Junior High (1220 Noe St., San Francisco)**, and **Mission High School (3750**

18th St., San Francisco)**, but struggled in all of his subjects except art.

He and his family moved again, to **704 14th Street**, just off Market. He got a dishwashing job at the **Tic Tock Drive-In (1000 3rd St., San Francisco ⊘)**, a job he held until he became a full-time musician in 1967, to pay for a white Gibson SG. During high school he began to form bands of his own with fellow students and other kids from the neighborhood, and became exposed to the rich variety of live music in the Mission. The population was a unique melange of cultures; Black, white, and a multitude of Latin-American nationalities, each of whom had a unique musical take on their immigrant roots.

Carlos and his friends also became frequent visitors to the **Fillmore Auditorium (1805 Geary Blvd., San Francisco)**, which had, under the stewardship of Bill Graham, built a following by deeply connecting it with the diversity of San Francisco culture. On any given night, rock, folk, soul, or some hybrid thereof was likely to be experienced, and all were welcome. This ethos became an essential ingredient of Carlos's musical direction, and he assembled the group around him with this in mind. Initially the band would coalesce around the name Santana Blues Band, or Santana Blues. Despite

Mission High School

704 14th Street

the name, however, and the fact that Carlos's guitar was the featured instrument, it was more of a collective, with no definitive leader. That would prove to be a recipe for creative growth and enormous success early on, but would also portend conflict and self-destruction down the road. David Brown (bass), Marcus Malone (percussion), Michael Carabello (congas), Jose "Chepito" Areas (timbales) and Gregg Rolie (keyboards and vocals), were critical early members that contributed to the innovative new sound of the band.

After a few fits and starts, Bill Graham, a closet Latin music aficionado, took the band under his wing, offering them free rehearsal space and regular slots headlining and opening for various acts at the Fillmore and **Fillmore West (10 S. Van Ness Ave., San Francisco)** through 1968. By January 1969, they were signed by Clive Davis to Columbia and began work on their first album. The initial sessions were disappointing, however, and after adding Michael Shrieve as drummer, they entered **Pacific Studios (1737 S. El Camino Real, San Mateo ⊘)** in May and successfully completed the album, *Santana*. Before its release in December, Bill Graham had sent them to the East Coast, culminating in their blistering performance at Woodstock, a revelatory coming-out party for a previously unknown band. Santana would ultimately hit #4 on the Billboard album chart, with the single "Evil Ways," a Bill Graham suggestion to their repertoire that had been a Latin hit for Willie Bobo, reaching #9 on the pop singles chart.

That first album would prove to be a breakthrough for Santana, but also a tipping point for Latin-American music. In an era of civil rights struggles and emerging ethnic pride, America's enthusiastic embrace of Santana was, in a sense, a form of cultural validation; the band's multicultural identity a talisman of what was achievable in a broader sense.

Poster by Lee Conklin, 1968. The image was later reconfigured for the first Santana album cover.

The band in this form would release two more classic albums over the next two years. *Abraxas*, released in 1970 and often regarded as this group's masterpiece, contained two signature Santana recordings: "Black Magic Woman," a reinvention of the Fleetwood Mac

Abraxas album cover by Mati Klarwein

tune, and "Oye Como Va," a similarly creative take on a Tito Puente record. The following release, 1971's *Santana III* featured the debut of teenage guitarist Neal Schon. As Carlos recalled in his memoir, *The Universal Tone*, "it was much more about adding more flames to the band, the sound and energy we had together. The fire that Neal brought was a white, white heat." Schon and Gregg Rolie would later form Journey.

What followed in 1972 was a perfect storm of events that conspired to tear Santana apart. Bad management, money, an embezzling accountant, the grind of touring, and rampant drug abuse among some of the band members threatened to destroy all they had built. Carlos's newfound spirituality with guru Sri Chinmoy was also alienating to some of the group. As Bill Graham related to *Rolling Stone* in 1972, "The Santana situation is so indicative of one of the major problems in rock. I've said it too many times: One of the challenges of life, challenges to your character, is what happens to you when you make it."

Carlos asserted his leadership in a novel way, by walking out on his own group, demanding some of the others be fired. After several dates playing to disappointed audiences, the band relented. Soon, Carlos would clean house even further, with only himself and Michael Shrieve remaining. Santana was now undeniably his band.

The work that followed for the next several years was often esoteric, reflecting Carlos's deepening spiritual enlightenment, much to the frustration of many of his fans. He and his new groups produced many acclaimed albums and were still a popular concert draw, but commercial success was erratic.

In 1999, Santana moved to Clive Davis's Arista Records and produced *Supernatural*, a huge hit that topped the charts and re-established him as a commercial force for the first time in many years. The single "Smooth" with vocalist Rob Thomas topped the Billboard Hot 100 for 12 weeks, easily Santana's biggest hit ever, introducing him to a new generation of fans. He followed this success in 2002 with *Shaman*, featuring another smash hit single, "The Game of Love," with vocalist Michelle Branch. In 2016, *Santana IV* reunited Carlos with several of the members from his classic early band, including Neal Schon, Gregg Rolie, Michael Carabello, and Michael Shrieve, and energetically recalls the fire and spirit of those early albums.

Carlos Santana may be a musical and cultural icon, but he has backed it up with dedication and perseverance toward his art. His success has fueled the Milagro Foundation, which helps children all around the world. With regard to his role as an innovator, he had this to say in *Voices of Latin Rock*, "For us, music was more of a matter of sounding like a street mutt, like a dog that's bred with everything. This is our contribution to the world: we gave birth to Chicano music, to a sound that is very alive today."

MORE SANTANA

NOTEWORTHY LIVE PERFORMANCES

California Hall (625 Polk St., San Francisco): Carlos Santana played for a few months with a local three-piece band the Mockers, and performed at a "School's Out" Band Battle on June 19, 1966.

Panhandle Park: Now renamed Mocker Manor Blues Band, the group played at the Love Pageant Rally, along with the Grateful Dead and Big Brother and the Holding Company, on October 6, 1966, in protest of the outlawing of LSD.

Glide Memorial Church (330 Ellis St., San Francisco): On October 9, 1966, Mocker Manor Blues Band played at the "2nd Artists Liberation Front Free Fair," a charity event. Country Joe and the Fish was also on the bill.

Fillmore Auditorium (1805 Geary Blvd., San Francisco): Carlos Santana's first time on the Fillmore stage is believed to have been this unbilled "audition" set with Mocker Manor opening for Country Joe and the Fish, Buffalo Springfield, and Bola Sete on November 13, 1966.

Santana also jammed with Michael Bloomfield on either January 22 or 29, 1967, after Paul Butterfield was incapacitated and his band couldn't play their scheduled set. Greatly impressed, Bill Graham offered his card and the opportunity to bring his band (which had yet to form) to play a future gig. On June 16, the Santana Blues Band opened for the Who and the Loading Zone. They showed up late the following night and were promptly fired by Graham.

The Ark (Gate 6, Sausalito): On March 1, 1967, the new Santana Blues Band played its first gig. The lineup included Santana (guitar), Tom Fraser (guitar, vocals), Gregg Rolie (keyboards, vocals), Danny Haro (drums), Gus Rodriguez (bass), and Michael Carabello (percussion).

Winchester Cathedral (3033 El Camino Real, Redwood City): Santana Blues Band shared a bill with the Chocolate Watchband and Sly and the Family Stone on March 17, 1967.

Straight Theater (1702 Haight St., San Francisco): Santana played the first of many shows at this movie theater over the course of the next several months. On some occasions, they were the opening act for a film, such as *La Dolce Vita*.

Avalon Ballroom (1244 Sutter St., San Francisco): On March 20, 1968, Santana performed at the KPMX Strike Fund Benefit, along with the Grateful Dead, Blue Cheer, and others.

The Rock Garden (4742 Mission St., San Francisco): In Carlos Santana's memoir, *The Universal Tone*, he cites this venue as a place the early Santana played. It later changed its name to the Ghetto.

Deno & Carlo's (728 Vallejo St., San Francisco): Santana played several gigs at this North Beach establishment during the summer of 1968, occasionally with Creedence Clearwater Revival.

Fillmore West (10 S. Van Ness Ave., San Francisco): On September 12–14, 1968, Santana shared a bill with Big Brother and the Holding Company and Chicago Transit Authority.

Cow Palace (2600 Geneva Ave., Daly City): Santana played the KYA San Francisco Holiday Rock Festival on December 26, 1968, with Steppenwolf, Buffalo Springfield, Blue Cheer, Three Dog Night, and others.

Poster by Rick Griffin, 1968

Altamont Speedway (17001 N. Midway Rd., Tracy): Santana opened the now-infamous concert that included the Jefferson Airplane, Flying Burrito Brothers, and the Rolling Stones on December 6, 1969. Santana chose not to participate in the filming of the event, which became the concert documentary *Gimme Shelter.*
Family Dog on the Great Highway (660 Great Highway, San Francisco): On February 4, 1970, Santana played with the Grateful Dead and Jefferson Airplane for a TV special "A Night at the Family Dog."
Berkeley Community Theater (1930 Allston Way, Berkeley): On February 6, 1970, Santana played a benefit for the Black Panther party.

"What I remember is walking in the building and being searched four times before getting to the backstage area, for weapons," Michael Shrieve recalled in *Voices of Latin Rock*, "Then going out to perform, being searched another four times, which I found very offensive."
Winterland (2000 Post St., San Francisco) ⊘: On March 26–28, 1971 Santana shared a bill with Eric Burdon and War, the J. Geils Band, Buddy Miles, and others.

NOTEWORTHY RECORDING SESSIONS

Wally Heider Studios (245 Hyde St., San Francisco): *Abraxas* was primarily recorded here in April and May of 1970.
Columbia Studios (827 Folsom St., San Francisco): *Santana III* was recorded here between January and July of 1971. *Caravanserai* was recorded here between February and May 1972.

OTHER NOTEWORTHY LOCATIONS

Grant and Green (1371 Grant Ave., San Francisco): Santana discovered bassist David Brown during a gig at this bar in North Beach, July, 1967.
Danny Haro's Garage (2606 21st St., San Francisco): The first incarnation of the Santana Blues Band rehearsed together for several weeks in the garage adjacent to their original drummer's home in early 1967.
Aquatic Park: A popular spot in the '60s for Latin conga jam sessions. Carlos and Michael Carabello liked to come here and check out the various musicians.
Mission Dolores Park: Another popular spot for weekend conga sessions in the '60s.

Nite-Life (2470 San Bruno Ave., San Francisco): Michael Carabello called Carlos one night and insisted he come to this club. It was here that they first saw Jose "Chepito" Areas, a Nicaraguan multi-instrumentalist in 1969 and asked him to join Santana.

88 Marin View Avenue, Mill Valley: Carlos Santana's main residence during the '70s, complete with tower. It sits atop a hill adjacent to the Muir Woods.

Dipti Nivas (216 Church St., San Francisco): Carlos and his wife Deborah opened this vegetarian restaurant at the instruction of their guru, Sri Chinmoy, one of the first in the city. It stayed in business until 1983.

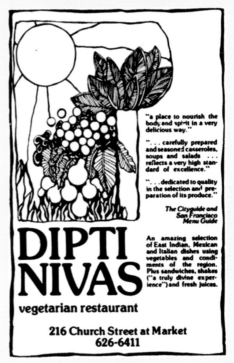

"a place to nourish the body and spirit in a very delicious way."

". . . carefully prepared and seasoned casseroles, soups and salads . . . reflects a very high standard of excellence."

". . .dedicated to quality in the selection and preparation of its produce."

The Cityguide and San Francisco Menu Guide

DIPTI NIVAS
vegetarian restaurant

An amazing selection of East Indian, Mexican and Italian dishes using vegetables and condiments of the region. Plus sandwiches, shakes ("a truly divine experience") and fresh juices.

216 Church Street at Market
626-6411

SYLVESTER

All men are created equal

Blue Thumb Records

"I'm not a drag queen, I'm *Sylvester*...
When I was little I used to dress up,
right? And my mother said, 'You can't
dress up. You *can't* dress up. You've
gotta wear these pants and these
shoes, and you have to, like, drink
beer and play football.' And, and I said,
'No, I don't,' and she said, 'You're very
strange,' and I said, 'That's okay.'"
—SYLVESTER ON *THE LATE SHOW*, WITH HOST
JOAN RIVERS, NEW YEAR'S EVE 1986

The late Sylvester James, Jr., known to the
world as Sylvester, was never one thing, never
always garish, never always effete, never always
effeminate, never always butch, sometimes
these things and more at once, and he seemed
to revel in following his own whims, regardless
of expectation. In the video for "You Make Me
Feel (Mighty Real)," a disco smash and longtime
gay anthem, Sylvester is if anything, sleek and
stylish, wearing a black leather jacket and
trousers and a long black blouse as he descends
a long, curved staircase; as the clip continues,
he's seen in a white suit, waving a white fan
as he casually saunters across a dance floor,
with five waiters wearing tank tops and silver
shorts walking in a circle behind him; the fan
remains in the next scene, but the suit is now a
sparkly kimono with matching toque; later, the
black blouse and leather trousers return, but are

accompanied by a gold coat and sash belt. None
of it appears incongruous on Sylvester.

Sylvester grew up in Los Angeles, where
he was known as Dooni, especially among
the Disquotays, a group of fellow gay teenage
boys who liked to dress up in drag, sometimes
glamorously, sometimes outrageously, to feel
themselves. Even among the Disquotays, the
tall, commanding Dooni stood out.

Enticed by a land where he could really be
himself, Sylvester headed up to San Francisco
in 1970, reportedly at the behest of a member of
the Cockettes, a psychedelic group of genderfuck
hippies who lived communally and had recently
begun putting on wild, loosely structured
midnight cabaret shows at the **Palace Theatre
(1731 Powell St., San Francisco)** with names
like *Tinsel Tarts in a Hot Coma*, *Elephant Shit—
The Circus Life*, and *Hell's Harlots*. The Cockettes
in 1970 had moved from a home at **2788 Bush
Street** to **944-948 Haight Street** after a fire.
It was at the "Haight Street Chateau" where
Sylvester was first asked to join the Cockettes
after they heard him playing a rickety piano and
singing during a party. He declined at first, but

Andi Sumpter

944–948 Haight Street

eventually joined the troupe, moving into the Haight Street Chateau and performing the theme to *The Mickey Mouse Club* as a sultry gospel number at the Palace.

By 1971, tiring of the Cockettes, Sylvester began branching out, sometimes performing as chanteuse Miss Ruby Blue at **Rickshaw Lounge (37 Ross Alley, San Francisco)** in Chinatown, along with a show called *Sylvester Sings! at the Palace*.

The final straw for Sylvester came during a disastrous three-week Cockettes engagement at the Anderson Theatre in New York City during November 1971. By now, he was performing with a group of rock musicians alternatively called the Hot Band and His Hot Band, and while the rest of the Cockettes' opening night performance received scathing reviews, Sylvester was marked for praise in the press. The next night he stepped onto the stage and issued a critical apology for the rest of the Cockettes; later in the week he again blasted the production, this time refusing to play. Though the Cockettes made it through the duration of their residency, Sylvester was finished.

Sylvester would remain with rock-heavy Hot Band for a few more years, embarking on tours and recording a pair of albums for the Blue Thumb label: *Sylvester and the Hot Band* and *Bazaar* were both recorded in Los Angeles, both comprised of reinterpreted covers, and both released to little fanfare in 1973. If the Hot Band were the right vehicle for Sylvester's emotive falsetto at the time, that would soon come to an end.

Reemerging as a solo artist in 1977 with a decidedly more polished R&B sound on the eponymously titled *Sylvester*, the singer was also presenting a more reserved public image; while the photograph on the back of the album sees Sylvester in a feminine ensemble, on the cover he wears a masculine black shirt and black trousers, yet inevitably evokes glamour. It was Sylvester's first album for Fantasy Records, and it featured an entirely new group of musicians, including plus-size singers Izora Rhodes and Marsha Wash, at the time called Two Tons o' Fun, later known the world over as the Weather Girls.

Sylvester was a modest hit for Fantasy, but the singer's path and the disco craze sweeping through dance clubs and onto the airwaves would soon converge. Sylvester had already recorded material for his 1978 followup album, *Step II*, before meeting keyboard player Patrick Cowley. The future-forward synthesizer overlays added by Cowley to "You Make Me Feel (Mighty Real)" and "Dance (Disco Heat)" were enough to set the tracks apart from other disco records, and they became instant dance floor classics.

Though its power to move butts, even today when mixed into a contemporary DJ set, is undeniable, "You Make Me Feel (Mighty Real)" is more than just a disco song; it's a multilayered gay anthem, whether one interprets realness as love at the most basic level or the more existential feeling of acceptance, of finding someone who gets us as we truly are, even in a world that doesn't.

Step II would go on to become Sylvester's greatest commercial success, hitting #28 on the Billboard 200 and #7 on the Billboard R&B chart. "You Make Me Feel (Mighty Real)" and "Dance (Disco Heat)" both topped Billboard's dance charts, and both went top 40, the latter reaching #19.

On March 11, 1979, Sylvester performed a sold-out show at the **War Memorial Opera House (301 Van Ness Ave., San Francisco),** backed by Two Tons o' Fun, his band, and the San Francisco Symphony Orchestra. The night unfolded in three rapturous acts and lasted nearly three hours, the venerable hall festooned with flowers. Sylvester was given a key to the city by Supervisor Harry Britt on what was decreed "Sylvester Day" by Mayor Dianne Feinstein. Before taking the stage, Sylvester washed down a hit of acid with champagne and chased it with a quaalude. Despite requests by Opera House management, Sylvester liberally threw glitter during his electrifying performance. A recording of the night was released later that year as the album *Living Proof.*

Sylvester's career would continue into the '80s, and though he survived the decline of disco, his singles were largely hits on the dance and R&B charts and didn't crack the Hot 100. He continued championing gay rights in marches and parades and by the very nature of his public persona as some conservatives began using the rising AIDS crisis in their attempts to vilify the LGBTQ community and its publicly perceived playground, San Francisco. The federal government under President Ronald Reagan vacillated between ignoring and—in the case of Reagan's acting White House Press Secretary Larry Speakes—ridiculing AIDS for years, but people within and outside of the gay community like Sylvester worked ceaselessly to ensure their voices be heard.

After seeing many friends, and his last great love Patrick Cranmer, succumb to complications from AIDS, Sylvester would himself catch the bug and pass away on December 16, 1988, at the age of 41. Sylvester's legacy lives on, not only as an LGBTQ icon, but also through his will: After money he'd borrowed against unpaid royalties was repaid, 75 percent of his posthumous royalties have been paid to **AEF (AIDS Emergency Fund) (170 9th St., San Francisco),** with the other 25 percent going to **Project Open Hand (730 Polk St., San Francisco),** which provides nutritious meals to the sick and vulnerable.

MORE SYLVESTER

NOTEWORTHY LIVE PERFORMANCES

Bimbo's 365 Club (1025 Columbus Ave., San Francisco): The Cockettes performed here on New Year's Eve 1970, a show primarily noteworthy as it was where Sylvester met and was enchanted by Michael Lyons, who he would marry in Spring 1971 in a ceremony at **Shakespeare Garden in Golden Gate Park**. The couple wore white tunics and flowered garlands.

Gold Street (56 Gold St., San Francisco): In the early '70s, Sylvester began performing one man shows backed by pianist Peter Mintun in clubs like Gold Street. Wearing a resplendent gown, Sylvester sang standards made famous by Billie Holiday, Bessie Smith, and Ethel Waters, along with more contemporary numbers by Hal David and Burt Bacharach, and Leonard Cohen.

Winterland Ballroom (2000 Post St., San Francisco ⊘): Though they mostly played local venues like **On Broadway (435 Broadway, San Francisco)**, the **Boarding House (960 Bush St., San Francisco)** and the **Orphanage (807 Montgomery St., San Francisco)**, Sylvester and His Hot Band supported David Bowie at a pair of shows at the comparatively massive Winterland Ballroom on October 27 and 28, 1972. In an effort to up the spectacle on the second night, Sylvester enlisted a harness and cables to take flight at the end of his set. The shows did not sell out, with Bowie reportedly claiming that San Francisco didn't need him since they already had Sylvester.

The Cabaret/City Disco (936 Montgomery St., San Francisco): After the dissolution of the Hot Band, Sylvester's career hit a low ebb. In 1975, he put together another band, added a pair of drag queens as backup singers and began playing two nights a week in the downstairs show room at The Cabaret. A few years later, now with Two Tons o' Fun and with dance music in full swing, Sylvester returned to the venue, recently renamed City Disco, to perform in the main room. By then, the reconstituted act was also playing **The Stud (1535 Folsom St., San Francisco)**, **The EndUp (401 6th St., San Francisco)**, and in 1976, **The Palms (1406 Polk St., San Francisco)**, where they picked up a steady gig.

The Elephant Walk (500 Castro St., San Francisco): Sylvester was playing regular gigs at The Elephant Walk when he was seen by Harvey Fuqua, cofounder of Cleveland doo-wop group the Moonglows, and later a record producer. Fuqua brought Sylvester, along with Two Tons o' Fun, to **Fantasy Records (2600 Tenth St., Berkeley)**, for whom he recorded his first six solo albums.

The Castro Theatre (429 Castro St., San Francisco): Despite the fact that he'd been singing onstage for longer than a decade, "One Night Only," a pair of ten-year anniversary shows, was put on by Sylvester at the Castro in February 1984.

Trocadero Transfer (520 4th St., San Francisco): Sylvester performed here numerous times, including his first 40th birthday party, held on September 6, 1985, when he was just 38. His reasoning for celebrating two years early was that it would make revelers remark how good he looked for his age.

One Market Plaza (1 Market St., San Francisco): On September 5, 1987, Sylvester turned in an emotional performance at a victory party for the Gay Softball World Series, one night after his partner Rick Cranmer passed away.

The I-Beam (1748 Haight St., San Francisco): Sylvester's 40th birthday bash, held on his actual 40th birthday this time, took place here on September 6, 1987. It was two days after the death of Cranmer. "My lover died Friday night, and I loved him so. And if he was here, he would love you," said Sylvester before performing "You Are My Friend," according to Joshua Gamson's *The Fabulous Sylvester: The Legend, the Music, the Seventies in San Francisco.*

OTHER NOTEWORTHY PLACES

324 Corbett Ave., San Francisco: Though he often moved from placed to place throughout the '70s, Sylvester and boyfriend John Maley settled in this three-floor condo in 1979. Though the relationship with Maley didn't last, Sylvester's residence did, at least until the mid-'80s.

Megatone Records (20 Landers St., San Francisco): Founded in 1981 by Patrick Cowley

and Marty Blecman, Megatone Records released Sylvester's *All I Need* the following year. He would release another two albums on the label, and Megaforce would produce Sylvester's final album, *Mutual Attraction* (1986), which was licensed and released by Warner Bros. "Do Ya Wanna Funk," Sylvester's 1982 Hi-NRG dance hit, was cowritten and produced by Cowley, and was heard in the Eddie Murphy/Dan Aykroyd comedy *Trading Places* the following year. Megatone was run from the home of Blecman.

San Francisco General Hospital, Ward 5B (1001 Portrero Ave., San Francisco): As the AIDS crisis grew in the '80s, Rita Rockett, a dancer friend of Sylvester's began visiting San Francisco General's Ward 5B, volunteering every other Sunday and doing everything from serving breakfast to tap-dancing in an effort to bring some light to patients who were stricken by the bug. Occasionally, Sylvester would come help. The unit moved into the larger Ward 5A in 1986, where a parlor at its west end was renamed the Rita Rockett Lounge.

Love Center Church (10440 International Blvd., Oakland): Sylvester began sporadically attending services at Love Center Church in the early '80s, where he found a much more accepting and nurturing atmosphere than in the church of his youth. Part of that was down to the Rev. Walter Hawkins, also a singer who prior to leading the Love Center Choir recorded with his brother's group, the Edwin Hawkins Singers, who had a crossover hit in 1967 with "Oh Happy Day." The Love Center Choir would appear on a handful of Sylvester tracks in his later years. When Sylvester died in 1988, his memorial service was held at the Love Center Church. Hawkins passed away in 2010 after a battle with pancreatic cancer.

SOUTH OF MARKET

GOLDEN STATE RECORDERS
665 Harrison St.

The Grateful Dead had their first group experience in a recording studio at Golden State Recorders in November 1965, booking time incognito as the Emergency Crew. Several tracks from the session were released in 2003 as part of the *Birth of the Dead* compilation, including an early version of "Caution (Do Not Stop on Tracks)," and rare originals like "Mindbender (Confusion's Prince)" and "The Only Time Is Now," neither of which stayed in the group's repertoire for very long. Golden State was also where the Beau Brummels recorded "Laugh Laugh" in 1964, the single peaking at #15 on the Billboard Hot 100, thus putting San Francisco firmly on the rock and roll map.

COAST RECORDERS/CBS STUDIOS/THE AUTOMATT
827 Folsom St.

Previously the second home of Coast Recorders and soon to become the Automatt, this Folsom St. studio was owned and operated by CBS Records. Most artists tended to prefer the laid back atmosphere at Wally Heider Studios at this time, but the Grateful Dead came here in 1974 to record *From the Mars Hotel*. Coast Recorders briefly reopened in San Francisco early in the 2000s at 1340 Mission Street.

SLIM'S
333 11th St.

Opened by musician Boz Scaggs in 1988, Slim's was a modestly sized club which didn't cater to any particular genre. Slim's was noteworthy for its wraparound bar and a few pillars in the middle of the floor, giving concertgoers either

Crispin Kott

something to lean on or lean around. During the COVID-19 pandemic, Slim's announced they were already planning to close by the end of 2020 and would not reopen even if the virus was gone before then.

Past performers at Slim's include Radiohead, Green Day, Jonathan Richman, Huey Lewis and the News, Curtis Mayfield, Bo Diddley, and Chris Isaak.

ROLLING STONE HEADQUARTERS
746 Brannan St.

Founded in 1967 by Jann Wenner and Ralph Gleason, *Rolling Stone* started life in second floor office space of a building at 746 Brannan Street, located across the street from a slaughterhouse. In its early years, *Rolling Stone* was published in newspaper broadsheet form and focused on expansive coverage of music and the surrounding scene. By the early '70s, politics were a key ingredient in the biweekly magazine, which took on a glossier, albeit larger, magazine format.

After a few years on Brannan, *Rolling Stone* moved its San Francisco base of operations to **625 3rd Street.** It maintained that office as an editorial bureau for a few years after moving its primary headquarters across the country to New York City, with the *San Francisco Chronicle* quoting Wenner as saying San Francisco had become a "provincial backwater."

Rolling Stone formally ended its presence in San Francisco, the city where it all began, when it closed its three-person office at **1700 Montgomery Street** in 2009.

Rolling Stone is still published today, changing from a biweekly to a monthly in 2018.

DREAMLAND
715 Harrison St.

A dancehall and performing arts center opened by Michael Maier, Dreamland's brief run as a live music venue included performances by Grace Jones, Chris Isaak, Ramones, Joan Jett and the Blackhearts, and local heroes, the Flamin' Groovies.

BOB DYLAN PRESS CONFERENCE

KQED STUDIOS (FORMER LOCATION)
525 4th St., San Francisco

Q: *"Do you think of yourself primarily as a singer or a poet?"*
A: *"Oh, I think of myself more as a song and dance man, ya know."*
Not a concert, but a performance all the same. Dylan had played the Bay Area a few times before, and as recently as April of that year, but much had changed since then. His controversial electric debut at the Newport Folk Festival in July and the many boos that greeted him during the following tour had made Dylan a polarizing figure, and in a time before serious rock journalism, the future Nobel laureate occupied a unique position somewhere between pop star and cultural icon.

Ralph Gleason, the enterprising San Francisco music critic and an early Dylan booster organized this TV event for December 3, 1965, ostensibly for the artist to promote his upcoming performances that evening and the next at the **Berkeley Community Theater (1930 Allston Way, Berkeley)**, and at the **Masonic Hall (1111 California St., San Francisco)** on December 11. What ensued proved to be an illuminating time capsule of a

moment in history as folk and rock were blending to become a dominant force in a rapidly evolving American culture.

In the audience was an amusingly eclectic combination of attendees. Along with a cadre of Dylan allies, including poets Allen Ginsberg, Lawrence Ferlinghetti, and Michael McClure, were a gaggle of high school contest-winners, promoters, photographers, and at least one hopelessly square news reporter. For nearly an hour, the 24-year-old Dylan held court casually smoking a cigarette and patiently answering each question in turn, many from Gleason himself. The broadcast is worth finding on the internet, and is a fascinating look at a quaintly bygone era in musical history.

BOZ SCAGGS

One of the most distinctive vocalists of the rock era, William Royce Scaggs first came to San Francisco in 1967, attracted by the psychedelic scene and answering the call from his compatriot Steve Miller. The two had been both classmates and bandmates in Dallas, where Scaggs grew up and acquired the schoolboy nickname "Boz." He and Miller also attended the University of Wisconsin and played in various bands in the area. Since then Scaggs had sought a solo career and eventually made his way to Sweden, where he recorded his first album, *Boz,* in 1965.

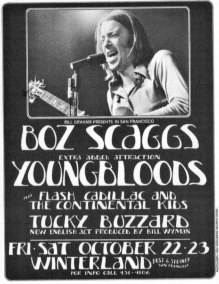

Poster by Randy Tuten with photo by Ken Greenberg, 1971

Scaggs lent his unique blues-inflected vocals to the Steve Miller Blues Band's first pair of albums, *Children of the Future* and *Sailor,* both released in 1968, before departing to reestablish his solo career. His ensuing albums achieved critical acclaim but sold slowly. In 1976, however, with the release of *Silk Degrees,* Scaggs emerged with a sleek, sophisticated R&B/Soul/Pop sound, and hit big with the singles "Lido Shuffle" and "Lowdown." His follow-up, *Down Two Then Left* (1977) was a musical departure that fared well but lacked the hits of *Silk Degrees. Middle Man* (1980), was a return to form, containing the hit singles "Jojo" and "Breakdown Dead Ahead." Scaggs also hit with "Look What You've Done to Me," included on the soundtrack to the film *Urban Cowboy.*

Seemingly at the height of stardom, Scaggs took a step back and essentially disappeared for the next eight years, reemerging with *Other Roads* in 1988, which yielded "Heart of Mine," a hit on the Adult Contemporary charts. That same year Scaggs opened **Slim's (333 11th St., San Francisco)**, originally a blues and R&B

club that rapidly evolved into one of the most important music venues in the city. Green Day, Metallica, and Radiohead all played Slim's in their formative years.

Slim's recently celebrated its 30th anniversary and until its 2020 closure during COVID-19 remained central to San Francisco's music community. Scaggs and his partners also acquired the **Great American Music Hall (859 O'Farrell St., San Francisco)** in 2002, an historic and similarly sized venue. Scaggs filmed and recorded *Greatest Hits Live* there in 2004. In 2010 he joined forces with Michael McDonald and Donald Fagen in the Dukes of September Rhythm Revue, which performed at the Hardly Strictly Bluegrass Festival October 1st in Golden Gate Park.

In recent years Scaggs has explored various forms of American music that have informed his own perspective, including standards, R&B,

and blues, most recently in 2018 with *Out of the Blues.*

ORACLE PARK
24 Willie Mays Plaza

Opened in 2000 as the new home of the San Francisco Giants, this China Basin ballpark has been known by a few different names over the years, starting with Pacific Bell Park and changing with new corporate sponsors. Renamed Oracle Park in 2019, the stadium is accessible by various forms of public transportation, including ferries, which disembark at the Giants Promenade as the San Francisco Bay meets the mouth of McCovey Cove.

Oracle Park has hosted numerous large concerts over the years, including the Rolling Stones, Metallica, Bruce Springsteen and the E Street Band, Paul McCartney, Pink Floyd, and Guns N' Roses. East Bay punk heroes Green Day brought their *American Idiot* tour to the ballpark on September 25, 2005, and they planned to return on July 20, 2021, as headliners of the Hella Mega Tour, sharing the stage with Weezer and Fall Out Boy, a date originally scheduled for the summer of 2020 but postponed by COVID-19.

"I wanted to be able for everyone to get a chance to sweat. By that I mean . . . if there was anything to be happy about, then everybody'd be happy about it. If there was a lot of money to be made, for anyone to make a lot of money. If there were a lot of songs to sing, then everybody got to sing. That's the way it is now. Then, if we have something to suffer or a cross to bear—we bear it together."

—SLY STONE, *ROLLING STONE*, MARCH 19, 1970

During their heyday, Sly and the Family Stone were the quintessential San Francisco band, a psychedelic soul outfit that drew inspiration from seemingly disparate sources to create a supremely funky and unified sound. The Family Stone was a family in both name and blood, a racially integrated collective of men and women, some actual siblings and others bonded by the music. Their live shows were an act of pure exuberance, sometimes spilling into the aisles, and on occasion out the door of the theater and into the streets. The Family Stone were equally adept at getting fans to "Dance to the Music" or "Sing a Simple Song" as they were at bringing social issues into the mix, as on "Don't Burn Baby" and "Don't Call Me Nigger, Whitey."

Born Sylvester Stewart, Sly Stone was the leader of the Family Stone, which not only included actual family members Freddie Stone (guitar & vocals), Rose Stone (electric piano and vocals), and Vet Stone (backing vocals as a member of Little Sister), but also the looser interpretation of family as the brother-and-sisterhood of humanity in Larry Graham (bass and vocals), Cynthia Robinson (trumpet and

vocals), Jerry Martini (saxophone), and Greg Errico (drums).

Family has always been important to Stone. Though he was born in Denton, Texas, the Stewart kids grew up in Vallejo, a bayside city where they were active in the Church of God in Christ; four of the five children sang gospel as the Stewart Four. Even in a musical family, Sly's proficiency on musical instruments before his teenage years was notable.

In high school, Sly and his friend Frank Arellano joined two other boys and two girls—all of whom were white—in the Viscaynes, making them the only racially integrated doo-wop group in the Bay Area. The Viscaynes had some measure of local success, including their 1961 single "Yellow Moon," a regional hit. The idea of different races and genders making beautiful music together would later go on to serve as the blueprint for the Family Stone.

Soon after high school, Sly was living in San Francisco and serving as staff producer and occasional songwriter for **Autumn Records (70 Dorman Ave., San Francisco)**, a label owned by KYA disc jockeys Tom Donahue and Bobby Mitchell; Sly produced singles for the Beau Brummels, the Vejtables, the Mojo Men, and the Great Society; he also helped rejuvenate the career of Bobby Freeman, for whom he cowrote and produced "C'mon and Swim" for Autumn, with the single peaking at #5 on the Billboard Hot 100 on August 29, 1964.

Sly's exuberance in the studio and association with Donahue and Mitchell helped convince him to become a radio DJ, first with KSOL, and then KDIA. His shows bucked the norm by mixing genres and following a "Black" record with a "white" one, because to Sly, these

sounds belonged together. In 1966, he would put together Sly and the Family Stone and put the theory to the ultimate test.

The utopian ideal of Sly and the Family Stone, a band bearing it together for a common purpose, would only last a few years, as its mercurial leader became more insular and began working on material in solitude. Sly and the Family Stone officially disbanded following a disastrously undersold concert at Radio City Music Hall in New York City in January 1975. The band split in different directions, occasionally coming together under the Family Stone umbrella, or working alongside one another in other groups, most famously the Graham-led Graham Central Station, which at times counted Robinson, Martini, and both Freddie and Rose Stone among its members. After a few comeback attempts, Sly famously became a recluse, occasionally appearing with his former bandmates over the years, including sporadic appearances during gigs by a reconstituted Family Stone.

MORE SLY AND THE FAMILY STONE

NOTEWORTHY LIVE PERFORMANCES

Winchester Cathedral (3033 El Camino Real, Redwood City): The first ever gig by Sly and the Family Stone took place at the Winchester Cathedral on December 16, 1966. The club was opened by Rich Romanello, who'd booked shows at his father's club the **Morocco Room (2010 S. El Camino Real, San Mateo),** including an appearance in 1964 by the Beau Brummels, who he would go on to manage. Wanting to make a name for himself, Romanello took over the lease at the Winchester Cathedral, augmenting its plush suburban opulence with contemporary touches such as four blocks of stained glass that spelled out the word LOVE.

Sly and the Family Stone were an instant hit, and Romanello, who would go on to briefly become the group's manager, booked them at Winchester Cathedral through much of the first half of 1967. It was during one of the Family Stone's late night sets that David Kapralik, an A&R man with Columbia Records, first saw the group. Kapralik had flown in from New York City at the behest of a colleague, Chuck Gregory. Spellbound by the typically hi-octane set, Kapralik began selling Sly on a record deal with Columbia subsidiary Epic later that evening at one of the few places still open before dawn, the **International House of Pancakes (491 Veterans Blvd., Redwood City).**

Fillmore Auditorium (1805 Geary Blvd., San Francisco): Sly and the Family Stone joined a stacked bill at the Fillmore on February 12, 1967. Billed as a birthday party for Abraham Lincoln, the group played alongside Moby Grape, Grateful Dead, and the New Salvation Army Band at this benefit for the Council for Civic

Unity. They would return to the fabled venue once more, supporting Quicksilver Messenger Service on June 21–23, 1968.

Fillmore West (10 South Van Ness Ave., San Francisco): Shortly after Bill Graham relocated his primary venue from Fillmore Auditorium to the former Carousel Ballroom—renamed Fillmore West—Sly and the Family Stone headlined a three-night stand from July 19–21, 1968, with the Jeff Beck Group and the Siegal Schwall Blues Band also on the bill.

Frenchy's (29097 Mission Blvd., Hayward): In the mid-'60s, Frenchy's was the sole rock club between Berkeley and San Jose, hosting shows by the Leaves, the Mojo Men, and supposedly for one unusual night in 1966, Neil Diamond backed by Frank Zappa's group the Mothers. Mistakenly called "Sly and the Family Stones" in newspaper ads, Sly and the Family Stone played Frenchy's on September 30–October 1, 1967 alongside blues legend T-Bone Walker.

Wayne Manor (199 South Murphy Ave., Sunnyvale): Briefly a satellite franchise of West Hollywood's celebrated Whisky a Go Go, Sunnyvale's Wayne Manor came to be after club owner Joe Lewis sought advice from the coolest kid he knew, his 11-year-old son. The Batman-themed club—complete with dancers dressed as Batgirl or Catwoman—opened in January 1966, quickly gaining recognition as a wave of Bat-mania swept across the nation thanks to the campy television series; Wayne Manor was featured in an article about the rising popularity of Batman in the March 11, 1966 issue of *Life Magazine*. Roughly one year later, Sly and the Family Stone turned in a pair of lengthy residencies there.

Fireside Lounge (2232 El Camino Real, San Mateo): Sly and the Family Stone played a brief run of shows at the Fireside Lounge in late-November and early-December 1967.

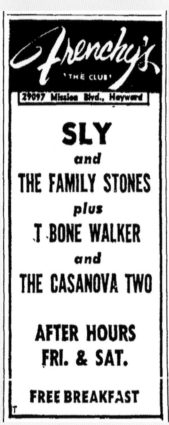

Both/And Club (350 Divisadero St., San Francisco): Though the Both/And Club primarily booked jazz artists, Sly and the Family Stone played here on March 18, 1968.

Circle Star Theatre (2 Circle Star Way, San Carlos): By 1968, Sly and the Family Stone were no longer just a local band, spending most of the year on the road, including a lengthy period in and around New York City. In a rare return to the Bay Area, the group played the Circle Star alongside Richie Havens on July 22, 1968.

San Francisco Civic Auditorium (99 Grove St., San Francisco): Not long after a show-stopping performance across the country at the Woodstock Music & Art Fair, Sly and the Family Stone came home to play San Francisco Civic Auditorium, now known as Bill Graham Civic Auditorium, on September 6, 1969.

Monterey Jazz Festival (2004 Fairground Rd., Monterey): One of the few Bay Area bands to not take part in the mythic Monterey Pop Festival two years earlier, Sly and the Family Stone finally played Monterey on September 19, 1969, headlining the opening night of the Monterey Jazz Festival, which also featured performances by the Miles Davis Quintet, Sarah Vaughn, Roberta Flack and Her Trio, and the Thelonious Monk Quartet.

Winterland Ballroom (2000 Post St., San Francisco ⊘): At perhaps the peak of their performing power, Sly and the Family Stone played a pair of late December 1969 shows at Winterland, returning the following December for two more.

Pepperland Auditorium (737 E. Francisco Blvd., San Rafael): A Beatles-themed hall with a quadraphonic sound system, the short-lived Pepperland played host to Pink Floyd, Hot Tuna, Captain Beefheart's Magic Band, and three months after its September 1970 opening, Sly and the Family Stone.

Berkeley Community Theater (1930 Allston Way, Berkeley): Sly and the Family Stone played the Berkeley Community Theater with support from Little Feat on August 19, 1973.

NOTEWORTHY RECORDING LOCATIONS

Coast Recorders (960 Bush St., San Francisco): Located in the building that would eventually become legendary comedy and music club the Boarding House, Coast Recorders—which had numerous addresses over the years—was one of two studios where Sly Stone (then still Sylvester Stewart) produced platters for Autumn Records. The other was **Golden State Recorders (665 Harrison St., San Francisco).**

Pacific High Recording (60 Brady St., San Francisco): Sly and the Family Stone cut their fourth LP, *Stand!*, at Pacific High during sessions in 1968 and 1969. The album was the group's first to crack the top 100, landing at #13 on the Billboard 200 on June 7, 1969.

Poster by David Singer, 1969

Record Plant (2200 Bridgeway, Sausalito):
In an alleged atmosphere of drug abuse and paranoia that led to the departure of Errico, Sly and the Family Stone recorded much of their 1971 album *There's a Riot Goin' On* at the Record Plant, augmented by tracks cut at Sly's home in Bel Air. Though credited to the band, *There's a Riot Goin' On* and its 1973 followup *Fresh*—also recorded at the Record Plant—were primarily the work of Sly, a drum machine, and extensive overdubs by various members of the Family Stone. Ike Turner, Billy Preston, and Bobby Womack also contributed to *There's a Riot Goin' On*, which hit the top spot on the Billboard 200 on December 18, 1971. *Fresh* yielded even less input from the Family Stone, with Graham appearing on just two tracks. Like its predecessor, *Fresh* was a smash, reaching #7 on the Billboard 200 on August 18, 1973.

OTHER NOTEWORTHY LOCATIONS

125 Denio St., Vallejo: K.C. and Alpha Stewart settled their family in this Vallejo home after moving to the Bay Area from Denton, Texas shortly after Sly was born in 1943.

Vallejo High School (840 Nebraska St., Vallejo): The Stewart kids went to Vallejo High, where Sly joined a doo-wop group, the Viscaynes.

Mission High School (3750 18th St., San Francisco): Greg Errico went to high school here around the same time as guitarist and bandleader Carlos Santana, and a few years after singer Bobby Freeman.

Castlemont High School (8601 MacArthur Blvd., Oakland): Originally known as East Oakland High School, Castlemont High was given its medieval name by students inspired by its architecture. Sly and the Family Stone bass guitarist Larry Graham is a Castlemont alum, as are June Pointer (Pointer Sisters), Raphael Saadiq (Tony! Toni! Toné!), and Randy Sparks (the New Christy Minstrels).

Vallejo Junior College (545 Columbus Pkwy, Vallejo): After graduating from high school, Sly moved on to Vallejo Junior College, where he spent three semesters, singing in the school choir. It was here that Sly studied under a music theory instructor named David Froehlich, a jazz pianist who Sly credited with helping him learn everything from reading notes to structuring chords. The school was renamed Solano Community College in 1966.

Chris Borden School of Modern Radio Technique (259 Geary St., San Francisco): Sly graduated from here in 1964 before launching his radio career.

700 Urbano Dr., San Francisco: With the proceeds earned from his work as a producer and sometime songwriter for Autumn Records, Sly Stone bought this house for his family in the mid-'60s. The basement of the home would effectively serve as a headquarters for Sly and the Family Stone during their formative

700 Urbano Drive

period, and was where in December 1966 Sly assembled what would become the first lineup of Sly and the Family Stone to share his vision of forming a group. The basement would sporadically continue its use as a Family Stone clubhouse through the remainder of the decade, its members coming together to jam and work on new material.

155 Haight St., San Francisco: During his time as a DJ and record producer in the mid-'60s, Sly had an apartment in this then-brand new building on Haight.

155 Haight Street

Mid-Century Monster (Lake Merritt, Oakland): Located along the shore of Lake Merritt just to the west of where Bellevue Avenue begins to curve away from the water sits what's been affectionately dubbed the "Mid-Century Monster." The recently renovated chartreuse sculpture was created by Bob Winston at the behest of Oakland Parks Superintendent William Penn Mott, Jr., the founder of nearby **Children's Fairyland (699 Bellevue Ave.)**, who imagined a structure along Lake Merritt for children to play on. For the cover of their 1968 album *Dance to the Music*, Sly and the Family Stone are seen sitting atop *Mid-Century Monster*, a subtle wink to East Bay residents who might have recognized the setting from the unique amoeba-like pseudopods in the lower half of the image.

THE FIREHOUSE
3767 Sacramento St. ⊘

Only in operation for a few months in 1966 before the building was razed to make room for a parking lot, The Firehouse, as its name implies, was formerly a fire station which housed the no. 10 truck and no. 26 engine for much of the first half of the century. By 1966, the top floor of the building was being used by local psych-rock band Sopwith Camel as a rehearsal space, while the ground floor was a live music venue which featured some of the city's earliest light shows. Concerts took place at The Firehouse on most Saturdays between February 12 and April 2, 1966, with the conveniently located Sopwith Camel almost always on the bill. Also playing The Firehouse were the pre-Janis Big Brother and the Holding Company, the Charlatans, the Great Society, and Wildflower.

Francisco). It was here that Robbie Robertson, who was ill with a temperature of 104 degrees, was hypnotized ahead of opening night. The Band would go on to play all three nights of their stand, with support from Sons of Champlin and the Ace of Cups.

BARBARY COAST ROOM
1650 Holloway Ave.

Renamed Jack Adams Hall in 1993, this space within the San Francisco State University Student Center used to host shows in the '70s and '80s, including the Jerry Garcia Band, Los Lobos, and the Red Hot Chili Peppers.

JOHNNY MATHIS'S CHILDHOOD HOME
346 32nd Ave.

Johnny Mathis, whose silky, mellifluous voice made him one of the most distinctive and successful romantic vocalists of the 20th century, grew up here and attended nearby **George Washington High School (600 32nd Ave.)**, and later **San Francisco State University**

SEAL ROCK INN
545 Point Lobos Ave.

This motor inn overlooking the Pacific Ocean from San Francisco's northwestern tip was where the Band stayed ahead of their live debut at **Winterland Ballroom (2000 Post St., San**

Amy Chase

Washington High School

(1600 Holloway Ave.), where he excelled at both basketball and track before embarking on a musical career in 1956. Early Columbia singles, including "Wonderful Wonderful" (1956) and "Chances Are" (1957) propelled him to stardom that would ultimately chart more than 70 albums over the next six decades. His *Greatest Hits* album, originally released in 1958, remained on the Billboard Top 200 until 1968, a record for most nonconsecutive weeks (490) that stood until eclipsed by Pink Floyd's *Dark Side of the Moon.* Now in his 80s Mathis is still going strong, recording and touring to the present day.

STEVE MILLER

"Well, San Francisco was the most vibrant music scene of the 20th century. So let's start right there. It was a complete change of how things worked in the world and when you're in something like that, you think it's great, you think it's going to last forever. You wake up one morning and it's gone. It was really magic."
—STEVE MILLER (*THE MORNING CALL*, ALLENTOWN, PA, 2014)

When 21-year-old Steve Miller first arrived in the Bay Area in 1965, he was already a remarkably accomplished guitarist and seasoned performer with bands in Texas and the Midwest. He spent his early years in Milwaukee and Dallas, where his mother was a jazz singer and his father was a doctor with a passion for recording jazz and blues performers, many of whom he befriended. As a youngster, Steve had the rare opportunity to learn at the feet of legends like Les Paul, Tal Farlow, and T-Bone Walker.

Miller's first musical impressions of San Francisco in 1965 were not very enthusiastic, however, and he decided to give college another try. As history has shown, Steve initially made the scene just a little early, but the siren call of rock and roll would lure him back soon enough.

By 1967 the Steve Miller Blues Band were an integral component of the San Francisco sound, gigging tirelessly at venues throughout the Bay

Poster by Victor Moscoso, 1967

Area, particularly the **Fillmore (1805 Geary Blvd., San Francisco)**. The group's performance at the 1967 **Monterey Pop Festival (2004 Fairground Rd., Monterey)** ultimately helped Miller land a record deal, and his first album *Children of the Future*, was recorded in London, after dropping "Blues" from the band's name.

Miller wound up recruiting bandmates from past groups, including guitarist Curly Cook, drummer Tim Davis, and bassist Boz Scaggs, his former schoolmate from Dallas. Scaggs would stick around for the first pair of Miller albums before embarking on a solo career. Miller recorded several landmark albums in the ensuing years, including *Sailor, Brave New World*, and *The Joker*, before achieving true superstar status in the late '70s with *Fly Like an Eagle* and *Book of Dreams*, both of which spawned timeless hits such as "Take the Money and Run," "Rock'n Me," "Jet Airliner,"

"Swingtown," "Jungle Love," and the title track from *Eagle*. All have been staples of Classic Rock radio ever since. His last major hit was the title track to 1982's *Abracadabra*, but he has continued to record and remains a concert draw to this day.

MORE STEVE MILLER

NOTEWORTHY LIVE PERFORMANCES

Fillmore Auditorium (1805 Geary Blvd., San Francisco): Miller famously jammed onstage with his friend Paul Butterfield and Jefferson Airplane on October 16, 1966. A few months later, after he had assembled his own group, the Steve Miller Blues Band, he became a regular performer here sharing bills with all the top San Francisco groups.

The Matrix (3138 Fillmore St., San Francisco): After playing gigs in Berkeley, the band was booked for a week at the pioneering club from December 16–22, 1966, a showcase for the emerging group.

Avalon Ballroom (1244 Sutter St., San Francisco): The Steve Miller Blues Band shared a bill with Moby Grape and the Grateful

Poster by Stanley Mouse, 1967

Dead December 23–24, 1966. They returned January 6–7, 1967 with Quicksilver Messenger Service.

California Hall (625 Polk St., San Francisco): On February 19, 1967, Miller and the group participated, along with Country Joe and the Fish and the San Francisco Mime Troupe in a benefit for the Port of Chicago Vigil, a massive demonstration intended to prevent weapons from shipping to Vietnam.

Muhammad Ali Festival (Hunter's Point, San Francisco): There is still some debate as to whether this event actually took place, but Miller is listed, along with the Mime Troupe, the

Poster by Victor Moscoso, 1967

Poster by Gomez, 1967

Loading Zone, and several other local acts in support of the legendary boxer on June 10–11, 1967. Ali had recently been stripped of his Heavyweight Champion title for refusing to honor the military draft.

Carousel Ballroom (10 S. Van Ness Ave., San Francisco): The Miller Band played here April 26–28, 1968, in support of their first album, *Children of the Future*. They returned May 10–12, and again June 12 with Jefferson Airplane.

Fillmore West (10 South Van Ness Ave.): The group performed at a benefit for the Peace and Freedom party on September 25, 1968, along with Santana, the Flamin' Groovies, It's a Beautiful Day, and several others.

The Forum (2455 Telegraph Ave., Berkeley): Upon his return to the Bay Area in 1966,

Miller settled in Berkeley, and beginning in December 1966, he secured a regular gig at this coffee house, established in a recently closed Lucky grocery store. To prepare for the stand, Miller hastily rehearsed his newly assembled group in an unlocked basement room at UC Berkeley's **Wurster Hall (Bancroft Way & College Ave., Berkeley)** over the Thanksgiving vacation. The stand would lead to better gigs at The Matrix and Avalon Ballroom. Today the site is home to Amoeba Music.

New Orleans House (1505 San Pablo Ave., Berkeley): Miller first played this popular Berkeley venue on February 17, 1967, but would return several times during the year.

Berkeley Community Theater (1930 Allston Way, Berkeley): On March 30, 1967, the Miller Blues Band shared a bill with blues greats Jimmy Reed and John Lee Hooker, along with jazzman Charles Lloyd.

KFRC Fantasy Fair and Magic Mountain Festival (Cushing Memorial Amphitheater, Mt Tamalpais State Park): On June 11, 1967, Miller, along with Jefferson Airplane, the Doors, the Byrds, and several others, played what is considered by many the first multiday outdoor rock festival, narrowly edging the Monterey Pop Festival.

NOTEWORTHY RECORDING LOCATIONS

Wally Heider Studios (245 Hyde St., San Francisco): Miller recorded his fourth album, *Your Saving Grace* here in 1969.

CBS Studios (827 Folsom St., San Francisco): Miller recorded his classic albums *Fly Like an Eagle* and *Book of Dreams* here from 1975–1977.

Book of Dreams album cover by Alton Kelly and Stanley Mouse, 1977

OTHER NOTEWORTHY LOCATIONS

Mrs Sherrill's Rooming House (2410 Russell St., Berkeley): When Miller first came to the Bay Area in the summer of 1965, he fell in with a loose collection of musicians living here and calling themselves "the Instant Action Jug Band," so named as they typically congregated at **The Jabberwock (2901 Telegraph Ave., Berkeley),** a popular coffee house and folk music venue practically next door. When an act was needed quickly to fill a slot or substitute for a cancellation, the gang sprung into action and played the gig. Among its regular members were Joe McDonald and Barry Melton, who later formed Country Joe and the Fish. It's possible that Miller sat in with them on a few such occasions.

Columbus Recorders (916 Kearny St., San Francisco): Miller signed a record deal with Capitol on December 10, 1967, and shortly thereafter brought his group to rehearse in the studio built by the Kingston Trio in the basement of Columbus Tower (AKA the Sentinel Building) through December and into January 1968. They later flew to London to record *Children of the Future*.

MediaPunch Inc./Alamy

"I remember that first show seeing fans that didn't care what they looked like. I mean they had cut-off denims and stuff. They didn't care. And they were at the front of the stage head-banging because the music did that for them. They weren't gathered around the bar scene, or anything. They were there for the music."

—JAMES HETFIELD, METALLICA, RECALLING HIS BAND'S FIRST BAY AREA GIG AT THE STONE IN THE 2019 DOCUMENTARY *MURDER IN THE FRONT ROW: THE SAN FRANCISCO BAY AREA THRASH METAL STORY.*

Metallica are undeniably a Bay Area band, though they didn't start out that way. Though they've lived in and around San Francisco for over three decades, Metallica began in Los Angeles in 1981. In Tinseltown the fledgling outfit quickly felt out of step with their aggressive guitars, fast rhythms, and total disinterest in ditching their denim and leather seemingly antithetical to the garish glam metal wave sweeping across the city. On September 18, 1982, they played **The Stone (412 Broadway, San Francisco)** with Hans Naughty and Bitch, and while they didn't move to the Bay Area for a few more months, it already felt like home.

In and around San Francisco, the heavy metal scene was already entrenched, with bands like Exodus getting started as early as 1979. The group shared with Metallica a fondness for British heavy metal bands like UFO, Judas Priest, and Motörhead, as well as an affinity for a good time both on- and offstage. By 1981, Exodus were led by a stocky singer named Paul Baloff, the explosive living embodiment of thrash metal, who'd been brought into the band by guitarist Kirk Hammett. On October 18, 1982, Metallica and Exodus played together for the first time at the **Old Waldorf (444 Battery St., San Francisco)** as part of the club's regular Metal Monday showcase.

"We played our show, then Metallica came on and they played," said Hammett in *Murder in the Front Row*. "And they were just fantastic. And that's when I first met James (Hetfield), and that's when I first met Lars (Ulrich, Metallica's drummer)."

Metal Up Your Ass, a live Metallica demo popular among tape traders, was recorded at the Old Waldorf on November 29, 1982.

Metallica had yet to consider a move up to the Bay Area, but that changed after they began courting bass guitarist Cliff Burton, who they'd seen play a Los Angeles show with Trauma. Burton, a skilled and innovative player,

would only consider joining Metallica if it didn't involve his relocating to Southern California.

"Cliff is the one that brought us to the Bay Area," said Ulrich in *Murder in the Front Row*. "'You want me in the band, you've gotta come up here.'"

Burton would officially join Metallica in late December 1982, after an audition-cum-rehearsal at the Metallica Mansion.

The Metallica Mansion (3132 Carlson Blvd., El Cerrito), named thus both ironically and alliteratively, would serve as the band's home and headquarters from late 1982 through 1986, a period during which they wrote and rehearsed many of the songs included on the *Ride the Lightning* and *Master of Puppets* albums in the since-removed garage. The group returned to the house in April 2016 to pay tribute to their humble roots, hosting an invite-only party and receiving a proclamation from the mayor.

"Thankfully, most of the things that went on in here are forgotten," said Metallica drummer Lars Ulrich at the ceremony. "But we had a lot of fun."

Burton made his live debut as a member of Metallica at The Stone on March 5, 1983, on a bill with Exodus and Lååz Rockit. Footage from a return to The Stone two weeks later appeared on a Metallica home video in 1987 called *Cliff 'Em All*.

Metallica headed off to the East Coast in April 1983 to record their debut album, *Kill 'Em All*; soon after arriving in New York, the band would fire guitarist Dave Mustaine and replace him with Hammett. On his bus ride back to California, a dejected but determined Mustaine planned his next band, Megadeth.

With Metallica embarking on world tours and spending less time around the local thrash metal scene, Exodus emerged as its premier group, with Vio-lence, Testament, Legacy, Possessed, and Death Angel among the other bands playing the local circuit, perhaps none

Crispin Kott

The former Metallica Mansion

more important than a long lost blues club in the East Bay.

Ruthie's Inn (2618 San Pablo Ave., Berkeley) was only open in its second life from 1983–1987, but it proved an invaluable nexus for two separate music scenes which probably had more in common than they realized. Promoter Wes Robinson saw the potential in punk, and after booking shows at **The Rio Theatre (140 Parker Ave., Rodeo)** and **Aitos (1920 San Pablo Ave., Berkeley)** a few years earlier, he breathed new life into old Ruthie's as a place he could call his own. But it wasn't just punk that needed a place to play in the East Bay, it was also thrash metal, a scene which treated Ruthie's like its own clubhouse.

Tales of thrash shows at Ruthie's are rife with reckless stage-diving, stifling air, broken glass, and the exploits of the Slay Team, who upon spotting a "poser"—often identified as someone openly supporting hair metal—would rip the offending T-shirt off their body, tear it into strips, then wear the strips around their wrists like war trophies.

Bonded by Blood, the first album by Exodus, opens with the title track, a visceral account of the Ruthie's scene. The song also inspired the title of the definitive book and subsequent documentary covering the Bay Area thrash scene, *Murder in the Front Row*.

While it was mostly Bay Area bands playing Ruthie's Inn, kindred spirits from elsewhere were also important pieces of the puzzle, including Slayer and Megadeth. Both bands were from Los Angeles—Mustaine having returned there after his departure from Metallica—but both fit into the Bay Area thrash scene much more fluidly than in the glam metal scene back home.

Metallica would play Ruthie's Inn just once, on August 24, 1985. It was a show sandwiched between appearances before significantly larger crowds at the Monsters of Rock Festival at Castle Donington in England and at Day on the Green at **Oakland-Alameda County Coliseum (7000 Coliseum Way, Oakland)**.

Day on the Green was an annual stadium series promoted by Bill Graham since 1973, and while the appearance of Metallica at one of the 1985 shows was viewed by some as a big win for the local thrash scene, punters had unofficially lampooned it the previous summer by dubbing Wes Robinson's two-day Eastern Front festival held at **Aquatic Park (80 Bolivar Dr., Berkeley)** "Day on the Dirt."

Held in mid-August, 1984, Eastern Front has since been hailed as the birth of the crossover scene, with metal and punk bands sharing the bill, and everyone involved getting along swimmingly. The seeds for the summit had already been planted at Ruthie's, which was holding punk and thrash shows almost from the beginning. But for many, seeing Suicidal Tendencies and Exodus on the same stage was a revelation. As a side note, one of the bands scheduled for the second day of Eastern Front—Beastie Boys—wound up canceling. Though they began life as a hardcore outfit, Beastie Boys had by 1984 already begun their transformation into a hip-hop trio, one which would make them famous two years later.

Metallica and Exodus are both still around, having long survived the deaths of key members: Cliff Burton was killed in the morning of August 27, 1986, when Metallica's bus overturned between tour stops in Sweden. Paul Baloff, who had recently returned to Exodus following a brief hiatus, fell into a coma after suffering a stroke in February 2002; he died of heart failure shortly thereafter.

Exodus most recently toured Europe in early 2020 with Testament and Death Angel on the Bay Strikes Back Tour, with a North American tour rumored to be in the works.

Metallica is one of the biggest bands in the world, selling out stadiums everywhere they go.

MORE METALLICA AND BAY AREA THRASH

NOTEWORTHY LIVE PERFORMANCES

Ducal Palace (1821 Webster St., Alameda):
Exodus headed to Alameda on September 16, 1982, sharing the bill with Blitzkrieg.

Mabuhay Gardens (443 Broadway, San Francisco): Though best known as the nerve center of the San Francisco punk scene, metal bands have also played the short stage. On October 30, 1982, Metallica and Exodus joined forces at the Mab for a *Metal Mania Magazine* fundraiser. It would be original Metallica bass guitarist Ron McGovney's final gig with the band. Metallica played Mabuhay Gardens once more, on July 20, 1984.

The Kabuki Theater (1881 Post St., San Francisco): Now a movie theater, in the '80s the Kabuki was a live music venue with shows promoted by impresario Bill Graham. Metallica played here with Armored Saint on March 14 and 15, 1985. Megadeth would also play the Kabuki that year, on May 31.

Bill Graham Civic Auditorium (99 Grove St., San Francisco): Then known as the San Francisco Civic Auditorium, Metallica headlined a New Year's Eve 1985 show here, sharing the stage with Exodus, Megadeth, and Metal Church.

Cow Palace (2600 Geneva Ave., Daly City): Metallica supported Ozzy Osbourne at the Cow Palace on June 17, 1986. They would return numerous times over the years, beginning with a pair of dates in mid-December 1988 alongside Queensrÿche. The Clash of the Titans Tour hit the Cow Palace on May 26, 1991, coheadlined by Megadeth, Slayer, and Anthrax.

Candlestick Park (602 Jamestown Ave., San Francisco): The Van Halen-headlining Monsters of Rock tour rolled into the since-demolished Candlestick Park on July 16, 1988, with Metallica, Scorpions, Dokken, and Kingdom Come also on the bill.

Shoreline Amphitheatre (1 Amphitheatre Pkwy., Mountain View): On Sept 15, 1989, Metallica brought their Damaged Justice tour to Shoreline, with support from Faith No More. The band would return on October 18 and 19, 1997 to play the annual Bridge School Benefit, performing an acoustic set each day on a bill with Neil Young, Lou Reed, Smashing Pumpkins, and others.

Hun Sounds Studios (647 Irwin St., San Rafael): Metallica invited a handful of lucky Met Club members to an intimate private rehearsal on August 17, 1995. More Met Club shows would

follow at **Slim's (333 11th St., San Francisco)** on June 9 and 10, 1996.

Berkeley Community Theater (1930 Allston Way, Berkeley): On April 21 and 22, 1999, Metallica engaged in their most ambitious project to date, playing two shows with symphonic accompaniment, which was composed by Michael Kamen, who also conducted the San Francisco Symphony. An album of performances from the pair of shows was released that November as *S&M*. On September 6 and 8, 2019, Metallica paid tribute to the album and to Kamen, who died in 2003, when they updated the original concept with *S&M2*. Metallica again performed with the San Francisco Symphony, working this time with music director Michael Tilson Thomas. They were

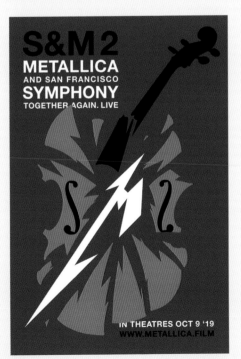

the first concerts ever held at the **Chase Center (1 Warriors Way, San Francisco).**

Kimo's Bar and Penthouse Lounge (1351 Polk St., San Francisco): Metallica played an intimate show on the tiny stage of this since-shuttered bar on June 4, 2002. With producer Bob Rock on bass guitar, the band opened their brief set with four Ramones covers.

San Quentin State Prison (Main St., San Quentin): One day after filming a video for the title track of 2003 album *St. Anger*, Metallica played an hour-long show for inmates in the prison yard on May 1, 2003. It was the first live show for the band's then-new bass guitarist Robert Trujillo, who would enjoy further intimate introductory shows later in the month when Metallica played four nights at the **Fillmore (1805 Geary Blvd., San Francisco).**

Marin Veterans' Memorial Auditorium (10 Ave. of the Flags, San Rafael): Metallica played a benefit concert for the Marin History Museum's then-new Marin Rocks Exhibition and Music Center on September 11, 2009. The band's headquarters are located in an undisclosed location in San Rafael.

Rasputin Music (2401 Telegraph Ave., Berkeley): In celebration of Record Store Day, Metallica played a nine-song set on April 16, 2016 at Rasputin.

Outside Lands Music and Arts Festival (Golden Gate Park, San Francisco): Metallica shared headlining duties with the Who and Gorillaz at the 2017 edition of the annual Outside Lands. Metallica closed out the festival's Saturday, August 12 performances, with Queens of the Stone Age, Solange, Thundercat, Royal Blood, Warpaint, Empire of the Sun, and the Avett Brothers also playing.

NOTEWORTHY RECORDING LOCATIONS

Record Plant (2200 Bridgeway, Sausalito):
Though they live in the Bay Area, Metallica
would not record an album there until their sixth
album, *Load*. Released on June 4, 1996, *Load*
was the product of roughly a year of recording
sessions. Its follow-up, *Reload,* was also cut
there. They have since largely recorded in a
studio in their headquarters at an undisclosed
San Rafael location.

**Prairie Sun Recording Studios (1039 Madrone
Ave., Cotati):** Exodus cut their seminal debut
album *Bonded by Blood* in July 1984 at Prairie
Sun's pastoral facility. For a variety of reasons,
the album would not be released until the
following April.

**Alpha & Omega Recording (245 Hyde St., San
Francisco):** Leased space located within Hyde
Street Studios, Alpha & Omega was where
Exodus convened to record their second album,
Pleasures of the Flesh, in 1987. It was the
first Exodus album to feature vocalist Steve
"Zetro" Souza, who joined the band following
the departure that year of Paul Baloff. After a
decade apart, Souza returned to Exodus in 2014.
Alpha & Omega has since relocated to **150
Bellam Boulevard in San Rafael**.

Fantasy Records (2600 Tenth St., Berkeley):
After recording their first two albums in Ithaca,
New York, Testament stayed closer to home,
cutting *Practice What You Preach* (1989) and
Souls of Black (1990) at Fantasy Studios. Death
Angel also recorded at Fantasy, producing their
second album *Frolic Through the Park* (1988)
there.

OTHER NOTEWORTHY LOCATIONS

Big O Tires (2625 San Pablo Ave., Berkeley):
Located directly across the street from Ruthie's
Inn, Big O Tires was often an ancillary hangout
for thrash metal fans spilling out of the packed
venue. Stories abound of everything from
vomiting to vandalism at Big O during the
period Ruthie's was in operation. Big O Tires
is still open today, but has likely been much
quieter at night in the decades since Ruthie's
shut down.

Record Vault (1920 Polk St., San Francisco):
Opened in 1982, Record Vault was a key record
shop where Bay Area metal fans could find
coveted imports and indie releases, as well as
having the occasional opportunity to have their
records signed by favorite bands. The shop
moved to **2423 Polk Street** in the midst of its
heyday.

**Tommy's Joynt (1101 Geary Blvd., San
Francisco):** After auditioning numerous
potential replacements for their late bass
guitarist Cliff Burton, the remaining members
of Metallica brought Jason Newsted to Tommy's
Joynt to ask him to join the band.

Crispin Kott

Barbary Coast Trail (corner of Broadway and Columbus Ave., San Francisco): A walking tour designed by the San Francisco Historical Society, the Barbary Coast Trail connects 20 historic sites and museums across the city, with around 180 bronze medallions embedded in the sidewalk along the 3.8-mile route. A memorial plaque dedicated to late Metallica bass guitarist Cliff Burton along the trail can be found just below the sign for the **Condor Club (560 Broadway).**

Kirk Hammett Former Homes (2505 Divisadero St./320 Sea Cliff/308 Sea Cliff): While his bandmates have preferred life in relatively quiet Marin County, Metallica guitarist Kirk Hammett has generally stuck with San Francisco. In 2009, Hammett sold his 10,000-square-foot Georgian mansion on Divisadero, moving into a Mediterranean-style home overlooking China Beach and the Pacific Ocean built in 1926 at **320 Sea Cliff,** which as seen in real estate listings when he sold the home was adorned with classic horror movie posters. Hammett also owned an adjacent home at **308 Sea Cliff,** which he has also sold.

Kirk Hammett Childhood Home (855 South Van Ness Ave., San Francisco): Prior to moving with his family to a Robin Hood-themed neighborhood in El Sobrante, Metallica guitarist Kirk Hammett lived in this apartment building

as a child. The move to the East Bay was difficult for Hammett, but would ultimately prove musically fruitful.

"We were far away from the city," he said in the 2019 film *Murder in the Front Row.* "We were isolated. There was nothing to do. All we had was music, you know?"

De Anza High School (5000 Valley View Rd., Richmond): Kirk Hammett, who cofounded Exodus before quitting to join Metallica, went to high school at De Anza, along with Exodus drummer Tom Hunting, and Les Claypool, singer and bass guitarist for Primus.

Castro Valley High School (19400 Santa Maria Ave., Castro Valley): Metallica bass guitarist Cliff Burton went to high school here, as did Jim Martin and Mike Bordin, guitarist and drummer respectively for Faith No More. The trio had a high school band called EZ-Street, named after a local topless bar. Burton and Martin would continue on to **Chabot College (25555 Hesperian Blvd., Hayward),** where they formed another band, Agents of Misfortune.

James Hetfield Former Home (35 Wali Trl., Novato): Metallica guitarist and frontman James Hetfield sold this four bedroom home with a saltwater swimming pool and timber outdoor kitchen in 2003. He's remained in Marin County ever since.

BERKELEY

AMOEBA MUSIC
2455 Telegraph Ave.
Though it's since gone on to take San Francisco and Los Angeles by storm, Amoeba Music was first founded in Berkeley in 1990 in a location once housed by the Forum Coffee House, one of the city's premier spots for countercultural life in the '60s. Amoeba boasts a wide selection of vinyl, compact discs and, with its recent resurgence, cassettes, along with T-shirts, movies, and other ephemera. Though the San Francisco location tends to book more shows, the Rubinoos, BEAK>, Al Jardine, Flipper, and the Melvins have all played the Berkeley store.

In 2018, Amoeba opened Hi-Fidelity, a legal marijuana dispensary next door to its Berkeley location at **2465 Telegraph Avenue**, selling a wide range of cannabis and cannabis-based products.

Mike Katz

BESERKLEY RECORDS
1199 Spruce St.
Boasting a roster brimming with power-pop and rock artists, Beserkley Records was an independent label founded by Matthew King Kaufman and some members of the group he managed, Earth Quake. Beserkley operated from 1973–1984, though it only served a single artist during the '80s: Greg Kihn.

Beserkley's most celebrated album may be the eponymous debut by the Modern Lovers, originally recorded in 1972 for A&M before being

licensed and released four years later. Other artists on the label included the Rubinoos, Jonathan Richman (of the Modern Lovers), and the Smirks. Kihn's three albums released in the '80s on Beserkley went top 40, and his single "Jeopardy" hit #2 on the Billboard Hot 100 on May 7, 1983.

BERKELEY SQUARE
1333 University Ave.
Open from the '70s through the '90s, Berkeley Square was a popular venue for touring bands like Red Hot Chili Peppers, Dream Syndicate, No Doubt, and Ramones; as well as local performers like Green Day, Primus, Flamin' Groovies, Chris Isaak, and the Mr. T Experience. Counting Crows' first live performance took place here in January 1992.

RALPH GLEASON RESIDENCE
2835 Ashby St.
Pioneering rock critic and journalist Ralph Gleason was born in New York City but moved to Berkeley in 1947 after working in the Office of War Information during World War II. Gleason was an early champion of the Bay Area rock scene and would go on to cofound *Rolling Stone* Magazine.

FINNISH BROTHERHOOD HALL
1970 Chestnut St.

Opened in the early 20th century as a mutual aid society, Berkeley Lodge 21 today, as it did then, hosts Finnish cultural events in its various rooms. It was also briefly the site of a handful of live rock gigs in the mid-'60s by Country Joe and the Fish, Wildflower, and Melvin Q. Watchpocket. A "Dance Benefit" for S.F. Newsreel and Liberation News Service held on March 19, 1969, headlined by the MC5 and featuring "funky porno flicks" was not held here as sometimes reported, but at the nearby **Finnish-American Cultural Hall (1819 10th St., Berkeley).**

BERKELEY COMMUNITY THEATER
1930 Allston Way

Built on the campus of Berkeley High School and opened in 1950, the Art-Deco style Berkeley Community Theatre's long history of performance has included some of the biggest names in rock and roll: Led Zeppelin, Bob Dylan, the Grateful Dead, Jimi Hendrix, Metallica, and Alice Cooper are among those who've played here.

Poster by Bob Masse, 1968

Berkeley Community Theater

PROVO PARK
1901-1999 Allston Way

In the shadow of Berkeley Community Theater and the City of Berkeley Civic Center sits Provo Park, site of numerous outdoor gigs and at least one organized draft card burning. Big Brother and the Holding Company, Country Joe and the Fish, the MC5, Silver Apples, Sons of Champlin and Loading Zone all played Provo Park in the late '60s.

SIERRA SOUND LABORATORIES
1741 Alcatraz Ave.

Founded in 1961 by Bob DeSousa, Sierra Sound Laboratories was a recording and mastering studio where everyone from Lightnin' Hopkins to the Blues Project recorded. Perhaps the most celebrated release to come out of Sierra Sound was *Electric Music for the Mind and Body*, the 1967 debut album by Country Joe and the Fish.

THE WILLIAM RANDOLPH HEARST GREEK THEATRE
2001 Gayley Rd.

Built in 1903 and named after the newspaper magnate who funded it, the Greek is an 8,500-seat amphitheater that began hosting rock shows in the '60s and continues hosting them today. The Grateful Dead, Country Joe and the Fish, Bob Dylan, the Beach Boys, Paul Simon, Santana, the National, and the Dave Matthews Band have all played the Greek.

JOHNNY OTIS'S CHILDHOOD HOME
2725 Dohr St.

The son of Greek immigrants, Otis (born Ioannis Veliotes) became an important and influential pioneer of R&B and early rock and roll as recording artist, producer, and general impresario. In addition to his many hits, which included "Willie and the Hand Jive," "Cupid's Boogie," and "All Nite Long," Otis discovered and promoted several important performers, including Etta James, Jackie Wilson, Big Mama Thornton, and the Coasters. In later years, in addition to touring, he hosted a radio show on Berkeley's KPFA. His son, Shuggie Otis, is an important R&B artist in his own right, having penned the hits "Strawberry Letter 23" and "Inspiration Information."

RATHER RIPPED RECORDS
1831 Euclid Ave.

This former Berkeley favorite was more than a record store, hosting occasional in-store loft gigs by the likes of the Patti Smith Group and the Cramps, and signings by the Police and Blondie. Musician Greg Kihn once worked at Rather Ripped, and Sonic Youth named their 2006 album in its honor. Rather Ripped closed in 1980 after a fire and the resulting emergency response in a next door building damaged most of their merchandise. But in 2012, original owner Russ Ketter reopened Rather Ripped in his hometown, Pittsburgh, Pennsylvania.

RASPUTIN MUSIC
2401 Telegraph Ave.

Originally opened in 1971 at 2523 Durant Avenue by Ken Sarachan, Rasputin moved into its current flagship location in the late '70s, simultaneously maintaining two Berkeley shops, with new location focusing on rock and the original specializing in jazz and soul. In 1982, the Durant Street location was irreparably damaged by a fire in a restaurant, forcing Rasputin's Berkeley operations into a single building.

Rasputin is the greater Bay Area's largest independent record store chain, with locations in Campbell, Fresno, Modesto, Pleasant Hill and San Lorenzo. In November 2019, Rasputin closed its last remaining San Francisco location at 1672 Haight Street.

Each Rasputin location has a wide range of new and used vinyl, compact discs, and movies, along with posters, T-shirts, and other ephemera. The Berkeley location famously hosted a performance by Metallica on Record Store Day on April 16, 2016.

MOE'S BOOKS
2476 Telegraph Ave.

One of America's landmark independent bookstores, Moe's has been a focal point of Berkeley's intellectual life since its establishment in 1959 by transplanted New Yorker Moe Moskowitz and his wife Barbara. Originally opened on nearby Shattuck Avenue as the Paperback Bookshop, it achieved legendary status after relocating to its current address in 1965. Moskowitz was an active advocate of the Free Speech Movement at the nearby UC campus and the store became a haven for the embattled left-leaning Berkeley community. Moskowitz was also a supporter of the burgeoning Berkeley music scene and helped Country Joe and the Fish by staging live performances and funding their eponymous EP in 1966. Moe's was also the original home of The Print Mint, a purveyor of psychedelic posters and underground comix.

Today Moe's comprises four floors of both new and used books, including a room for rare

and collector volumes, and is run by Doris Moskowitz, daughter of the original owners.

NEW ORLEANS HOUSE
1505 San Pablo Ave.

Open from the mid-'60s through the mid-'70s, this former restaurant and live music venue is perhaps best known as the location where Jefferson Airplane offshoot Hot Tuna recorded their eponymous debut album. Flamin' Groovies, Country Joe and the Fish, the Steve Miller Blues Band, Notes from the Underground, and Quicksilver Messenger Service were among the many artists to play New Orleans House.

Poster by Tom Weller, 1966

TRILON RECORDS
3123 San Pablo Ave.

Initially established in 1946 as a record pressing plant and named for the signature pointed "Trylon" tower of the 1939 New York World's Fair, Trilon quickly branched out into recording artists of its own, most notably the Vagabonds, a theatrical Italian-American quartet that also operated a nightclub on Geary Boulevard in San Francisco. Significantly, Trilon also had production relationships with both Bob Geddins's Oakland-based Big Town Records and Dave Rosenbaum's Rhythm label, important pioneers in the recording and distribution of Rhythm & Blues artists of the postwar period. When Geddins ran into financial difficulty, Trilon gained control of his business and inherited several of the Big Town stable of artists, including Lowell Fulson and Jimmy McCracklin, issuing many of their early recordings. Other important artists who released discs on Trilon included the Paramount Gospel Singers and the Wright Brothers Jubilee Singers. By 1948 Trilon had overextended itself and ultimately sold out to Mercury Records.

PRUNE MUSIC
1345 Grove St.

Founded in 1967 by Randall Smith and Dave Kessner, Prune originally established itself here as the music equipment repair shop of choice for the flourishing Bay Area scene, catering to the likes of Country Joe and the Fish, Moby Grape, Quicksilver Messenger Service, the Grateful Dead, and many others. Its specialty was repairing and fine-tuning amplifiers, and by 1969, Smith developed his own, based originally on the Fender Princeton. This ultimately blossomed into the legendary Mesa Boogie line of amplifiers, initially championed by Carlos Santana. In the ensuing years many notable artists, including Keith Richards, Mick Jones, Al DiMeola, Bruce Springsteen, Ron Wood, Bootsy Collins, Andy Summers, and Neal Schon embraced Mesa Boogie, which moved its operations to Petaluma in 1980 and where they are manufactured today.

GREEN DAY

Green Day at 924 Gilman

Murray Bowles

"I grew up in a town called Rodeo. It's right off the 80 at Willow. And it was the inspiration for this next song. This is 'Jesus of Suburbia.'"
—BILLIE JOE ARMSTRONG, GREEN DAY, THE WARFIELD ON OCTOBER 13, 2005

Punk trio Green Day have traveled all around the world, but they always come back to the East Bay. It's where two of them—singer-guitarist Billie Joe Armstrong and bass guitarist Mike Dirnt—grew up, and where all three cut their teeth playing gigs at house parties, in bowling alleys and warehouses and clubs, and most importantly, at **924 Gilman Street**, the all-ages, DIY, nonprofit music and art community space that was the crucible for the punk scene from which Green Day emerged in the early '90s.

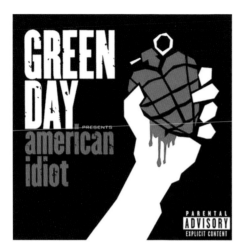

How much of "Jesus of Suburbia,"—the first of two suites on Green Day's epic 2004 album *American Idiot*—is based on the members of Green Day themselves or people they might have known or observed is unclear. But as with many of the band's lyrics, the lion's share written by Armstrong, the setting is local but the appeal universal. Early on there were numerous songs about teenage suburban malaise, a feeling hardly exclusive to Rodeo, California.

Though filmed in Los Angeles, the **7-11** referenced in "Jesus of Suburbia" was real, likely the location at **2869 Pinole Valley Road in Pinole**, not far from where Armstrong grew up. But there are convenience stores everywhere, along with countless other places kids go to find a sense of community, to hang out, to get fucked up, to not feel so alone.

The tracks in the lyrics of "Christie Road" (from 1991 album *Kerplunk*) are actual railroad tracks along a rural stretch of Christie Road off the John Muir Parkway in Martinez where, for lack of anything better to do, Armstrong, Dirnt, and their friends would hang out. Corbett Redford is the director, producer and cowriter of *Turn It Around: The Story of East Bay Punk*, the 2017 documentary executive produced by Green Day and then-manager Pat Mangarella.

"There's literally nothing to do," said Redford. "And so what they would do was they would all get in (early Green Day bass guitarist) Sean Hughes's Volvo and they would go out to this place called Christie Road."

"Tight Wad Hill" (from 1995 album *Insomniac*) is an actual hill at **John Swett High School (1098 Pomona Street, Crockett)**, from where Armstrong transferred after his freshman year.

"This is where all the losers, the cheapskates, would come up and watch the football games without paying for them," said Armstrong in a *Rolling Stone* cover story from December 28, 1995. "It's actually the best view in the whole place. . . . A lot of tweakers come and hang out up here, the crank victims and stuff."

The song also references kids growing up stultified in the shadow of the C&H Sugar Factory in Crockett.

Green Day's lyrics provide a roadmap to their youth: The corner in "Stuart and the Ave." is **Stuart Street and Telegraph Avenue** in Berkeley; "Homecoming" mentions Jingletown, an Oakland community adjacent to the Oakland Estuary where Green Day once had a recording studio **(Jingletown Recording, 829 27th Ave., Oakland)**; "Going to Pasalacqua," though slightly misspelled, is at least partly about

the **Passalacqua Funeral Chapel (901 W. 2nd St., Benicia)**. They even found room for a local reference in a song recorded for *Short Music for Short People*, a 1999 compilation released by San Francisco punk label Fat Wreck Chords featuring 101 bands playing songs averaging 30 seconds in length; Green Day's "The Ballad of Wilhelm Fink" is about the likely sticky end of a clandestine rendezvous at **Berkeley Marina (201 University Avenue, Berkeley)**.

For the members of Green Day, the East Bay isn't just a well of memories from which to draw inspiration for their spiky anthems; it's where they chose to remain despite fame and fortune at an early age making it possible to live almost anywhere in the world. It's where they're raising their own families, and where they've established side hustles, like Oakland Coffee Works, an organic, fair-trade, environmentally conscious coffee company.

Dirnt is also the co-owner of **Rudy's Can't Fail Cafe (4801 Hollis Street, Emeryville)**, an award-winning retro-styled diner with killer milkshakes and a BLAT (thick-cut bacon, lettuce, avocado, tomato), name-checked in a 2012 Lonely Planet "Field Guide to 20 Great American Sandwiches."

Broken Guitars (423 40th St., Oakland), co-owned by Armstrong, is an aptly named guitar shop specializing in used American models. In addition to being Green Day's bass technician and tour crew manager, Broken Guitars co-owner Bill Schneider is a musician who's played

Crispin Kott

alongside Armstrong in Pinhead Gunpowder and the Coverups.

In the '90s, Green Day's music first connected with disaffected teenagers across the country and around the world. They blended the fury of punk with an innate understanding of pop-craft, their lyrics about angst or boredom or even love often painting a distinctly local portrait that was universally recognizable. Green Day are still around, and though they've grown up and matured, adding global issues to their palate, they've never shed the unbridled East Bay energy that was an integral piece of their puzzle from the very beginning.

MORE GREEN DAY

NOTEWORTHY LIVE PERFORMANCES

924 Gilman Street (Berkeley): In his 2015 Rock Hall of Fame acceptance speech, Billie Joe Armstrong said: "So we come from this place called Gilman Street. It's a club. It's in Berkeley. We are so fortunate to be able to play there because it's all-ages and it was nonprofit. It was just all of these goofballs. It was like Romper Room for degenerates. It was so great. And what a great scene. We got to watch our friends' bands, and they got to watch us play, and they got to heckle us. We tried to heckle back, but they had one better. So, then I got to see Operation Ivy, and I got to see Crimpshrine, and I got to see Sewer Trout, Nasal Sex. These far out there bands. I'm truly fortunate."

It would be impossible to overstate the importance of 924 Gilman on the East Bay punk scene, and despite what turned into a complicated relationship after the group signed with Reprise Records ahead of their commercial breakthrough *Dookie*, that very much includes Green Day. The band, then known as Sweet Children, initially had a hard time getting to play the club they'd already fallen under the spell of, supposedly because their demo had been deemed "too poppy" by Tim Yohannon, founder of *Maximumrocknroll* magazine, and one of the primary instigators of the Alternative Music Foundation at 924 Gilman.

Green Day were eventually allowed on a bill at 924 Gilman, and they would go on to play there a great many times through September 1993, when they signed with Reprise Records, breaking one of the club's rigid principles. They officially returned to 924 Gilman on May 17, 2015, to play a Fire Relief Benefit for AK Press, 1984 Printing, and others displaced by a fire that March.

Rod's Hickory Pit (199 Lincoln Rd. West, Vallejo ⊘): The first ever Green Day gig, when they were still known as Sweet Children, took place on October 17, 1987, at Rod's Hickory Pit, a diner where Armstrong's mother worked.

Club Psycospecific (966 Market St., San Francisco): Green Day were bottom of the bill on April 14, 1989, at this short-lived venue, playing ahead of Sweet Baby and Samiam.

Cloyne Court Hotel (2600 Ridge Rd., Berkeley): Green Day played a couple of times during their formative years at this co-op campus housing at the University of California, Berkeley.

935 W. 6th St., Benicia: Green Day played a house party here with Monsula on May 21, 1989.

Benicia Historical Museum at the Camel Barns (2060 Camel Rd., Benicia): Listed on gig flyers as **2024 Camel Rd.**, the official address of the museum where Green Day played with Separate Ways, Bumblescrump, and Blatz on June 8, 1989, is **2060 Camel Rd.** It's unlikely you'll have trouble finding your way there using either address.

Los Robles Lodge (1985 Cleveland Ave., Santa Rosa ⊘): Green Day played a Halloween 1989 show at this since-demolished restaurant/hotel/nightclub, once a Santa Rosa mainstay. The headliners were Victim's Family, with Toast, Cliche of Copulation, and Double Ugly also on the bill.

1821 1st St., Benicia: With Fifteen also on the bill, Green Day played a house party here on November 25, 1989. Rumors abound that Green Day's set was cut short when the cops came because of a noise complaint.

Santa Rosa High School (1235 Mendocino Ave., Santa Rosa): Green Day played an afternoon set

on the senior steps in the midst of a teacher-student protest walkout in 1991.

Komotion (2779 16th St., San Francisco): Green Day played a benefit at this former art gallery and occasional live music space on February 13, 1991. They would return there in September 1992 with Pung.

Pony Express Pizza (2114 Broadway, Redwood City): This metal-punk club and pizza parlor was home to countless gigs, including a performance by Green Day with Plutocracy and the Dread on March 15, 1991.

Bear's Lair (2465 Bancroft Way, Berkeley): With headliner Mr. T Experience and Samiam also on the bill, Green Day played this on-campus bar at the University of California, Berkeley on April 6, 1991.

Oasis (298 11th St., San Francisco): Creature Feature Night on April 7, 1991, featured Green Day, Trunk and Little My for a $4 cover.

Chameleon (853 Valencia St., San Francisco): Green Day played this former club a few times between 1992–1993.

Slim's (333 11th St., San Francisco): Serving as a bridge between their early days and massive fame, Green Day played this venerable San Francisco club a handful of times in 1993 and 1994. Live footage shot during a February 17, 1994 show was used in the "Welcome to Paradise" video.

Cactus Club (417 S. 1st St., San Jose): Green Day played at this now-shuttered club on February 20, 1994.

Shoreline Amphitheatre (1 Amphitheatre Pkwy., Mountain View): By now huge stars by way of MTV and alternative radio, Green Day opened the main stage for two straight days of traveling music festival Lollapalooza. Other bands on the tour included Smashing Pumpkins, Beastie Boys, George Clinton and the P-Funk All-Stars, the Breeders, and many more. They would return to Shoreline in October 1999, for the 13th Annual Bridge School Benefit Concert, playing an unplugged set on each of the festival's two days.

Henry J. Kaiser Auditorium (10 10th St., Oakland): Green Day played a pair of benefit shows at the since-shuttered Henry J. Kaiser Auditorium on May 1995, with Pansy Division opening. All proceeds from the shows were donated to Food Not Bombs, the Berkeley Free Clinic, the Haight Ashbury Free Clinic, and the SF Coalition on Homelessness.

Oakland-Alameda County Arena (7000 Coliseum Way, Oakland): The Pop Disaster Tour with coheadliners Green Day and Blink-182 stopped here on April 29, 2002.

Bottom of the Hill (1233 17th St., San Francisco): By the time Green Day first played this small San Francisco rock club, they were already selling out arenas. On April 17, 1998, they played a secret show with tickets given away to members of the group's official fan club, the Idiot Club. The concert was filmed for MTV's Live @ the 10 Spot, and the group played for a further two hours after the cameras stopped rolling.

The Fillmore (1805 Geary Blvd., San Francisco): For their final shows of 1997, Green Day played a three-night mid-December stand at the Fillmore, with support from New York punks D Generation. Armstrong and D Generation's Jesse Malin have since become lifelong friends.

Piers 30-32, San Francisco: Green Day joined the Vans Warped tour in the summer of 2000,

sharing the bill with Weezer, the Donnas, Jurassic 5, NOFX, the Mighty Mighty Bosstones, and many others. The tour made its Bay Area stop on a pier in the shadow of the San Francisco-Oakland Bay Bridge on July 1.

Civic Center Plaza, San Francisco: On November 5, 2000, Green Day joined Metallica's Kirk Hammett, the Blind Boys of Alabama, Mark Eitzel, Creeper Lagoon, and others to play Take Back San Francisco, a protest against rising rents.

Bill Graham Civic Auditorium (99 Grove St., San Francisco): Green Day performed alongside Papa Roach, the Deftones, AFI, and Disturbed as part of Live 105's annual Not So Silent Night concert on December 15, 2000.

Oracle Park (24 Willie Mays Plaza, San Francisco): Green Day first played the home of the San Francisco Giants, then known as SBC Park, on September 24, 2005, with support from Flogging Molly and Jimmy Eat World. They planned to return in July 2021, headlining the Hella Mega Tour with Weezer and Fall Out Boy.

Cybelle's Pizza (El Cerrito): To get a sense of what an early Green Day set might have been like, search the internet for video shot by BayAreaPunkShows of the group playing this pizza parlor in 1991.

Marx Meadow (Golden Gate Park, San Francisco): On June 30, 1991, Marx Meadow bore witness to Filthfest, with sets from Green Day, 23 More Minutes, Smog, Blister, Insaints, Blatz, Fifteen, and Jack Acid.

Marsugi's (399 S. 1st St., San Jose): A young Green Day played a handful of shows at this now-shuttered San Jose club.

The Phoenix Theater (201 Washington St., Petaluma): Green Day played here in

March 1990 on a bill with the Mr. T Experience and Victim's Family. Primus was the headliner.

The Starry Plough (3101 Shattuck Ave., Berkeley): On September 20, 1990, Green Day played this Irish pub and live music venue. Armstrong would return here over a decade later for an intimate gig by one of his other bands, Pinhead Gunpowder.

The Women's Building (3543 18th St., San Francisco): Green Day played an early show with new drummer Tre Cool at this women-led nonprofit arts and education community center

on October 19, 1990. Also on the bill were the Mr. T Experience, Creamers, and Bad Town Boys.

Berkeley Square (1333 University Ave., Berkeley): Green Day supported the Mr. T Experience on November 10, 1990, their first time playing the since-shuttered Berkeley Square.

The Playground (9029 San Leandro St., Oakland): Green Day joined Blatz, Still, and Separate Ways to play a party at The Playground, within Paradigm Studios, on November 17, 1990. They would return to Paradigm Studios almost a year later to play a show with Econochrist, Fifteen, and Wynona Riders.

Lower Sproul Plaza (University of California, Berkeley): Green Day joined the ranks of countless other bands when they played this campus plaza on October 4, 1991. They'd play there once more the following February.

American Legion Hall (1240 Pearl St., Napa): On December 9, 1990, Green Day played on a bill with several other bands, including 3 Legged Dog, the Wynona Riders, and Public Humiliation.

Sonoma Community Center (276 E. Napa St., Sonoma): For one of their final shows of 1990, Green Day played the Sonoma Community Center on a bill with Toast, Chomphard, and the Henry David Rhythm Section in late December.

Kingman Hall (1730 La Loma Ave., Berkeley): Green Day played a house party at this UC Berkeley student co-op sometime in 1992. The 45-minute set supposedly took place in the living room, with some residents angry that it interrupted a broadcast of *The Simpsons*.

Your Place Too (5319 Martin Luther King, Jr. Way, Oakland): Green Day played this former club on March 4, 1992, sharing the bill with Rancid and the Wynona Riders.

UC Santa Cruz-Porter College (1156 High St., Santa Cruz): Green Day and Samiam played the quad at this residential college in the afternoon of March 7, 1992.

Mary Ward Hall, San Francisco State University (800 Font Blvd., San Francisco): A dorm room party with music performed by Green Day took place in Mary Ward Hall on March 12, 1992.

Casa Zimbabwe (2422 Ridge Rd., Berkeley): There are seemingly few student housing co-ops at UC Berkeley which Green Day didn't play during their formative years, including Casa Zimbabwe, where they performed with Chill Factor on April 4, 1992. Hip-hop DJs DJ Nickie, DJ Top, and DJ Beehive were spinning in another room at Casa Zimbabwe on the same night.

940 Wood St., Oakland: Green Day and Lungbutter played a house party benefit for the homeless in the afternoon on July 26, 1992.

Saratoga Lanes (1585 Saratoga Ave., San Jose ⊘): Since demolished and replaced by a residential property, Saratoga Lanes was a former San Jose bowling alley where Green Day played a back room with North American Bison, Model Citizens, and the Curbs in August 1992.

Benicia Youth Center (150 E. K St., Benicia): Green Day and the Wynona Riders were on the bill for a show here on September 5, 1992.

Uncle Charlie's (5625 Paradise Dr., Corte Madera): Perhaps best known as being the incubator for the group that became Huey Lewis and the News, Uncle Charlie's also played host to Green Day, Overwhelming Colorfast, Elysium, and others on September 6, 1992. The gig was apparently a disaster, with the band saying later tensions with the owner made it among the worst places they've ever played.

The Catalyst (1011 Pacific Ave., Santa Cruz): Bad Religion headlined a show at The Catalyst on October 19, 1993, with support from Green Day and Seaweed.

The Warfield Theatre (982 Market St., San Francisco): Still on tour supporting Bad Religion, Green Day played the Warfield on October 20, 1993. They returned here for a marathon 35-song gig on October 13, 2005, with support from the Network, a brief side-project featuring, among others, the members of Green Day themselves.

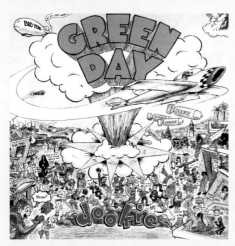

Paradise Lounge (1501 Folsom St., San Francisco ⊘): A little over two weeks after the release of their major label debut, *Dookie*, Green Day headlined this now-demolished club.

Stork Club (2330 Telegraph Ave., Oakland): Green Day side project the Foxboro Hot Tubs played a show in this club on May 15, 2008.

Toot's Tavern (627 2nd Ave., Crockett): The Foxboro Hot Tubs, a group comprised of the members of Green Day among others, played here on May 16, 2008.

The Independent (628 Divisadero St., San Francisco): Green Day played a secret show at this 500-capacity club on April 7, 2009.

DNA Lounge (375 11th St., San Francisco): As part of their gonzo run of secret shows ahead of the release of *21st Century Breakdown*, Green Day played DNA Lounge on April 9, 2009.

Fox Theater (1807 Telegraph Ave., Oakland): Green Day played the Fox on April 14, 2009, running through new album *21st Century Breakdown* followed by a hit-laden encore.

The Uptown Nightclub (1928 Telegraph Ave., Oakland): One night after their show at the Fox, Green Day played a surprise show at the significantly more intimate Uptown, with tickets being sold at the door.

1-2-3-4 Go! Records (420 40th St., #5, Oakland): Rumors abound of Armstrong and his son Joey helping build the stage in this

Crispin Kott

crucial Oakland record shop, which sits across the street from Broken Guitars. Perhaps the clearest sign that Green Day truly loves this shop is their decision to play a Bay Area music fan appreciation event here on September 22, 2011. The sweaty set was open to a handful of Idiot Club members, friends, and family. Shop here for records by Green Day and many, many others.

Mezzanine (444 Jessie St., San Francisco): Green Day joined Ty Segall and Kut U Up here on November 1, 2011 for a benefit for the Surfrider Foundation.

The William Randolph Hearst Greek Theatre (2001 Gayley Rd., Berkeley): Green Day brought their Uno! Dos! Tre! tour to the Greek Theatre on April 16, 2013.

Eli's Mile High Club (3629 Martin Luther King, Jr. Way, Oakland): Green Day side project, the Foxboro Hot Tubs played a show here on October 26, 2013.

The UC Theatre (2036 University Ave., Berkeley): Green Day played a typically lengthy show at this theater on October 20, 2016, with "Forever Now" making its live debut.

Starline Social Club (2236 Martin Luther King Way, Oakland): Green Day played a private set here for family and friends on December 17, 2017.

Ivy Room (860 San Pablo Ave., Albany): Armstrong and Dirnt played a handful of shows across 2018 at the Ivy room as members of the Coverups, who blast through marathon sets of covers by everyone from the Rolling Stones to the Replacements, the Damned to the Beastie Boys. Armstrong most recently played the Ivy Room with his band the Longshot.

Thee Parkside (1600 17th St., San Francisco): The Coverups played this longtime dive bar

and live music venue on March 8, 2018. Armstrong's band the Longshot also played here in April 2019.

NOTEWORTHY RECORDING LOCATIONS

Art of Ears Studio (1213 Fell St., San Francisco): Green Day recorded their first two EPs—*1,000 Hours* and *Slappy*—and their first album—*39/Smooth*—at Art of Ears. The studio has since moved to **21087 Cabot Boulevard** in Hayward.

Fantasy Studios (2600 Tenth St., Berkeley): *Dookie*, Green Day's debut album for Reprise Records, was recorded at Fantasy in September and October 1993. Released on February 1, 1994, *Dookie* was a worldwide smash which would go on to sell over 10 million copies in the United States alone. Armstrong had already

LOOK FOR LOVE

"Billie Joe"

Recorded by "Billie Joe" on Fiat Records

Lyrics by James J. Fiatarone
Music by Marie-Louise Fiatarone

$1.25

recorded here once before, cutting his debut single "Look for Love" at Fantasy in 1977 when he was just five years old.

Hyde Street Studios (245 Hyde Street, San Francisco): Green Day's fourth studio album *Insomniac* was recorded at Hyde Street Studios in San Francisco's Tenderloin. The space was formerly occupied by Wally Heider Studios, one of the premier Bay Area recording studios of the late '60s and early '70s.

Studio 880/Jingletown Recording (829 27th Ave., Oakland): Green Day has a long history with this recording studio, beginning in early 2000 when they began recording their sixth studio album, *Warning*. It was Studio 880 at the time, and would remain so when they returned to record some of their 2004 concept album *American Idiot* and some of 2009's *21st Century Breakdown*. By the time they began recording the tracks that would become their *¡Uno!, ¡Dos!, ¡Tré!* album trilogy in 2012, they owned the studio, which they renamed Jingletown Recording after the neighborhood in which it was located. Green Day have since sold Jingletown Recording, and they recorded 2016 album *Revolution Radio* at OTIS, a small clubhouse and studio in Oakland used exclusively by the group. The exact location of OTIS is not known to the general public.

OTHER NOTEWORTHY LOCATIONS

Carquinez Middle School (1099 Pomona St., Crockett): Armstrong and Dirnt attended middle school here.

"Our school district went bankrupt, so they closed down the junior high and combined two elementary schools," said Armstrong during his Rock and Roll Hall of Fame speech in 2015. "I think in fifth grade, I was like the class clown, but Mike was like the class clown, so it was kind of like these dueling banjos that was going to go back and forth. What you get is *Deliverance*."

Pinole Valley High School (2900 Pinole Valley Rd., Pinole): Armstrong transferred from John Swett High to Pinole Valley, where Dirnt was already a student. An early version of Green Day played outdoors during the school's annual Foreign Foods Day on May 10, 1990. Armstrong dropped out of Pinole Valley, but Dirnt stayed long enough to earn his diploma.

Fiat Music Company (2722 Pinole Valley Rd., Pinole): A young Armstrong would take piano and singing lessons in this shop owned by James and Marie-Louise Fiatarone. The shop is still open and still roughly in the same location it was in the '70s, but the plaza was rebuilt at some point.

The Nantucket (501 Port St., Crockett): Dirnt worked in longtime seafood restaurant The Nantucket during high school, coming back to the Armstrong family home where he was living stinking of fish. The Nantucket, in the shadow of the Carquinez Bridge, closed for business in February 2019.

Foxboro Village (Willow Ave. & Viewpointe Blvd., Hercules): The Foxboro Hot Tubs, a side project featuring all three members of Green Day, was named after this Village suburban townhouse development south of Rodeo. When they were teenagers, Armstrong, Dirnt and other friends used to sneak into the property to hang out in the hot tubs with booze and, preferably but perhaps not often, girls.

"Welcome to Paradise" (1640 7th St., Oakland): Armstrong and Dirnt once squatted in a warehouse on 7th Street in Oakland,

the address of which they confirmed during an October 2016 appearance on the *Howard Stern Show*. The warehouse was the subject of "Welcome to Paradise," a song which first appeared on the group's second album *Kerplunk* before being recut for *Dookie*.

"It's about West Oakland, living in a warehouse with a lot of people, a bunch of artists and musicians, punks and whatever just lived all up and down, bums and junkies and thugs and gang members and stuff that just lived in that area," said Armstrong in the June 2005 issue of *Guitar Legends* magazine. "It's no place you want to walk around at night, but it's a neat warehouse where you can play basketball and stuff."

Ruby Room (132 14th St., Oakland): "Ruby Room," a song about getting sloshed by Green Day side band the Foxboro Hot Tubs, is about this Oakland dive bar and nightclub. The cover of *The Donnas Turn 21*, the fourth studio album by Palo Alto garage rock band the Donnas, was shot in a booth here.

Berkeley Repertory Theatre (2015 Addison St., Berkeley): The staged musical production of *American Idiot* had its world premiere at Berkeley Rep, running in the Roda Theatre from September 4–November 15, 2009, shattering box office records for the theater.

Powell Street Station (899 Market St., San Francisco): Scenes for the video for "When I Come Around," the fourth single from *Dookie*, were shot at this shared Muni Metro and Bay Area Rapid Transit (BART) station. The station's distinctive circular tiling is seen throughout the video.

Warning (133 Waverly Place, San Francisco): The album cover for Green Day's sixth album

Warning were shot roughly here as the band walked through Chinatown.

Billie Joe Armstrong Former Residence (6076 Manchester Dr., Oakland): Armstrong and his wife Adrienne Nesser built this house in 1998, raising their family here until they sold it in 2009. The property was the former location of Red Gate, designed by renowned architect and engineer Julia Morgan in 1911. Red Gate was destroyed in the Oakland Hills firestorm in the summer of 1991. As seen in real estate listings around the time the Armstrongs sold their home in 2009, the most personal touch of its most famous resident was a bathroom covered in punk flyers.

Taking the Longview (2243 Ashby Ave., Berkeley): Green Day's preparation for their first album on Reprise Records, *Dookie,* included shooting the video for lead single "Longview" in the rundown Victorian home they lived and rehearsed in. Over two days in January 1994, the band was filmed in the house, which with the exception of a couch brought in for singer-guitarist Billie Joe Armstrong to destroy, appears exactly as it always did.

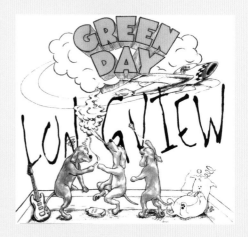

Mike Katz

2243 Ashby Avenue, Berkeley

"The whole house was communal living," said Armstrong in a *Rolling Stone* interview in 2014. "And we rehearsed there every day."

According to an interview with Green Day drummer Tré Cool in Ben Myers's *Green Day: American Idiots and the New Punk Explosion*, record label reps would visit the house to try and sign the group.

"The record company guys would come to see us rehearse in the basement and their wives would go shopping on Telegraph Avenue," Cool said. "And when we went on tour we would come back to discover these crusty punks had squatted our place, and every single thing we owned was gone. And my love letters ended up on the internet. . . ."

EAST BAY PUNK

Operation Ivy at 924 Gilman

Murray Bowles

"Community making decisions, not just one person. Man, that is a beautiful thing."
—TIM ARMSTRONG, OPERATION IVY/RANCID, *TURN IT AROUND: THE STORY OF EAST BAY PUNK*

Most music scenes need a nerve center, an incubator for young bands to play and kids to come together. The Cavern Club. CBGB. The Hacienda. 924 Gilman Street.

924 Gilman, the all-ages, DIY, nonprofit music and art community space that has long served not only as an East Bay Punk venue, but also as its symbol, is unlike most other important rock clubs around the world, in part due to its location not far from countercultural epicenters from bygone eras in Berkeley and San Francisco. Though sometimes ideologically aligned, punks generally rejected their hippie forebears. In the November 13, 1976 issue of now defunct British music weekly *Melody Maker*, the Clash's Joe Strummer summarized the punk ethos thusly: "The hippie movement was a failure. All hippies around now just represent complete apathy. There's a million good reasons why the thing failed, OK. But the only thing we've got to live with is that it failed.

At least you tried. But I'm not interested in why it failed."

If Tim Yohannan, founder of *Maximumrocknroll*—originally a punk radio show on Berkeley-based **KPFA (1929 Martin Luther King Jr. Way, Berkeley)** and later a not-for-profit monthly zine—was ever a hippie, he was on the far left of the spectrum, an ideologue who also happened to love rock music. That made for an easy transition when punk music reared its snarling head in the late '70s, and Yohannan used his bully pulpit on the radio as a means of battling cultural sacred cows, most famously Bill Graham, who'd cemented his place in local legend as the most renowned rock concert promoter of the San Francisco Scene of the '60s.

Though Graham had presented on January 14, 1978, the first Bay Area appearance—and ultimately last ever show until a reunion two decades later—of the Sex Pistols at **Winterland**

Ballroom (2000 Post St., San Francisco ⊘) he had a reputation for being anti-punk, a feeling that carried over into the '80s. And like the San Francisco punks did in the '70s by turning **Mabuhay Gardens (443 Broadway, San Francisco)** into their unofficial, un-Graham headquarters, Yohannan crossed paths with like-minded Victor Hayden and settled on a warehouse space at **924 Gilman Street**, which after months of renovation held its first show on December 31, 1986.

Perhaps 924 Gilman is most renowned outside of the East Bay for the commercially successful acts who've played its stage during their formative years. But for every Operation Ivy, Green Day, Rancid, or Jawbreaker, there are innumerable other bands who've rocked the Gilman rafters, most, but by no means all, somewhere beneath the expansive punk umbrella. The Mr. T Experience (who released the quintessential musical anthem "At Gilman

Crispin Kott

924 Gilman Street

Street" in 1989), Crimpshrine, Isocracy, Pansy Division, Yeastie Girlz, Neurosis, Fang, Blatz, the Lookouts, NOFX, Beatnigs, Sewer Trout, Samiam, Special Forces, Kamala and the Karnivores, Spitboy, Sweet Baby Jesus, Kwik Way; they were among many other early and often dissimilar Gilman groups, and that doesn't even begin to scratch the surface.

"It was pretty much a conduit for the entire underground around here since its inception in 1986," said Corbett Redford, director of *Turn It Around: The Story of East Bay Punk*, and founding member of acoustic folk-rock duo Bobby Joe Ebola and the Children MacNuggits.

For kids in the East Bay, 924 Gilman became a haven, a place where they were not only able to get flattened by the propulsive energy of a live gig by a new favorite band, but where they were also largely accepted, even if they weren't in almost any other corner of their lives. In keeping with the DIY aesthetic and what remains of the anti-capitalist, left-of-center philosophies initially imbued by Yohannan, Gilman is an all-ages independent collective with no owner, with volunteers working together to keep it afloat. According to the club's website, the "annual $2 membership card is required of everyone that pays to attend a show. The purpose of requiring everyone to become a member is to introduce you to the communal atmosphere encouraged here and to get you to agree (with your signature) to abide by the rules posted at the front door of the club, which were democratically agreed upon (and are constantly refined) at the membership meetings."

Over the years, 924 Gilman has updated but ultimately abided by its original set of rules, the current iteration of which can be found just inside the doorway: No alcohol. No drugs. No violence. No stagediving. No dogs. No fucked-up behavior. No racism. No misogyny/sexism. No homophobia. No transphobia.

Chris Appelgren, former owner and president of Bay Area record label Lookout! Records, first visited Gilman as a young teenager.

"At the time Gilman had this rule where because people were only going to certain shows and where popular bands were playing, they stopped saying who was playing on any given night, so you'd just have to go," Appelgren said in 2019. He went to the show with the son of a friend of his aunt. "He had no interest in music at all, but was just sort of like a nice older teenager. And by the end of the night he was working the door . . . he was very interested in the way that the club was run, even if he wasn't interested in the music."

As has been the case for many teenagers since 1986, the atmosphere at Gilman hooked Appelgren.

"It was sort of a very inviting place, you know, despite kind of looking a little intimidating when you first go, or at least when you first go as a 14-year-old or 15-year-old," he said, adding that while teenagers have a reputation for breaking rules, it happens less frequently at Gilman because rules are part of the reason the place functions at all. The inside is still covered in graffiti, the music is still loud and often aggressive, but the kids who come to Gilman generally follow its rigid principles. "The ways that it's rigid are understandable. You think about it, it's a place that caters to

youth. And so you have to be hard and fast with those rules that are gonna keep it a place that's appropriate for younger people."

Many of the faces have changed since Gilman first opened its doors, but the basic philosophies haven't, somehow managing to stay in the now without feeling like a relic of the past. It's why Gilman still matters.

"It's about weird, lost people coming to someplace and finding themselves," said Billie Joe Armstrong of Green Day in the 2017 documentary *Turn It Around: The Story of East Bay Punk*. "That's what so great about where Gilman is at now, and why it's been going on for so long. It's because you get these new people, young people and old people, all ages people. And they're making a community, and it's working."

But it hasn't always worked. Following the departure of Yohannan and the *Maximumrocknroll* contingent, 924 Gilman suddenly closed in September 1988; a note left on the door by Yohannan claimed "apathy and taking Gilman for granted" as the cause, though the collective had also recently been hit with a $16,000 judgment after being sued by someone who'd broken their arm in the pit during a show. Gilman reopened a few weeks later with the same core principles, the same meeting-based opportunity for volunteers to have their voices heard, and the same basic idea of giving kids—of all ages—a place to come together.

While 924 Gilman Street is the generally acknowledged epicenter of the East Bay Punk scene that exploded in the late '80s and early '90s, it was hardly the only place where shows took place. Punk happened at parties in backyards and warehouses, all following a hands-on DIY philosophy. It also went beyond *Maximumrocknroll*, with Aaron Cometbus's zine *Cometbus* and compilation tapes of local bands, including *Get Off My Guts;* and Robert Eggplant's *Absolutely Zippo* zine essential to the story of the

LOOKOUT! RECORDS

Founded by Larry Livermore and David Hayes in 1987, Lookout! Records was for years the unofficial independent label of the East Bay Punk scene, releasing crucial albums, EPs and singles by Green Day, Operation Ivy, the Mr. T Experience, Rancid, and a great many others. Also on Lookout! was Livermore's band the Lookouts, which shared its name not only with the label, but also the zine which preceded it.

Hayes officially left the label on January 1, 1990, in part due to philosophical differences, and Livermore was eventually joined by employees Chris Appelgren and Patrick Hynes as junior partners. Though Livermore was splitting his time between his home outside of Laytonville in Mendocino County and Berkeley, it was in the latter where the label's East Bay headquarters was located within Livermore's studio apartment **(1829 Berkeley Way, Berkeley)**. It was less than glamorous.

"There was one key which had 'Do not duplicate' stamped on it, so we always literally had to meet up," said Appelgren in 2019. "If there was anyone that was going to be out, I'd have to be like, 'Okay, I'll meet you at the cafe and get the key.'"

Even after managing to get copies of the key made, the apartment-cum-office lacked the feel of a traditional place of business.

"There was no doorbell so if anybody from bands came to visit, they would throw rocks or pennies up at the window so we'd come down and let them in," Appelgren said. "It was a small room with filing cabinets and a door across them as the desk. One computer, and then at another point we got a second one. Larry had a futon that he'd sort of unfold to sleep on

the dingy carpet. This was like kind of before a lot of desktop publishing. So we were doing a majority of the album cover and advertisement and poster layouts on the floor. And there was an attached bathroom . . . with like one of those accordion doors. So it was really horrible if you had to use the bathroom, not a sense of privacy."

In late 1994, Lookout! Records moved into a third-floor office at **1942 University Way in Berkeley**, but after years spent in Livermore's studio apartment, they struggled with giving it the professional touch.

"I had this kind of ridiculously ornate but also particleboard desk in my office and somehow a denim covered couch," Appelgren said. "We were kind of trying to seem really serious and legitimate but didn't quite know how to do it the right way."

In 1997, with its fortunes still soaring as it retained the rights to Green Day's first two albums after they signed with Reprise Records three years earlier, Lookout! opened a record store on the ground floor of the building which held their offices; that same year, Livermore and Hynes left the label, leaving Appelgren, Molly Neuman, and Cathy Bauer in charge.

"There was the continuous growth that we'd experienced for those first few years where it was, you know, 60 percent growth year over year," Appelgren said. "And then in the wake of Green Day, it was like 600 percent (growth); that was certainly not sustainable."

Also unsustainable was the Lookout! Records shop, which in addition to records and merchandise, also housed the label's mail order operation and had a small stage which occasionally hosted live shows.

"It was a little bit of a clubhouse," said Appelgren. "We sold mostly our own stuff, and then other titles that we would take on consignment, or friends' bands or things that sort of felt part of the same scene. But it was a hard business to justify in the same city as **Amoeba Music (2455 Telegraph Ave., Berkeley)**, and at the time there was a great record shop just a few blocks up the street, **Mod Lang (2136 University Ave., Berkeley; since relocated to 6328 Fairmount Ave., El Cerrito).**

The Lookout! offices and record shop shared a building with a number of therapists, which didn't help.

"At a certain point in the life of the record shop, we had to really scale down the number of loud volume events that we did because we did get some complaints . . . they would have sessions in booked into the evening."

In 1999, Lookout! Records shut the shop and moved off of University Way altogether, buying a building at **3264 Adeline Street in Berkeley**, which remained their office and warehouse until the label folded several years later.

developing scene. Important too were the songs cut not in professional recording studios, but wherever a band could set up, drop a cassette in a boom box, and make their own unique noise.

"This music that we made in our basements or garages, without any parents, without any teachers, that was a profound thing to happen to us a young age," said Tim Armstrong (Operation Ivy/Rancid) in *Turn It Around: The Story of East Bay Punk*. "Because it made us realize that anything was possible if you just do it yourself."

In the years since, the neighborhood has become increasingly gentrified, with craft breweries, restaurants, and a Whole Foods all within spitting distance of 924 Gilman. This has occasionally led to friction, with some of the new neighbors wary of the kids spilling out onto the streets during and after Gilman shows. Claims of vandalism have sometimes been leveled by nearby businesses. Threats of closure have come and gone, but Gilman still survives, hosting shows a few times a week,

and giving "weird, lost people" someplace to find themselves.

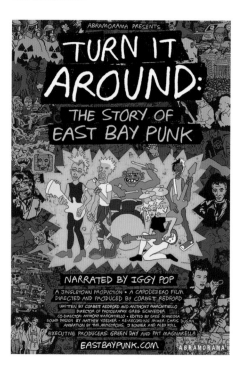

MORE EAST BAY PUNK

NOTEWORTHY LIVE PERFORMANCES

Ruthie's Inn (2618 San Pablo Ave., Berkeley):
In a former life, Ruthie's Inn was a blues club
that hosted both touring and local musicians,
including B.B. King and Bobby "Blue" Bland.
Thanks to visionary impresario Wes Robinson,
Ruthie's became one of the early East Bay spots
to put on punk shows, with the Dead Kennedys,
Bad Brains, Social Distortion, Flipper, and Black
Flag all playing its stage a few years before
924 Gilman Street opened its doors. Robinson
first brought San Francisco punk bands like the
Avengers and the Dead Kennedys across the
bay for shows in 1979 at the **Rio Theatre (140
Parker Ave., Rodeo),** then promoted punk gigs
at **Aitos (1920 San Pablo Ave., Berkeley),** which
came to an end after the venue was trashed.
Robinson has also been largely credited with
helping the nascent local thrash scene thrive as

well, with Ruthie's becoming a crossover home
to punk and metal in the mid-'80s.

"Some people will tell you it's Gilman," said
Redford of the debate over the most important
East Bay punk venue. "And then some people
will tell you it's Ruthie's."

**New Method (3623 Adeline St., Emeryville
⊘):** New Method was an abandoned
warehouse space that was part sprawling
squat, part DIY venue named after the previous
tenant, New Method Laundry.

"By the time I was 16 or 17, a lot of people
were living in a warehouse called New Method,"
said Dave Ed of Neurosis in *Turn It Around: The
Story of East Bay Punk.* "It basically became
like a squat. And they took over a section of the
warehouse and did a show space there. We did
a lot of super DIY shows."

Operation Ivy, Neurosis, 7 Seconds, Soul
Asylum, and Das Damen are among the bands
who played New Method in the '80s and '90s.

Own's Pizza (3308 Adeline St., Berkeley): A show at Own's Pizza on May 29, 1986, headlined by Canadian punk band No Means No, and featuring Victim's Family, Complete Disorder, the Mr. T Experience, and the Lookouts, was later credited as planting the seeds for what became the East Bay Punk scene, with no one getting hurt, no one destroying anything, and everyone having a good time.

Barrington Hall (2315 Dwight Way, Berkeley): A former student housing cooperative, the graffiti-covered Barrington Hall was known in the '80s for its occasional "Wine Dinners," which included an LSD-laced bowl of punch and performances by punk bands like Operation Ivy, NOFX, Flipper, Black Flag, Dead Kennedys, and Camper Van Beethoven. The former Barrington Hall is now known as Evans Manor.

Punks With Presses (1255 26th St., Oakland): More than just another graffiti-festooned warehouse squat, Punks With Presses was also an operating printing press. Seemingly every East Bay punk band had at least one member who lived there for a spell, many of which played shows in the small kitchen, including Jawbreaker, Rancid, Econochrist, Pinhead Gunpowder, and visiting Riot Grrrl group Bikini Kill.

Your Place Too (5319 Martin Luther King, Jr. Way, Oakland): Long since shuttered, Your Place Too was a bar that began hosting punk shows in the early '90s, with the Gr'ups, Bumblescrump, Your Mother, and One Man Running playing there.

"It was basically just like an old local bar that had a stage," said Appelgren. "The proprietors would let some of the kind of crusty punks book shows there. And even before I was 21, it was a place that was not very concerned about ID'ing people as they came in. I can remember seeing a lot of bands, like Jawbreaker, there."

Paradigm Studios (9029 San Leandro St., Oakland): A rehearsal space with a large open area for live shows, Paradigm Studios hosted gigs by Pansy Division, Bratmobile, Lagwagon, and DRI.

NOTEWORTHY RECORDING LOCATIONS

Dangerous Rhythm (3700 E. 12th St., Oakland): The majority of the tracks on *Turn It Around*, the October 1987 double 7-inch vinyl compilation covering the Gilman scene, were recorded at Dangerous Rhythm, with one band beginning as soon as another finished. Operation Ivy, Crimpshrine, Isocracy, No Use for a Name, and

Sweet Baby Jesus were all on the compilation. A few tracks, including those by Corrupted Morals **(Art of Ears Studio, 1213 Fell St., San Francisco)** and Yeastie Girlz **(924 Gilman St., Berkeley)** were recorded elsewhere. Operation Ivy also recorded *Hectic E.P.* at Dangerous Rhythm.

Art of Ears Studio (1213 Fell St., San Francisco): East Bay punk bands often traveled to San Francisco to record at Art of Ears, including Rancid, Stikky, the Lookouts, and the Wynona Riders.

Sound and Vision (684 Indiana St., San Francisco): Operation Ivy, Neurosis, the Mr. T Experience, Spitboy, Monsula, and Econochrist were among the East Bay punk bands to record at Sound and Vision.

Razor's Edge Recording (503 A Divisadero St., San Francisco): NOFX, Jawbreaker, Samiam, and post-Beatnigs outfit the Disposable Heroes of Hiphoprisy are all Gilman alum who've recorded at Razor's Edge, a former studio owned and operated by Jonathan Burnside inside this 1888 Victorian. Years earlier, author Anne Rice set scenes from her celebrated 1976 novel *Interview with the Vampire* there; the titular interview takes place in the house's front room, with the novel's opening paragraph mentioning Divisadero Street.

Dancing Dog Studios (1500 Park St., Emeryville): Run by producer Kevin Army, Dancing Dog was an East Bay studio where Operation Ivy, Spitboy, the Mr. T Experience, Blatz, Monsula, Crimpshrine, and many other local punk bands cut records.

OTHER NOTEWORTHY LOCATIONS

The Ashtray (3242 Adeline St., Berkeley): "Ashtray," a 1988 song by Screeching Weasel, is about this notoriously squalid punk house with a fitting name where Jesse Michaels (Operation Ivy), and members of Filth and Alkaline Trio lived. The apartment was directly above J&B Fine Foods Market, a liquor store that was in operation in the age of the Ashtray.

523 20th St., Oakland ⊘: Since demolished, this address was once the site of a rehearsal space used by Operation Ivy, Rancid, and the PeeChees.

7-11 (1540 Solano Ave., Albany): This nondescript chain convenience store was where punk kids from Albany and Berkeley would gather, and is reportedly where Jesse Michaels and Tim Armstrong met before forming Operation Ivy.

"When Operation Ivy and Rancid were growing up here, it was not the kind of affluent place that it is now," said Redford. "It was more of a bedroom community for the Richmond shipyards during World War II. It was very, very working-class place at the time. So those kids would meet up with the Berkeley kids right here."

CREEDENCE CLEARWATER REVIVAL

Pictorial Press Ltd./Alamy

"I think there are four things that make a record great. There's the title. There's the sound of the actual recording. The third thing is the song itself—but many great records have actually been made out of average songs. And the last thing, for me, is that if a record has a great guitar hook, then that's the very top of the mountain."

—JOHN FOGERTY (BMI MUSIC WORLD, 2010)

Unlike most of their Bay Area contemporaries, Creedence Clearwater Revival came together far from the collegiate folk dens and psychedelic streets of San Francisco. El Cerrito was East Bay suburbia; a cultural backwater, but it spawned what was arguably the most successful American band of its time. By honoring and extrapolating the rich texture and mythology of the American musical experience, they produced a prolific string of classic hits, including "Proud Mary," "Bad Moon Rising," and "Fortunate Son" in a relatively brief span, appealing to both top 40 listeners and serious critics. It's a story as old as the music business. A quartet of hard working guys who paid their dues, refined their craft, and ultimately hit the big time. It is also a cautionary tale about how creativity and ambition can be thwarted by naivete, recrimination, and unrepentant greed.

By the time they recorded their first album together as Creedence in 1968, John Fogerty, Stu Cook, and Doug Clifford had been playing together, on and off, for the better part of a decade. They first met at **Portola Junior High School (1021 Navellier St., El Cerrito ⊘)** in the 8th grade, and continued through **El Cerrito**

High School (540 Ashbury Ave., El Cerrito).
With John on guitar, Doug on drums, and Stu
on piano they played sock hops and Boys Club
dates as the Blue Velvets, an instrumental
group steeped in Duane Eddy, Freddie King,
Link Wray, and the Ventures. They occasionally
played with John's older brother Tom, who had
musical experience of his own and was a pretty
fair singer. They even recorded a few singles
on the diminutive Orchestra label as Tommy
Fogerty and the Blue Velvets. The records made
little impact, but they did give John his first
opportunity to record original work. "Have You
Ever Been Lonely" from 1961 is very much pop-
rock of its time, but pretty impressive work for
a 16-year-old. He was also learning the basics
of recording from Bob DeSousa at **Sierra Sound
Studios (1741 Alcatraz Ave., Berkeley)**. John
had simply phoned and asked if he could come
by and pick up some of the basics; a kind of
high school internship. Eventually the Velvets
wound up recording a few demos there.

In March 1964, KQED aired a three-part
program entitled *Anatomy of a Hit* with host
Ralph Gleason, the respected jazz critic. It
profiled San Francisco's Fantasy Records, a
small jazz label that scored a surprise hit the
previous year with Vince Guaraldi's "Cast Your
Fate to the Wind." Guaraldi, a local jazz pianist,
would enjoy even greater success in 1965
with the score for *A Charlie Brown Christmas*.
Until that point, Fantasy's most important
recording artist was probably Dave Brubeck,
but he had left almost 10 years before for
greener pastures, feeling he'd been swindled.
The Fogerty brothers were fascinated by the
show, which revealed the inner workings of a
small record label and featured the owners, the
Weiss brothers. John decided the time was ripe
to cross the bridge to the big city across the
bay and visit the Fantasy offices at **855 Treat
Avenue**, a decidedly unglamorous address in
the Mission. There he was welcomed by Max

855 Treat Avenue

Weiss. At this point it was April 1964, and
Beatlemania was in full swing, and it probably
made good business sense to give a few
minutes to a high school kid with a rock and
roll band. Soon the Blue Velvets had a contract
and were recording songs in Fantasy's dingy
ramshackle studio. John also secured a job as
a shipping clerk at Fantasy, giving him a close-
up look at the operation.

After some months, the Blue Velvets had
recorded several tracks, but were still waiting
for something to be released. Stu went off
to San Jose State, and the rest fended for
themselves in various ways. John took a month-
long gig at a club in Portland with some U.C.
Berkeley students. It was there that he worked
on improving his singing, eventually taking
over the lead. When the group returned to
Berkeley, they secured a gig at a local college
hangout, **The Monkey Inn (3105 Shattuck Ave.,
Berkeley)**, adding Doug Clifford on drums.
When that group called it quits, he called in his
fellow Blue Velvets to continue the residency.
This would be a new incarnation of the Velvets
however, one where John Fogerty was the
undeniable leader. He ordered Stu Cook to get a
bass and encouraged his brother Tom to learn
some basic chords on the guitar. The Monkey Inn
would prove to be critically important to their
development. It was here that they honed their

Mike Katz

3105 Shattuck Avenue, Berkeley

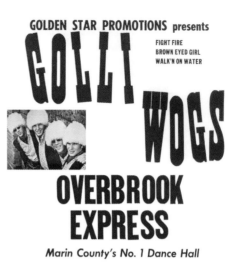

GOLDEN STAR PROMOTIONS presents

GOLLIWOGS

FIGHT FIRE
BROWN EYED GIRL
WALK'N ON WATER

OVERBROOK EXPRESS

Marin County's No. 1 Dance Hall

FAIRFAX PARK
PAVILION

FRI. NITE DEC. 30

8 p.m. to 12 Midnight

DRESS CASUAL   **ONLY $2.00**

Note the fashionable yak hats

skills together through 1964–1965 and evolved into a classic rock and roll formation.

Max Weiss, however, was not enamored of the name Blue Velvets and told the group to come up with a new moniker, so they became the Visions. When their new singles were finally ready they rushed over to Fantasy only to find the name Golliwogs on the label. In some kind of demented logic, Golliwogs was supposed to be "mod," and more in tune with the British Invasion. It was a moment of enormous frustration, but one of clarity as well. The conception, identity, and sound of this band would have to come from within, and John Fogerty took it upon himself to supply those elements, a move that would sow the seeds of both success and internal rancor.

Tom sang lead on the first pair of singles, but then John began to employ his newly honed grittier vocals on the third, "You Can't Be True," and the fourth "Brown-Eyed Girl" became something of a regional hit, opening more doors for them professionally. As Stu Cook remembered unromantically for *Uncut* in 2012 "The four of us spent the next few years putting out unsuccessful records and touring around Central and Northern California, playing little towns and military bases. We had a variety of names: The Visions, Tommy Fogerty and the Blue Velvets, the Golliwogs. We put out half a dozen singles on the Scorpio label, a subsidiary of Fantasy. They got airplay in towns like San Jose, Lodi, Merced, all the little stations in Central Valley."

For a brief time, they were even hoodwinked into wearing ridiculous matching white Himalayan yak hats. As John recounts in his 2015 memoir *Fortunate Son*, "Later on there'd be a point of just ripping that furry hat off and throwing it in the audience. . . . I know I don't have mine. Because I hated it."

By mid-1967, a confluence of events began to tilt matters in their favor. Firstly, John and Doug finished with the Army and Coast Guard Reserves, respectively, and Saul Zaentz, the sales manager at Fantasy, had teamed with a group of investors and acquired the company. He wanted to give the band another shot. They insisted on coming up with a new name, of course, and eventually settled on Creedence Clearwater Revival. The origins of the name are somewhat nebulous, but they involve a local custodian, Native Americans, and a beer commercial. Suffice to say, they knew what they were doing. On January 5, 1968, the group signed a new contract with Zaentz and Fantasy. They didn't know it at the time, but the substance of that contract would haunt and torment them for decades to come.

This time the band got to record in a proper studio, the venerable **Coast Recorders (960 Bush St., San Francisco)**, where they set about producing a new single. They chose the Dale Hawkins classic "Suzie Q," rather than another Fogerty original, as those had failed to make an impact, at least as Golliwogs records. In an attempt to put a new spin on an old tune, and to appeal to the progressive DJ's at **KMPX (50 Green St.),** they constructed an extended double-sided single, complete with multiple guitar solos and sound effects. It didn't hurt that they performed in support of the staff at the KMPX strike on March 18, on the back of a flatbed truck. The strategy worked, and the record became a legitimate hit, eventually reaching #11 on the Billboard Hot 100. At the same time, they secured a steady weekly gig at **Deno & Carlo's (728 Vallejo St., San Francisco)**, a North Beach club that became their first regular foray into San Francisco. They held the gig until the summer of 1968, well after their first album *Creedence Clearwater Revival* had been released. Midway through the year, they'd be playing at the big venues in town, such as the **Avalon Ballroom (1244 Sutter St., San Francisco), Fillmore West (10 S. Van Ness Ave., San Francisco),** and the **Cow Palace (2600 Geneva Ave., Daly City)**, often sharing the bill with the likes of Quicksilver Messenger Service, Santana, Canned Heat, Vanilla Fudge, and Steppenwolf.

In 1969, Creedence released three smash albums and produced three double-sided hits, an astonishing tally. Their second album, *Bayou Country*, consisted almost entirely of

songs written by John Fogerty, including two of his most well-known, "Proud Mary" and "Born on the Bayou," released together as a single and reaching #2 on the Billboard Hot 100. Even Fogerty was surprised by his songwriting breakthrough. As he told the *Boston Globe* in 2019 with regard to "Proud Mary": "That song was by far, way-up-in-the-clouds better than anything I had done before. And I recognized it right away. It was like, 'What happened to me?'"

The touring and recorded output continued at a breakneck pace, with Fogerty keeping a steady eye on the charts. If he sensed Creedence slipping he would lock himself in a room and produce new material, often to the consternation of his wife and family. "I was very driven," he told *The Guardian* in 2013, "It was life and death. I could see we didn't have a publicist, we didn't have a manager, we didn't have a producer, and we were on the tiniest label in the world, so we had to do it with music. And that kind of meant me." Clearly, the many years of toiling in obscurity had impressed upon him the

impermanence of life on the pop charts, and he, as well as the rest of Creedence, were determined to make it. "You'd have the Grateful Dead and Jefferson Airplane talking like: 'We don't want to be successful, maaaaan.'" he continued, "I wasn't embarrassed that I was ambitious. We wanted to be the best we could be."

Successive albums *Green River* and *Willy and the Poor Boys* were even more successful, containing the classic hits "Bad Moon Rising"/"Lodi," "Green River," and "Down on the Corner"/"Fortunate Son." Fogerty's songwriting was continuing to gain in sophistication as well, embracing the passions of the times. "Fortunate Son," lashed out at the Vietnam War

and patriotism in general, gaining the band a certain amount of street cred but generating plenty of resentment from Middle America as well. It was one thing for radical hippie bands to be against the war, but to hear Creedence blasting the same sentiments from their AM radios was hard to take. Their next album *Cosmo's Factory* would include "Run Through the Jungle," frequently perceived as another Vietnam tune, but actually a screed against the proliferation of guns.

1970's *Cosmo's Factory*, was named both for Doug and the rehearsal studio **(1230 5th St., Berkeley)** that served as their headquarters, and the album cover is the actual rehearsal space the band used at that time. It spawned two more double-sided hits, "Travellin' Band"/"Who'll Stop the Rain," "Up Around the Bend"/"Run Through the Jungle," and the playful "Lookin' Out My Back Door," inspired by John Fogerty reading Dr. Seuss's *And to Think That I Saw It on Mulberry Street* to his kids. The following album, *Pendulum*, would prove to be the last for Creedence as a quartet. Tom Fogerty had grown weary from the band's dissension and his brother's domineering ways and left for a solo career upon its completion. The internal fracturing would grow worse, and Creedence would produce only one more album, 1972's *Mardi Gras*, generally considered something of a dud. Out of appeasement, or perhaps disgust, John had Stu and Doug produce their own material, so that each group member was represented roughly equally. The record was met with puzzled negativity by critics and has largely been disavowed by John Fogerty. Creedence called it quits shortly thereafter.

Unfortunately no history of Creedence Clearwater Revival, even a brief one, is complete without some description of the legal quagmire that engulfed all four members in the years since the breakup. When the group signed its contract with Fantasy in 1968, they unwittingly signed away any rights to the songs they produced. Since John Fogerty wrote nearly all of the songs, he found that he had given away his musical legacy. Additionally, there were specific output requirements that bound him to the contract for years to come. As he recounted in his memoir: "Fantasy Records had not only chiseled me out of a fortune, they still owned my future. I was enslaved." It got even worse. Mysterious offshore investments set up by Saul Zaentz on their behalf had largely pilfered the band's earnings in the interim. Lawsuits and ugliness ensued, and relationships between former bandmates disintegrated. Only after Fantasy was sold following Saul Zaentz's death in 2014 was there even partial recompense.

Meanwhile, John Fogerty embarked on a solo career, releasing a couple of albums, 1973's *The Blue Ridge Rangers*, and 1975's *John Fogerty* which met with some acclaim but nowhere near the commercial success of the past. He adamantly refused to perform any Creedence material live, lest he continue to line the pockets of his archnemesis, Saul Zaentz. He remained largely silent for a decade, absorbed in legal hoodoo and his own personal funk, finally reemerging triumphantly in 1985 with *Centerfield*, recorded at **The Plant (2200 Bridgeway, Sausalito)** returning him to the top of the charts for the first time since his tenure with Creedence. He was promptly sued by Zaentz for the track "Zanz Kant Danz," (later changed to Vanz Kant Danz), and for plagiarizing *himself* on "Old Man Down the Road." The seemingly eternal legal nightmare continued, but he rode that success with several more successful albums.

Unfortunately the bitterness between former bandmates continues to this day. In an era where seemingly everyone reunites to cash in on past glory, the three surviving members of Creedence seem no closer to doing so than they did in 1972. For several years beginning in the 1990s Doug and Stu toured with a group of musicians as Creedence Clearwater Revisited, but a legal challenge from Fogerty forced them to briefly employ the name Cosmo's Factory. John Fogerty has fully embraced his own Creedence legacy these days and continues to tour worldwide, making it a family affair with his sons as part of the band.

MORE CREEDENCE CLEARWATER REVIVAL

NOTEWORTHY LIVE PERFORMANCES

AS THE GOLLIWOGS:

The Brass Rail ⊘ **(160 Mountain View-Alviso Ave., Sunnyvale):** In what was billed as their "1st Bay Area Performance," the Golliwogs played the Sunday "Under 21 Club" at this legendary strip joint on January 23, 1966. The street was later named Persian Drive.

Solano County Fairgrounds (900 Fairgrounds Dr., Vallejo): On Friday, October 28, 1966, the group shared a bill with the New Breed. They are featured on the poster wearing their signature Himalayan yak hats.

Poster by Randy Tuten, 1969

Strand Theatre (1021 10th St., Modesto): The group opened for the Sir Douglas Quintet, another band that sort-of pretended to be from England, here on November 23, 1966.

Fairfax Park Pavilion (142 Bolinas Rd., Fairfax): On Friday, December 30, 1966, the yak-hatted band shared a bill with Overbrook Express.

AS CREEDENCE CLEARWATER REVIVAL:

Avalon Ballroom (1244 Sutter St., San Francisco): Creedence Played the KMPX Strike Fund Benefit on March 20, 1968, two days after the impromptu performance at the station, with the Grateful Dead, Kaleidoscope, the Santana Blues Band, Blue Cheer, Clover, and others. Another benefit concert followed on March 27.

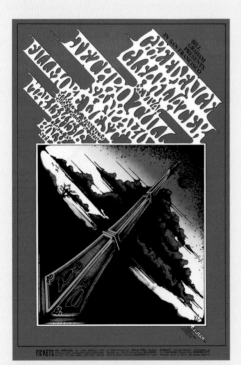

Poster by Randy Tuten, 1969

The New Monk (2119 University Ave., Berkeley): Creedence played this club April 5–7, 1968. The venue was later known as the Keystone.

The Committee Theater (836 Montgomery St., San Francisco): On August 24–25, 1968, Creedence played this theater, better known as a venue for avant garde satirical comedy.

Fillmore West (10 S. Van Ness Ave., San Francisco): Creedence shared the bill with Fleetwood Mac and Albert Collins on January 16–19, 1969.

Oakland-Alameda County Arena (7000 Coliseum Way, Oakland): On January 31, 1970, Creedence was filmed and recorded here for a television special, which has only been aired sporadically over the years. A live album was also recorded and released, labeled erroneously as *The Royal Albert Hall Concert*. It has since been renamed *The Concert*. Booker T and the MG's opened the show and are seen in the TV special jamming with Creedence in the Factory

in Berkeley. The band's last official performance in the Bay Area was in this same venue October 16, 1971.

NOTEWORTHY RECORDING LOCATIONS

Dick Vance Recording Studio (3249 Grand Ave., Oakland): In 1959, John, Tom, Doug, and Stu recorded at least two tracks, including: "Yes, I Love You," and "Oh Yes, I Know" as Tommy Fogerty and the Blue Velvets. These are the first known recordings of the group that would become Creedence Clearwater Revival.

Coast Recorders (960 Bush St., San Francisco): John, Tom, Stu, and Doug accompanied singer James Powell on his recording session for "Beverly Angel" released on the Christy label in 1960.

Wally Heider Studios (245 Hyde St., San Francisco): Creedence recorded the albums *Green River, Willy and the Poor Boys, Cosmo's Factory, Pendulum,* and parts of *Mardi Gras* here. John Fogerty recorded his second solo effort *John Fogerty* here in 1975.

Fantasy Studio A (2600 Tenth St., Berkeley): Referred to as "the house that Creedence built," the band recorded the bulk of their last album, *Mardi Gras* here in 1971–1972. John Fogerty recorded his first solo album, *Blue Ridge Rangers* here as well in 1972.

OTHER NOTEWORTHY LOCATIONS

7251 Eureka Avenue, El Cerrito: The first home for Tom and John Fogerty's family in El Cerrito. They lived here until approximately 1951.

226 Ramona Avenue, El Cerrito: The family moved here after Eureka Avenue, and this was the Fogerty brothers' home until they grew up. John initially had the room over the garage but

eventually moved down to the basement, which flooded every winter. As he remembered in his memoir, "There would be an inch and a half of water on my floor, and I got to laying two-by-fours so I could get from outside my room to my bed without stepping in the water."

School of the Madeleine (1225 Milvia St., Berkeley): John Fogerty attended first grade here. It was a long commute from home, and he was frequently late, drawing the ire of the faculty.

Harding Elementary School (7230 Fairmount Ave., El Cerrito): Where John Fogerty attended school from approximately 1952–1956. The current building was erected in 1980.

1325 Brewster Drive, El Cerrito: Stu Cook grew up here with his family. Many practice sessions for the pre-Creedence band members took place in the family rumpus room downstairs.

St. Mary's College High School (1294 Albina Ave., Berkeley): Tom Fogerty attended high school here, but John managed only the 9th and half of the 10th grade before transferring to El Cerrito High School. Paul Kantner of Jefferson Airplane also attended St. Mary's around the same time. The current building is of more recent vintage.

Richmond High School (1250 23rd St., Richmond): After struggling through his junior year, John Fogerty was required to attend summer school here, where he was reunited with Mrs. Starck, his music teacher from Portola Junior High. It was in Mrs. Starck's class that he originally got together with Doug and Stu and formed the Blue Velvets. She was an enthusiastic supporter of his musical aspirations when most of his teachers offered little to no encouragement. The current school building dates from 1969.

Contra Costa College (2600 Mission Bell Dr., San Pablo): John Fogerty was accepted to the University of San Francisco, but couldn't afford the tuition, so he entered Contra Costa instead. He attended classes until he went into the Army Reserve.

Duck Kee Market—Former Location (3219 Peralta St., Oakland): Creedence used this small neighborhood grocery store as the backdrop for the cover of *Willy and the Poor Boys* in 1969, as photographed by Basul Parik. The building remains, but the market and all recognizable signage are long gone.

Fantasy Records Headquarters (1281 30th St., Oakland): Saul Zaentz moved the Fantasy offices here after leaving the Treat Street location in San Francisco.

John Fogerty's Former Studio (842 Key Route Blvd., Albany): This small complex served as Fogerty's studio and office for several years following the demise of Creedence. He wrote songs and worked on demos for his first few albums on the premises, including *Centerfield* in 1984. Today the facility is a child care center.

OAKLAND

FOX THEATER
1807 Telegraph Ave.
Opened as a cinema in 1928, the 2,800-seat Fox Theater with its terra cotta tiling, lush paintings, and golden gods has hosted live music since an extensive renovation in 2009. Its life as an opulent movie palace with occasional performances by popular crooners began waning in the '60s, and in the subsequent decades the theater survived decay, neglect, and arson.

Since reopening, the Fox has seen Sonic Youth, Brian Wilson, David Byrne, Neil Young, the National, and many more grace its stage.

The Oakland Fox

Crispin Kott

PARAMOUNT THEATRE
2025 Broadway
Built as a grand Art Deco movie palace in 1931, the Paramount is currently home to the Oakland East Bay Symphony and Oakland Ballet. It's also a popular concert hall, hosting music from a wide range of genres. The Paramount closed as a cinema in 1970 with the Beatles' warts-and-all documentary *Let It Be*, but as

it began expanding its offerings later in the decade began including rock concerts on its calendar. Bob Dylan, Bruce Springsteen and the E Street Band, Prince, James Brown, Tom Waits, Jeff Beck, and Ringo Starr have all played the Paramount.

THE SPORTSMAN AND THE SHOWCASE
Sportsman: 5319 Grove St. (since renamed Martin Luther King Jr. Way)
Showcase: 3228 Telegraph Ave.
Born and raised in Oakland, Don Barksdale might best be remembered as an African American pioneer during his playing days in the NBA, and as the first Black athlete to play for the US men's basketball team in the 1948 Olympics. Barksdale was no less a trailblazer off the court, and during his time as a DJ in the Bay Area on stations like KDIA and KROW he also owned a pair of popular nightclubs, The Sportsman and The Showcase.

Both clubs were open in the '60s, with touring performers like Marvin Gaye, Jackie Wilson, B.B. King, Ike & Tina Turner, the Marvelettes, and the Temptations performing there.

OAKLAND SCOTTISH RITE CENTER
1547 Lakeside Dr.
Completed in 1927, this freemason's lodge overlooking Lake Merritt has occasionally seen live music played in both its auditorium and banquet hall. Fugazi, Suicidal Tendencies, M.C. Hammer, and Hüsker Dü have all played the Scottish Rite Temple.

BURGER BOOGALOO/T.B.A.
Mosswood Park, 3612 Webster St.
Hosted most recently in the summer of 2019 by filmmaker John Waters, Burger Boogaloo is an annual two-day festival produced by Oakland's Total Trash Productions through a partnership with Fullerton-based Burger Records. Since

WEST OAKLAND

Another neighborhood that once lay legitimate claim to the title "Harlem of the West" is West Oakland. Not unlike the Fillmore across the bay, much of it has been expunged by aggressive civic redevelopment. The Cypress Street Viaduct, construction of the BART station, and a mammoth postal facility all combined to isolate the district and crush its cultural vitality. In the last decade or so, however, a greater historical appreciation for the vibrant musical culture of the past has created renewed interest in what once was a thriving, exciting entertainment and nightlife destination.

Seventh Street can trace its roots as a musical hub at least as early as 1919, when trombonist Kid Ory came from New Orleans and regularly performed at the **Creole Cafe (1740 7th St. ⊘)**. By 1922, however, the club was failing, prohibition notwithstanding. After prohibition and particularly during the war years when the area was brimming with shipyard workers, Seventh Street was one of the hottest destinations in the Bay Area, with clubs,

restaurants, theaters, and bars lining a street abuzz with life and excitement.

Bob Geddins left behind a life in Texas picking cotton in search of greater opportunity on the West Coast. He performed a variety of jobs, and even collected garbage for a time before opening his own record store in South Central Los Angeles. On a trip to Oakland in 1942 he came upon the thriving musical scene on Seventh Street and saw an opportunity. Very few manufacturers of "race music" as African American music was then called, operated out of Northern California, so Geddins eventually embarked on a new career scouting talent and recording artists at various radio studios around the Bay Area, ultimately cutting records himself for his Big Town label at a homemade record pressing plant in a garage on **Eighth and Center Street ⊘** in 1944. His first success was the Rising Stars, a popular gospel group. He later recorded Lowell Fulson and produced his first national hit in 1948, "Three O'Clock Blues." Geddins established a family of labels, including Down Town, Cava-Tone, Art-Tone, Bro-Tone, and Irma (named for his wife), as well as his own publishing company, B-Flat Music. What recordings he didn't distribute himself he leased to other labels like Modern and Aladdin. He eventually set up his own recording studio at **Seventh and Center Street ⊘**, where the BART station now sits. He established his headquarters at **711 Seventh Street**, and his last recording studio was at **539 11th Street** near Lafayette Square. A litany of Bay Area blues legends worked with Geddins, including Jimmy McCracklin, Roy Hawkins, Jimmy Wilson, Johnny Fuller, and Sugar Pie DeSanto, who had a big hit with "I Want to Know" in 1960. He

produced records on and off into the '80s and died in 1991, his legacy as a true Bay Area musical pioneer assured.

SLIM JENKINS SUPPER CLUB
1748 7th St. ⊘

Shortly after prohibition's repeal, Louisiana native Harold "Slim" Jenkins opened a liquor store at **1740 Seventh Street** and eventually the now-legendary Supper Club, ushering in a golden age of first-class entertainment for a mixed-race, but primarily African American clientele. For more than three decades, Jenkins hosted topflight performers, including Duke Ellington, Louis Jordan, B.B. King, Nat King Cole, Dinah Washington, the Ink Spots, T-Bone Walker, Big Mama Thornton, and Ivory Joe Hunter, who released his R&B hit "Seventh Street Boogie" in 1945. Saunders King, the first local artist

to score a major hit with his "SK Blues" in 1942 was also regular. Jenkins's enterprise came to encompass the entire corner at Wood, consisting of the night club, a coffee shop and cocktail lounge, a luxurious restaurant with banquet hall, and the liquor store. He also operated a Bar-B-Que spot down the street at **1541 Seventh Street**, as well as several other businesses up and down the coast. He became active in the Republican Party and welcomed several prominent political figures over the years, including President Franklin D. Roosevelt, who moored his yacht, the *Potomac,* nearby. Slim hung on through 1962, when he relocated his club to **310 Broadway** at Jack London Square; sadly, that didn't last. Jenkins passed away in 1967. Just down Seventh Street is the recently built Slim Jenkins Court apartment complex named in his honor.

ESTHER'S ORBIT ROOM
1724 7th St.

Esther Mabry had been a waitress at Slim Jenkins's place after arriving from Texas in 1942, and opened her own restaurant, Esther's Breakfast Club in 1950. She expanded by opening a cocktail lounge in 1961, and after Jenkins's departure in 1962, the Orbit Room at 1753, creating a new home for West Oakland's R&B and blues community. Cozier and more casual than Jenkins's establishment, the Orbit Room became a landmark venue that featured nationally recognized performers, such as Aretha Franklin, Ike & Tina Turner, Bobby "Blue" Bland, Lou Rawls, and Al Green, as well as local artists Etta James, Lowell Fulson, and "Terrible" Tom Bowden. She crossed over to **1724 Seventh Street** when work on the new post office began

Here He Is!!!
The King of the Blues
SAUNDERS KING
and
ALADDIN
got HIM!

First Release Out Next Week

"ST. JAMES INFIRMARY BLUES"
and "LITTLE GIRL"
ALADDIN NO. 3027
Order From Your Distributor!

Aladdin
RECORDS
HOLLYWOOD 27, CALIFORNIA

in 1973. Esther's outlasted every other nightspot in the area and survived into the 21st century before finally succumbing in 2005. Esther herself died five years later at age 90.

LINCOLN THEATRE
1620 7th St. ⊘

Built in 1919, the Lincoln served as a live performance venue, movie theater, and church into the 1950s before being abandoned and left to decay. Billie Holiday is said to have performed here several times in her career. Unfortunately after years of neglect and a roof collapse, the Lincoln was demolished in 2003.

JESSE FULLER'S HOME
1679 11th St.

Known primarily for his classic "San Francisco Bay Blues," Fuller had a colorful life that brought him across the country from Jonesboro, Georgia, in the 1920s. He worked a variety of odd jobs for many years, including hot dog vendor and even as a film extra before settling in Oakland in 1929, where he worked for the Southern Pacific Railroad. Always a musician at heart, Fuller became a full-time performer in the '50s, billing himself as "The Lone Cat." He recorded his first album in 1958 at the age of 62, and typically performed as a one man band, with guitar, harmonica, and "fotdella," a foot-operated contraption of his own invention. He reached his greatest success in the '60s as the blues and folk revival was in full swing and his tunes were covered by many contemporary artists, including the Grateful Dead, Janis Joplin, Johnny Cash, and Peter, Paul, and Mary. Fuller lived in this house for the latter part of his life and died in 1976.

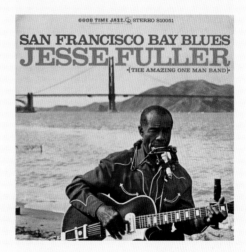

THE MUSIC THEY PLAYED ON 7TH ST.—OAKLAND WALK OF FAME
1451 7th St.

Just outside the BART station on Seventh Street is the first phase of a project that honors the musical legacy of West Oakland. The product of many years of campaigning by Ronnie Stewart of the Bay Area Blues Society, the 84

plaques installed commemorate many of the great performers and contributors who made West Oakland an historic musical destination, including national stars like Billie Holiday, Aretha Franklin, and B.B. King, as well as those who first made their mark in the Bay Area, such as Etta James, Lowell Fulson, Johnny Heartsman, and Saunders King.

severed ties with Burger Records and promised to bring the festival back in July 2021. As of October 2020, the festival has yet to be renamed.

HARLEM QUARTER
708 Franklin St.

This pagoda-styled structure was built in 1924 as a Chinese restaurant and has remained one for most of its lifetime, but for at least a few years beginning in 1948 it was the Harlem Quarter, a swanky nightclub featuring African American entertainment, including Billy Eckstine and the young Sammy Davis, Jr. The location is probably best known as the location of the Legendary Palace for many years before becoming the Cinnamon Tree.

2013, the festival has been held in Oakland's Mosswood Park. Past performers include Iggy Pop, Buzzcocks, Shannon and the Clams, the Jesus and Mary Chain, Psycotic Pineapple, Oh Sees, and Jonathan Richman. The 2020 festival was postponed by the COVID-19 pandemic, and was shortly thereafter caught up in the reckoning brought upon since-shuttered Burger Records by numerous women who claimed the label and many of its bands fostered an atmosphere conducive to sexual harassment and sexual assault. Total Trash Productions

OAKLAND-ALAMEDA COUNTY COLISEUM
7000 Coliseum Way

As with other stadiums in the Bay Area, Oakland-Alameda County Coliseum has suffered from a bit of an identity crisis over the years, beginning in 1998, over 30 years after it opened, when it was renamed Network Associates Coliseum. The Coliseum has been home to the Oakland Athletics since 1968, after the franchise left Kansas City. It was also home to the Oakland Raiders football team for two long stretches separated by over a decade in Los Angeles, the last few begrudgingly as the franchise completed its move to Las Vegas for the 2020 season. The A's too are hoping to leave the Coliseum in the near future, though they'll stick with Oakland with a new baseball-friendly stadium in the works for Howard Terminal.

In addition to the annual Bill Graham–produced Day on the Green series starting in 1973, Oakland Coliseum also hosted Amnesty International's Human Rights Now! benefit concert on September 23, 1988, with performances by Bruce Springsteen and the E Street Band, Peter Gabriel, Sting, Joan Baez, Tracy Chapman, and others.

Metallica and Guns N' Roses brought their coheadlining tour to the Coliseum on September 24, 1992. Other concerts staged by Green Day and U2 have also taken place here.

OAKLAND-ALAMEDA COUNTY ARENA
7000 Coliseum Way
Known today as simply Oakland Arena, this indoor stadium adjacent to the much larger outdoor Oakland-Alameda County Coliseum was with the exception of a mid-'90s renovation period the home of the Golden State Warriors from 1971–2019, after which point they moved to the brand new **Chase Center (1 Warriors Way, San Francisco)**.

Oakland Arena has hosted many concerts over the years, including the Grateful Dead, Prince, Van Halen, Nine Inch Nails, Megadeth, Kendrick Lamar, and Paul Simon.

TUPAC SHAKUR'S APARTMENT
275 MacArthur Blvd., Apt. H
Tupac Shakur, one of the most revered and influential figures in hip-hop history, has roots in New York City and Baltimore, but it was in the Bay Area that his career took full flight.

In an attempt to escape the violence and poverty of Baltimore, Afeni Shakur dispatched her 16-year-old son and his step-siblings to Black Panther associates in Marin City in 1988, then a notorious crime and drug haven. Tupac briefly attended nearby **Tamalpais High School (700 Miller Ave., Mill Valley)**, but dropped out when that living situation, exacerbated by his mother's arrival and descent into drug addiction, disintegrated into chaos.

He had experimented with hip-hop earlier in Baltimore, but he developed his chops in the Bay Area and eventually met a sympathetic poetry teacher, Leila Steinberg, who agreed to manage him and got him a gig performing at the 1989 Marin City Festival with his group, Strictly Dope. That led to an introduction to

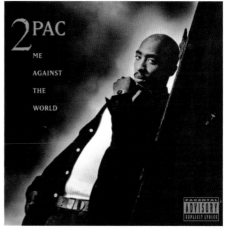

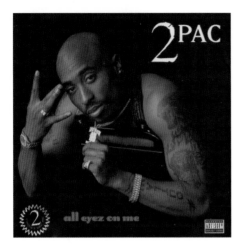

Atron Gregory, who managed the Oakland-based hip-hop collective Digital Underground led by Shock G. Digital Underground initially employed Tupac as a roadie before making him a full-fledged member of the group in 1990. He debuted on the tune "Same Song" on the soundtrack to the 1991 Chevy Chase/Dan Aykroyd film *Nothing but Trouble*, in which Tupac appears with the rest of the group. The film bombed, but the song appeared again on the D.U. recording *This Is,* an EP Release in January, 1991.

Shakur appeared on one more Digital Underground release, *Sons of the P* (1991) before embarking on his solo career that same year with the release of *2Pacalypse Now*, establishing him as a deeply political and thoughtfully unflinching social commentator. In October of that year, Shakur had one of his early run-ins with the law when he was cited for jaywalking at Broadway and 17th Street in Oakland and badly beaten by police. Tupac sued the city for $10 million and was eventually awarded $42,000. He moved into the MacArthur Boulevard apartment shortly thereafter and would reside there for another couple of years, sharing space with his step-brother Mopreme who would appear on some of Tupac's recordings before establishing his own career.

Shakur's second album, *Strictly 4 My N.I.G.G.A.Z. . . .* contained a pair of now-classic tracks "I Get Around" and "Keep Ya Head Up," and proved to be Shakur's commercial breakthrough, reaching #4 on the Billboard Top R&B/Hip-Hop chart. That success ultimately took him from Oakland to Los Angeles, where his career reached even greater heights before his untimely death by violence at age 25.

In 2016 the city of Oakland declared June 16 (his birthday) "Tupac Shakur Day." The official declaration reads in part: "he cherished his time in Oakland as his home, stating that he got his 'Game' from Oakland." Tupac once said: "I give all my love to Oakland, if I'ma claim somewhere I'ma claim Oakland."

TOWER OF POWER RISES
I.D.E.S. Hall
1105 C St., Hayward
Saxophonist Emilio Castillo hailed from Detroit, but grew up in Fremont where he closely identified with the Oakland soul tradition, and by his teenage years was already fronting a horn-driven R&B cover band known as the Motowns. He met up with baritone sax man Steve "Doc" Kupka over Fourth of July weekend, 1968, at the **Alameda County Fairgrounds (4501 Pleasanton Ave., Pleasanton)**, and the

THE POINTER SISTERS

They emerged from a devoutly religious home (1176 18th St. ⊘) in West Oakland to become one of the hottest and most versatile acts of the '70s and '80s, but the path to success for the Pointer Sisters was a tortuous one.

The Reverend Elton Pointer of the **West Oakland Church of God (1003 Myrtle St. ⊘)** imposed his parochial will on the family, and the girls all chafed under their father's judgmental eye. They did enjoy singing both in and out of the sanctuary, though, creatively absorbing a world of influences, including jazz, country, rock and roll, big band, pop, and R&B, a flexibility that would eventually serve them well.

By the early '60s the Pointers moved to **524 E 17th St.** in Lake Merritt, and the three eldest sisters, Ruth, Anita, and Bonnie attended **Oakland Technical High School (4351 Broadway).** The youngest, June, attended

Castlemont High School (8601 MacArthur Blvd., Oakland), but dropped out at 16 when she and Bonnie kicked off their musical careers as "Pointers, a Pair" in 1969. Anita joined not long afterward and they renamed themselves the Pointer Sisters. By 1971 the three shared an apartment at **422 Gough Street, San Francisco** (now numbered as 414). They had some success performing around the Bay Area and eventually got steady work as backup singers. They even cut a pair of singles for Atlantic which went nowhere, but were able to secure lucrative session work with artists such as Sylvester, Taj Mahal, Grace Slick, Dr. Hook, and Elvin Bishop. Ruth occasionally subbed for June, who was not always up for performing, and ultimately joined the group full time. Things finally began to coalesce for the sisters in 1972, and they recorded their first album, *The Pointer Sisters,* for new Blue Thumb label in 1973 at **Wally Heider Studios (245 Hyde St., San Francisco).** The musically eclectic debut was widely acclaimed and produced two hit singles, the Alan Toussaint-penned "Yes We Can Can" and a celebratory reimagining of the Willie Dixon classic "Wang Dang Doodle." The Sisters' colorful retro style made for good television as well, and they made appearances on the Helen Reddy, Flip Wilson, and Carol Burnett shows. Their follow-up album, *That's a Plenty,* provided another hit, the countrified "Fairytale" written by Anita and Bonnie, which earned them their first of three career Grammy awards. On April 21, 1974, they recorded what became their third album, *Live at the Opera House* in San Francisco's **War Memorial Opera House (301 Van Ness Ave., San Francisco).**

The year 1977 would prove to be a watershed year for the sisters. Hard living and the L.A. party scene had taken a severe toll. June was barely present on their album *Having a Party*, which tanked, and Bonnie left for a solo career. As Ruth recounts in her 2016 memoir *Still Excited*: "The original Pointer Sisters were kaput. I was just about broke and severely addicted to cocaine. I had no life plan, no fallback position, no career prospects, and no idea how to get out from under." Perseverance and new management got them to producer Richard Perry, who helped them craft a new contemporary sound and enticed June back to form a trio. The resulting 1978 album *Energy* was a triumph, fueled by their smoldering rendition of Bruce Springsteen's "Fire." The newly reinvented Pointer Sisters proved to be bigger than ever, releasing several classic era-defining hits over the next several years, including "He's So Shy," "Slow Hand," "I'm So Excited," "Jump (For My Love), and "Neutron Dance." The string of chart successes didn't last forever, but the Pointers Sisters carried on. Sadly, June passed away in 2006, succumbing to years of ill health, and Anita retired in 2015. Ruth continues to tour internationally with her daughter Issa, who joined in 2002, and granddaughter Sadako. After several years of ill health, Bonnie passed away in 2020.

pair would transform and funkify the band into Tower of Power, which debuted at the I.D.E.S. Portuguese social hall in Hayward on August 13, 1968. Tower of Power was originally signed by Bill Graham's San Francisco label and released their first LP, *East Bay Grease* in 1970. Greater success followed in the '70s, and Tower of Power had a string of now-iconic soulful brassy hits, including "So Very Far to Go" and "What Is Hip?" in 1973 alone. After years of recording and touring, as well as numerous personnel changes, Tower of Power is still going strong beyond their 50th year, true to their Oakland musical roots. On May 31, 2018, Mayor Libby Schaaf and the city of Oakland officially honored the band on "Tower of Power Day," recognizing them as "pillars and signatures of the Bay Area music scene."

SHEILA E'S CHILDHOOD HOME
920 E 21st St.

Sheila Escovedo, better known as virtuoso percussionist Sheila E, grew up here and attended nearby **Franklin Elementary School (915 Foothill Boulevard., Oakland), Montera Middle School (5555 Ascot Drive, Oakland), and Oakland High School (1023 MacArthur Boulevard, Oakland)**. She grew up in an

sextet, and played with Santana before founding the big band ensemble Azteca. Sheila gained notoriety working with George Duke in the '70s and Prince in the '80s, as well as launching her own successful solo career. Her breakout 1984 LP *The Glamorous Life* and its hit title track are irresistibly funky dance classics. She has performed with many top musicians, including Ringo Starr and Beyonce, as well as collaborating with film composer Hans Zimmer. In 2009 President and Mrs. Obama welcomed Sheila with a stellar lineup of musical luminaries for "Fiesta Latina" at the White House.

illustrious musical family; her father Pete Escovedo and Uncle Coke had their own jazz

DPA Picture Alliance/Alamy

"We're from San Francisco, and we think it's the greatest place in the world."
—HUEY LEWIS (*ROLLING STONE*, MAY 17, 2013)

The meteoric ascent of Huey Lewis and the News is a tale that can be told through two local bars, one which isn't around any longer, the other of which remains in many ways exactly as it was a few decades ago when its interior appeared on the cover of one of the most popular rock albums of the '80s: **Uncle Charlie's (5625 Paradise Dr., Corte Madera)** and **The 2 AM Club (382 Miller Ave., Mill Valley)**.

Truth is, Huey Lewis and the News didn't just appear overnight, it only *seemed* like they did. By the time the harmony-laden rocker "Do You Believe In Love" hit #7 on the Billboard Hot 100 on April 17, 1982, the News had already been a band for around three years, first calling themselves Huey Lewis and American Express before fear of a copyright infringement lawsuit led to Huey Lewis and the News.

But first there was Clover, a country-fried Mill Valley rock band who either had lousy timing or an undiagnosed allergy to commercial success. Lewis and keyboardist Sean Hopper joined Clover close to 10 years after the group got started, just in time for their final two albums. *Unavailable* and *Love on the Wire*, both released in 1977, were recorded while the group was in the U.K. trying to reverse their fortunes, which included a gig—minus Lewis, but including Hopper—backing Elvis Costello on his debut album, *My Aim Is True*.

Clover was nothing if not persistent, playing the same venues year after year. **The Lion's Share (60 Redhill Ave., San Anselmo)**, the **Scoreboard (San Rafael)**, **River City (52 Bolinas Ave., Fairfax)**, **Old Mill Tavern (106 Throckmorton Ave., Mill Valley)**, **Sweetwater Music Hall (19 Corte Madera Ave., Mill Valley)**, and **Brown's Hall (390 Miller Ave., Mill Valley)** were among the places Clover routinely rocked. The band played its final gig before splitting in 1978 at **Throckmorton Theatre (142 Throckmorton Ave., Mill Valley)**.

Another venue not unfamiliar to Clover was Uncle Charlie's, a wild rocking bar in a suburban Corte Madera shopping center. Sometime after Clover dissolved, Lewis was asked to organize a regular jam session at Uncle Charlie's, dubbed Monday Nite Live, bringing in among others Hopper, along with three members of the Sound Hole, another Marin County band cut from a similar cloth as Clover, which had spent time backing local resident Van Morrison: Drummer Bill Gibson, guitarist and saxophonist Johnny Colla, and bass guitarist Mario Cipollina, younger brother of Quicksilver Messenger Service guitarist John Cipollina. With the addition of guitarist Chris Hayes, the now-classic Huey Lewis and the News lineup was complete. (The band would soon return to their roots, shooting the video for 1985 single "The Power of Love" during a pair of intimate live shows at Uncle Charlie's.)

In an October 2017 interview for the *Mill Valley Oral History Project*, Lewis said that in putting the News together, a sense of community was crucial.

"We were friends first," Lewis said. "We came from Marin County. Sean is from Sausalito, Billy's from Mill Valley, Mario's from Mill Valley, Johnny's from Fairfield, but he was living in Mill Valley, and I'm from Strawberry Point. We were a very, very local band. We didn't answer ads in newspapers or music papers or any of that stuff. This was our thing."

Huey Lewis and the News, the group's self-titled debut for Chrysalis Records recorded

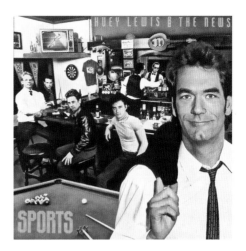

in Los Angeles in late 1979, was released the following June, falling just outside the Billboard 200 chart before fading away. The group's next album, 1982's *Picture This*, was recorded closer to home at **The Automatt (827 Folsom St., San Francisco)**. *Picture This* hit #13, thanks largely to the Mutt Lange-penned "Do You Believe in Love" and its video, which showcased the band's collective sense of humor and everyman good looks. It was a step in the right direction, but the best was yet to come.

Like its predecessor, Huey Lewis and the News' third album, *Sports*, was produced by the band, returning to The Automatt for some of the sessions, but also cutting tracks at two of the Bay Area's preeminent recording studios, the **Record Plant (2200 Bridgeway, Sausalito)** and **Fantasy Studios (2600 Tenth St., Berkeley)**. With songs honed to pop perfection on club stages, and with a slew of impossibly catchy singles and accompanying videos, *Sports* took the world by storm upon release in September 1983, hitting the top of the charts in the United States, Canada, and New Zealand, and going top 10 in several other countries. The album eventually went 7× Platinum in the United States, and four of the album's five singles broke the top 10 in America, including "I Want a New Drug," which went gold.

Filmmaker David Rathod helped bring *Sports* to the small screen, directing the videos for the first two singles off the album, "Heart and Soul" and "I Want a New Drug."

"Heart and Soul" features Lewis flirting with a woman played by Signy Coleman at a wild party, with the pair stealing away into the night. The News, including Cipollina as a vampire waiter, are seen circulating among the guests. The clip was filmed entirely in San Francisco, with the party scenes shot in a spacious loft on Folsom Street in the Mission.

"All the dancers were friends and friends of friends," said Rathod in 2019. "It was an actual party, but designed for the video. We started pre-lighting in the morning, people arrived in the early evening, and we wrapped at dawn. Grueling."

The door of the party as seen near the beginning and end of the video was the entrance to Rathod's production and edit studio at **66 Broadway**, while the final shot of Lewis and Coleman took place somewhere in Portrero Hill.

"I Want a New Drug," which sees Lewis making his way to a gig with the News, had its live footage filmed at **Sherwood Hall (940 N. (940 N. Main St., Salinas)** during an actual concert. Coleman, the costar of "Heart and Soul," also featured in "I Want a New Drug."

"We put her in the front row so Huey could drop to his knees and sing to her," said Rathod.

"He performed the song twice in that show so we had a couple of chances to get the moment right."

According to Rathod, the triple-shot of Colla playing his sax solo was shot on the Sherwood Hall stage beforehand.

In the video, Lewis, in a sleek cherry red suit and black T-shirt, is seen making his way to Sherwood Hall by means of car, boat, and helicopter, with glimpses of Coleman throughout. The boat scenes were shot on the Golden Gate Ferry, which departed from a pier at San Francisco's **Ferry Terminal** and traveled round trip to Sausalito.

"We just purchased tickets for the cast and crew and did the shoot," said Rathod. "Again, Signy was put on the deck of the speed boat and they pulled up alongside the ferry and we took the shot."

The videos from *Sports* went a long way to selling Huey Lewis and the News as a fun-loving, earnestly rocking alternative option in a world seemingly overrun by hyperstyled heavily made-up acts; so did the album's sleeve art. The now-iconic image was shot inside The 2 AM Club, a modest Mill Valley bar that even today looks as it did in 1983, with a pool table, long wooden bar, rows of booze lined up beneath a toilet-seat guitar. Lewis is in the foreground, ready to relax, his top button open and his jacket thrown over his shoulder. Sitting at the bar are Colla, Hopper, Gibson, and Hayes, while Cipollina prepares to sling drinks.

In a 2007 interview with Marin Nostalgia, an online interactive museum, Lewis explained that the cover of *Sports* was meant to evoke the music within the grooves.

"I thought it was a funny notion," Lewis said. "I can't explain how it happened to be honest. I wanted a place that looked and felt like what I thought we were and sounded like. And that was kind of it. It juxtaposed against the title *Sports* because sports are on the television but we're in kind of a sports bar."

MORE HUEY LEWIS AND THE NEWS

NOTEWORTHY LIVE PERFORMANCES

Knight's Bridge (1618 2nd St., San Rafael): The Monday Nite Live sessions at Uncle Charlie's that led to the formation of Huey Lewis and the News branched out, including performances at this San Rafael dive bar.

Rancho Nicasio (1 Old Rancheria Rd., Nicasio): During their brief time as Huey Lewis and American Express, the group played a few gigs in late 1979 here, including one that September supporting Van Morrison.

The Old Waldorf (444 Battery St., San Francisco): Chrysalis Records threw Huey Lewis and the News a big bash at the Old Waldorf on June 16, 1980. Lewis fell on his ass during the set and the band received mixed reviews from the press. "It seemed to me I'd heard all the riffs before; seen all the gestures somewhere," wrote Philip Elwood of the *San Francisco Herald-Examiner.* Though the performance wasn't prime time News, it was the first time members of the band noticed girls waiting for them outside after a gig. They would return to the small venue a few times over the next year or so.

Frost Amphitheater (365 Lasuen St., Stanford): Huey Lewis and the News played Stanford University's Frost Amphitheater on August 3, 1980.

The Stone (412 Broadway, San Francisco)/ The Keystone (2119 University Ave., Berkeley)/ The Keystone (260 California Ave., Palo Alto): Huey Lewis and the News played this trio of linked clubs numerous times in the early '80s, sometimes jumping from one to the next.

Bill Graham Civic Auditorium (99 Grove St., San Francisco): Formerly known as the San Francisco Civic Auditorium, Huey Lewis and the News were regulars at the annual Bammies, an awards show with winners chosen by readers of free monthly music magazine *BAM* (*Bay Area Music*). Their first Bammies appearance took place on March 3, 1982, with the band performing "Workin' for a Livin'" and "Hope You Love Me Like You Say You Do."

Kabuki Theater (1881 Post St., San Francisco): Now a movie theater, in the '80s the Kabuki was a live music venue with shows promoted by impresario Bill Graham. Huey Lewis and the News first played here on October 8 and 9, 1982.

The William Randolph Hearst Greek Theatre (2001 Gayley Rd., Berkeley): By 1984, Huey Lewis and the News were superstars, selling out three nights at the Greek Theatre from July 8–10.

Oakland-Alameda County Arena (7000 Coliseum Way, Oakland): Huey Lewis and the News first played this massive arena on October 16 and 17, 1980, as the opening act for the Doobie Brothers. They were the headlining act when they returned for a pair of sold out dates on December 30 and 31, 1984. They'd double that with four shows at the arena between December 27–31, 1986.

Berkeley Community Theater (1930 Allston Way, Berkeley): Huey Lewis and the News played a pair of benefit shows at Berkeley Community Theater on November 22 and 23, 1985, with Nick Lowe opening the second night. It was the band's first show at the theater since their American Express days, when they opened for Van Morrison on October 21, 1979.

Slim's (333 11th St., San Francisco): Bay Area musicians came together in 1989 for a series of benefit shows as part of the In Concert Against AIDS series. Huey Lewis and the News played a series of intimate shows at the 500-capacity club Slim's between May 21–23, with proceeds from the $125 tickets going to charity. They would return to Slim's that November for another benefit show, this time for earthquake relief. The band played other Bay Area club shows in late 1989 for earthquake relief, including **New George's (842 4th St., San Rafael), The Catalyst (1011 Pacific Ave., Santa Cruz),** and **The Cotati Cabaret (85 La Plaza, Cotati).**

The Hilton Hotel (333 O'Farrell St., San Francisco): Tracks from Huey Lewis and the News' forthcoming album *Hard at Play* were unveiled at the Hilton during a short set at a convention for the National Association of Recording Merchandisers on March 24, 1991.

Shoreline Amphitheatre (1 Amphitheatre Pkwy., Mountain View): Huey Lewis and the News first played Shoreline as part of their *Hard at Play* tour on October 18, 1991.

Concord Pavilion (2000 Kirker Pass Rd., Concord): The *Hard at Play* tour hit Concord Pavilion for a pair of dates on October 19 and 25, 1991.

Mountain Winery (14831 Pierce Rd., Saratoga): This majestic amphitheater first hosted Huey Lewis and the News for a three night stand between June 24–28, 1998. The group would return here numerous times over the years, often making it their sole Bay Area tour stop.

Stern Grove (19th Ave. & Sloat Blvd., San Francisco): Huey Lewis and the News played this natural amphitheater in Sigmund Stern Recreation Grove in the Sunset on June 17, 2007.

Sweetwater Music Hall (19 Corte Madera Ave., Mill Valley): Huey Lewis and the News returned to Mill Valley for an intimate sold-out show at Sweetwater Music Hall on October 15, 2017.

NOTEWORTHY RECORDING LOCATIONS

Different Fur Studios (3470 19th St., San Francisco): Still going by Huey Lewis and American Express, the group cut a three-song demo at Different Fur in 1979. The demo impressed Pablo Cruise manager Bob Brown, who took the group on as clients after catching them play Uncle Charlie's.

Studio D Recording (425 Coloma St., Sausalito): *Fore!*, the fourth album by Huey Lewis and the News, was cut at Studio D shortly after it opened in the mid-'80s. They returned here for its follow-up, 1988's *Small World*, as well as some of their 1994 covers album *Four Chords & Several Years Ago*.

Skywalker Sound (5858 Lucas Valley Rd., Nicasio): Located on filmmaker George Lucas's sprawling Skywalker Ranch, Skywalker Sound is where Huey Lewis and the News cut 1991 album *Hard at Play.*

OTHER NOTEWORTHY LOCATIONS

Natural Foods Express (767 Lincoln Ave., San Rafael): Somewhere between the demise of Clover and the success of Huey Lewis and the News, Lewis opened a health food store in San Rafael.

Strawberry Point Elementary School (117 E. Strawberry Dr., Mill Valley): After his family moved to the area, Lewis—born Hugh Cregg III—attended elementary school here.

Edna Maguire Junior High School (80 Lomita Dr., Mill Valley): Lewis was at Edna Maguire for 7th and 8th grades. Edna Maguire became an elementary school in the early '70s.

Tamalpais High School (700 Miller Ave., Mill Valley): Cipollina, Gibson, and Hopper all went to high school at Tam High. Lewis took a machine shop summer school course between junior high and high school here before moving on to a prep school in New Jersey. The album art for *Fore!* (1986) which sees Huey Lewis and the News casually standing against a wall was shot here.

Mountain Theatre (Mount Tamalpais State Park, Fern Creek Trail, Mill Valley): The video for "Don't Ever Tell Me That You Love Me" from the debut album by Huey Lewis and the News was shot in and around this rustic amphitheater.

MOBY GRAPE

"The first group tonight is kind of like in a more difficult position than other groups because everybody's getting settled, and someone has to start the show. And this next group, I think, were very happy that they decided because nobody else wanted to go first. It's a difficult position, and let's have a warm hand . . . really . . . let's make it extra warm . . . for Columbia Recording artists Moby Grape."
—TOMMY SMOTHERS, THE MONTEREY POP FESTIVAL, JUNE 17, 1967

For many, Moby Grape were simultaneously the greatest and unluckiest band of the '60s San Francisco scene. Legal issues with former manager Matthew Katz that raged on for decades have left some of their music, including most of their eponymous 1967 debut, out of print and unavailable on digital streaming services. Additionally, Alexander "Skip" Spence, one of three guitarists in the classic lineup, suffered from a combination of mental health issues and drug addiction, and spent six months in New York City's Bellevue Hospital after wielding an axe to chop his way through a bandmate's hotel room door.

Even minor controversies managed to disrupt Moby Grape's momentum: Shot outside of a Marin County antique shop called **Junktiques (341 Bolinas Rd., Fairfax)**, the photograph on the cover of *Moby Grape* features drummer Don Stevenson slyly flipping the bird

against an old washboard; the offending middle finger was airbrushed out on many subsequent reissues. An American flag over Spence's left shoulder was airbrushed red for the initial release, airbrushed black for the first round of reissues, and restored to its original state along with Stevenson's middle finger on vinyl and CD reissues by London-based Edsel Records.

Moby Grape was recorded in Los Angeles, but the chemistry forged during wild guitar jams and live rave-ups across the Bay Area is what's found in the grooves. Columbia Records sought to capitalize on the sounds of San Francisco with the Grape, though their initial marketing strategy of simultaneously releasing five different singles from the debut album backfired, with radio stations veering between being confused and irritated by the gimmick. Only "Omaha" managed to crack Billboard's Hot 100, peaking at #88.

Poster by Heinrich Kley, 1966

Box sets of the five singles were among the plush perks for attendees at a lavish party thrown at the **Avalon Ballroom (1268 Sutter St., San Francisco)** on June 6, 1967. The Grape were no strangers to the venue, having played the hall numerous times over the previous year. But this time around revelers and journalists flown in for the soiree slipped around on purple orchids which blanketed the floor after being dropped from the ceiling; guests were given bottles of specially made—or at least specially labeled—Moby Grape wine, though no one had thought to provide corkscrews.

The evening had more surprises in store for Moby Grape's trio of guitarists, as Spence, Peter Lewis and Jerry Miller were arrested in a Marin County park in the wee small hours and charged with contributing to the delinquency of a minor, a misdemeanor, when a few of the girls in a group of people they were hanging out with turned out to be 17 years old; Miller was also booked on possession of marijuana, a felony, but all of the charges were later dropped.

Eleven days later, the group played the **Monterey Pop Festival at the Monterey County Fairgrounds (2004 Fairground Rd., Monterey)**, which focused the eyes of the world on artists like the Jimi Hendrix Experience, Janis Joplin, and the Who, and which has since gone on to be revered as a touchstone of rock festivals and the hippie generation. After having their time slot moved from just before Otis Redding's electrifying headlining set on the Saturday to the very beginning of the evening session, Moby Grape's performance was excluded from the subsequent film and live audio releases, they allege, because Katz demanded a fortune in return. Moby Grape's rousing performance of "Hey Grandma," including an almost apologetic introduction from Tommy Smothers, was later included in the Criterion Collection's 2017 Blu-Ray reissue of *The Complete Monterey Pop*, and audio of most of the other songs from their set were released on a Sundazed Music compilation of songs recorded onstage between 1966–1969, called *Moby Grape Live*.

Whatever crackling energy Moby Grape had on the Monterey Pop stage was all but drained from the group over the following year as they decamped to New York to record their sophomore album. It was a period not only marked by madness, but also loneliness and disenchantment. Spence was the first to leave the group, his forced exile into Bellevue meaning the Grape had to roll forward without him. Bass guitarist Bob Mosley left the following year, and by late 1969 Moby Grape were no more. They would come together in various incarnations over the years, then break apart again; the original five members reconvened in 1971 to record an album and play some shows, and they reunited once more in 1987 for a couple of gigs. As of October 2020, the Grape is still around, with original members Lewis, Miller, and Mosley still in the band, with Stevenson occasionally sitting in. Spence, who suffered from mental illness, and drug and alcohol addiction for much of his adult life, died of lung cancer on April 16, 1999, just two days shy of his 53rd birthday.

MORE MOBY GRAPE

NOTEWORTHY LIVE PERFORMANCES

The Ark (Waldo Point Harbor, Gate 6, Sausalito): The disused and permanently docked S.S. *Charles Van Damme* ferry may seem a curious spot for a rock and roll venue, but such was the Ark, which hosted shows by everyone from Bob Dylan to Jimi Hendrix, along with Bay Area groups like the Charlatans and Big Brother and the Holding Company. Moby Grape cut their teeth as a live act on the Ark, playing their first gigs here in October 1966; they used the Ark as a rehearsal space and also signed their management contract with Matthew Katz on board. Many Ark shows lasted long into the night, with bands performing as the sun rose behind them across Richardson Bay.

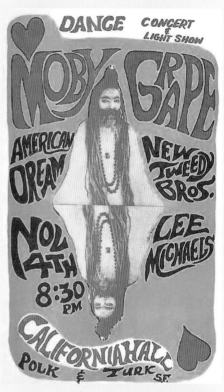

Poster by Lichtenwalner, 1967

California Hall (625 Polk St., San Francisco): The Grape's first show outside the Ark took place at California Hall on October 28, 1966, and was by all accounts an undersold letdown. Some of the attendance issues may have stemmed from the gig poster not including the actual show date. Also on the bill were Lee Michaels, the West Coast Branch, and American Dream. A poster for a return to California Hall on November 4 of the same year exists, but there's some question as to whether the gig actually happened.

Avalon Ballroom (1268 Sutter St., San Francisco): Moby Grape first played the Avalon Ballroom on November 11 and 12, 1966, supporting the 13th Floor Elevators. They

Poster by Victor Moscoso, 1967

Poster by Wes Wilson, 1967

returned two more times that year, including a two-night stint to close out the year on a bill with Grateful Dead and the Steve Miller Blues Band.

Goman's Gay '90s (345 Broadway, San Francisco): As with Moby Grape's second appearance at California Hall, a poster exists for a November 12, 1966, show at Goman's Gay '90s, this time supporting Buffalo Springfield. But with the Grape definitively playing Avalon Ballroom and Buffalo Springfield at Fillmore Auditorium that night, it would either have gotten off to a very late start or it didn't happen at all.

Fillmore Auditorium (1805 Geary Blvd., San Francisco): The Grape played a pair of three-night stands at the Fillmore in late autumn of

1966, sharing the stage with Jefferson Airplane and the James Cotton Blues Band for the first run of shows, and Love and Lee Michaels during the second.

The Matrix (3138 Fillmore St., San Francisco): Moby Grape played the Matrix from December 6–8, returning for another short residency between December 13–15, 1966.

Santa Venetia Armory (153 Madison Ave., San Rafael): A National Guard Armory that hosted numerous teen dances in the mid-'60s, gigs at the Santa Venetia Armory included Moby Grape, who first played there on December 23, 1966, alongside the Sons of Champlin, Morning Glory, Freedom Highway, and others. They returned six

days later, sharing the Wilson, with the Grateful Dead and Morning Glory.

Sausalito Auditorium (120 Central Ave., Sausalito): This charmingly rustic hall has long since gone back to being known as the Sausalito Woman's Club, but for at least one night on February 18, 1967, it was Sausalito Auditorium, home of the "Totally Odd Ball," an event—at least according to the poster—featuring the music of the Loading Zone and Moby Grape. The Grape also supposedly played the Ark that same evening alongside California Girls and the Sparrow.

Winterland Ballroom (2000 Post St., San Francisco): The Grape played the "First Annual Love Circus" on March 3, 1967, a show produced at Winterland by the Love Conspiracy Commune. Also on the bill were the Grateful Dead, Love, Loading Zone, and the Blue Crumb Truck Factory. Radical activists the Diggers picketed the show due to the high price of tickets—$3.50—and at least some were let in for free after the Dead said they wouldn't play until the issue was resolved.

Kezar Stadium (670 Kezar Dr., San Francisco): Moby Grape played a "Peace Fair" at Kezar Stadium on April 15, 1967. Also on the bill were Judy Collins, the Steve Miller Blues Band, and Malvina Reynolds.

Golden Gate Park Bandshell, San Francisco: In 1967, The *San Francisco Examiner* sponsored a series of free Thursday afternoon concerts. Moby Grape headlined one of the free shows on July 20, 1967, with support from Melvin Q. Watchpocket and the Cleanliness and Godliness Skiffle Band.

Concord Coliseum (1825 Salvio Rd., Concord): The Grape played this short-lived venue in early November 1967.

Carousel Ballroom//Fillmore West (10 South Van Ness Ave., San Francisco): Moby Grape played the Carousel Ballroom, with support from It's a Beautiful Day and Sweet Rush, on April 12 and 13, 1968. Three months later the venue was renamed the Fillmore West, where the Grape would play a handful of times during their brief reunion in 1971.

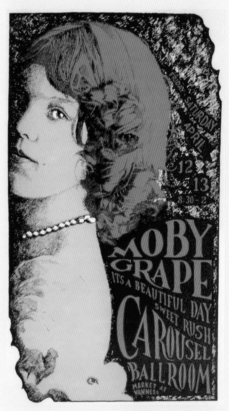

Poster by L. Kent Hollister, 1968

Chateau Liberté (22700 Old Santa Cruz Highway, Los Gatos): A rock and roll biker bar with a swimming pool, a bar cut from timber and an eclectic clientele, Chateau Liberté was a crucial venue through most of the '70s for groups like the Doobie Brothers, Quicksilver Messenger Service, and in 1971, the reunited Moby Grape.

Brooks Hall (Southern Half of Civic Center Plaza, San Francisco): This disused event space beneath Civic Center Plaza was the unlikely site of a reunion show by Moby Grape on May 22, 1971. After over a decade of declining use due to more modern convention options cropping up in the city, Brooks Hall closed to the public in April 1993, due to construction of the new Main Library and never reopened.

Drag'on A' Go-Go (49 Wentworth Place, San Francisco): This awkwardly named teen rock club in the heart of Chinatown was only open for a couple of years in the mid-'60s, but it hosted groups like pre-Moby Grape outfit the Frantics, the Beau Brummels, and from England—but not actually Liverpudlian—the Liverpool Five. Wentworth Place was also known as Wentworth Alley, and decades earlier, as Salty Fish Alley.

The Syndrome (1310 Old Bayshore Hwy., Burlingame): Opened in 1966 by Joe Gannon, the former road manager of the Kingston Trio, The Syndrome was one of many short-lived clubs to crop up across the Bay Area attempting to stretch the San Francisco sound to the suburbs. Most notable among the acts to play The Syndrome was Luminous Marsh Gas, a short-lived group featuring former members of the Frantics, who would soon go on to form Moby Grape. The Syndrome lasted for about one year before closing.

NOTEWORTHY RECORDING SESSIONS

Moby Grape House (20 Granite Creek Rd., Santa Cruz): For their first few albums, Moby Grape decamped to Los Angeles or New York to record. But when they reunited in 1971, they opted to stay in Northern California to cut their next LP. This sprawling Victorian home is where Moby Grape recorded much of *20 Granite Creek*, for Reprise Records. Various members of the group lived in the house during the recording, reportedly seeing ghosts of past residents.

Pacific Recording Studios (1737 S. El Camino Real, San Mateo): When they were finished recording at home in Santa Cruz, Moby Grape brought *20 Granite Creek* to Pacific Recording, where it was mixed and received overdubs.

Action Records (2207 South El Camino Real, San Mateo): The Frantics, a group featuring future Moby Grape cofounders Jerry Miller, Bob Mosley, and Don Stevenson, recorded their final single, "Human Monkey" for Action Records in 1966.

OTHER NOTEWORTHY LOCATIONS

Matthew Katz's Office (1725 Washington St., San Francisco): The office of the notorious former manager of the Jefferson Airplane and Moby Grape was located in a since-demolished building. It was at this address that the members of Moby Grape reportedly played music together for the first time in 1966.

Jerry Miller Home (503 Pineo Ave., Mill Valley): According to an arrest report in the June 9, 1967 issue of the *Daily Independent Journal* (San Rafael), Moby Grape guitarist Jerry Miller lived in this apartment house.

Peter Lewis Home (370 Sunset Way, Mill Valley): Moby Grape guitarist Peter Lewis lived

here in 1967. The paper incorrectly identifies the address as being in Tamalpais Valley, but Lewis's home was actually here, a short walk away from Jerry Miller's place.

Skip Spence Home (110 Redwood Ave., Corte Madera): In 1967, Moby Grape guitarist Alexander "Skip" Spence lived in this Corte Madera house roughly five miles north of his bandmates Peter Lewis and Jerry Miller.

COW PALACE
2600 Geneva Ave., Daly City

Opened in 1941 as the California Livestock Pavilion, the Cow Palace sits along the southern border of San Francisco but is technically located in Daly City. Emerging as a multi-purpose arena, the Cow Palace over the years has hosted everything from basketball to boxing, wrestling to rodeos, political conventions to circuses. The NBA's San Francisco—now Golden State—Warriors called the Cow Palace home during two multiyear stretches, most recently between 1966–1971.

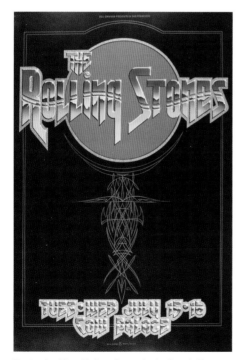

Poster by Alton Kelley, Crazy Arab, Randy Tuten, and Stanley Mouse, 1975

The Cow Palace has also been the site of many concerts by premier touring musical acts, including the Beatles, the Rolling Stones, the Allman Brothers, the Supremes, Van Halen, Prince, Grateful Dead, Elvis Presley, Journey, Pink Floyd, Nirvana, the Jackson 5, Fleetwood Mac, and Kiss.

The concert the Cow Palace may be most renowned for was a performance by the Who on November 20, 1973. Drummer Keith Moon, who'd reportedly taken horse tranquilizers, passed out onstage during "Magic Bus," and Pete Townshend apologized, then asked, "Can anybody play the drums?" followed a beat later by "I mean somebody good." Nineteen-year-old Scot Halpin was enlisted from the crowd, playing on three songs before the concert ended.

FANTASY FAIR AND MAGIC MOUNTAIN MUSIC FESTIVAL AND MONTEREY INTERNATIONAL POP MUSIC FESTIVAL
Fantasy Fair: Sidney B. Cushing Memorial Amphitheatre, Mount Tamalpais, Mill Valley
Monterey International: 2004 Fairground Rd., Monterey

Around 150 miles and five calendar days separated the Fantasy Fair and Magic Mountain Music Festival and the Monterey International Pop Music Festival in June 1967. Both were pioneers in effectively presenting the blueprint of what has by now become commonplace, the music festival as an immersive experience, with lineups representative of the best—or at least most popular—sounds of the era. Fantasy Fair (June 10 and 11) actually happened first, while Monterey Pop (June 16–18) followed closely behind. Yet it's the latter most often cited as being the cultural apex of the Californian Summer of Love, while the former, at least in the greater consciousness, has been almost forgotten.

That might be at least partly due to what happened later. By the end of December 1968, *Monterey Pop*, a documentary by esteemed filmmaker D.A. Pennebaker, was airing in cinemas, and ever since various home video and television broadcasts have allowed the festival to echo across time; years later, audio performances from the festival were also released, allowing the experience to remain fresh. Fantasy Fair has comparatively faded from memory, even in the internet age, with the few clips circulating on YouTube disjointed montages, some shot by an audience member on 8mm film.

Sponsored by San Francisco radio station KFRC Fantasy Fair was modeled after a renaissance festival, with the stage of the Sidney B. Cushing Memorial Amphitheatre

bedecked in flags. The lineup boasted a handful of artists who would go on to play Monterey Pop, including Jefferson Airplane, Country Joe and the Fish, the Steve Miller Blues Band, the Byrds, and Canned Heat. Also playing Fantasy Fair were the Doors, Captain Beefheart and the Magic Band, Tim Buckley, the Seeds, the Grass Roots, and many others. Performances took place primarily on the main stage of the historic 4,000-seat amphitheater, with a second stage also pulled into service to allow for relatively seamless live music for the duration of the festival.

In order to accommodate the roughly 18,000 attendees for each day of the festival, chartered buses (dubbed Trans-Love Bus Lines) departed from surrounding communities and wound their way up the mountain roads, with occasional motorcycles running back and forth. In at least one instance, that of Jefferson Airplane guitarist Jorma Kaukonen, the journey was made on foot. Tickets for the festival were $2 apiece, with proceeds benefiting the Hunter's Point Child Care Center. Tom Rounds and Mel Lawrence, who produced Fantasy Fair, would go on to put together the Miami Pop Festival in December 1968, not to be confused with the wholly unconnected Miami Pop Festival which took place in May 1968.

Monterey Pop took place in a setting already accustomed to live music festivals, albeit one significantly less amplified; the Monterey Jazz Festival was on the cusp of its ninth straight year at the time of Monterey Pop. Even so, estimates ranging between 25,000–90,000 people attended a festival with an enclosed live music arena that was approved to hold just 7,000.

Organized by John Philips of the Mamas and the Papas, record producer Lou Adler, entrepreneur Alan Pariser, and publicist Derek Taylor, Monterey Pop drew its roster from further afield. In addition to a host of local groups,

Poster by Tom Wilkes, 1967

like Grateful Dead, Big Brother and the Holding Company, and Jefferson Airplane, Monterey Pop also showcased southern soul music (Otis Redding), British imports (the Who; the Jimi Hendrix Experience, who despite their American leader were based at the time in England), and for a lengthy Sunday afternoon set, Ravi Shankar, who for many in attendance played the first sitar they'd heard outside of a pop music context. Monterey Pop even had its own theme song, "San Francisco (Be Sure to Wear Flowers in Your Hair)" by Scott McKenzie, which peaked at #4 on the Billboard Hot 100 on July 1, 1967, and which ignored the fact that the intersection of Haight and Ashbury streets in San Francisco was over 100 miles north of the Monterey County Fairgrounds. In addition to happening slightly earlier, Fantasy Fair also had proximity on its

side, being situated fewer than 40 winding miles away from the perceived ground zero of the Summer of Love.

Unlike Fantasy Fair, Monterey Pop was credited with turning a few of its performers into superstars, with Redding, Big Brother and the Holding Company's mesmeric singer Janis Joplin, and the Jimi Hendrix Experience receiving ecstatic reviews in the emerging rock and counterculture media.

Considered together, the Fantasy Fair and Magic Mountain Music Festival and the Monterey Pop Music Festival set the table for larger fetes in the near future, like the Isle of Wight Festival (held between 1968–1970), the Atlanta International Pop Festival (held between 1969–1970), and most famous of all, the Woodstock Music & Art Fair (August 15–17, 1969). A direct line can also be traced back to Fantasy Fair and Monterey Pop from contemporary annual festivals like Coachella Valley Music and Arts Festival, Lollapalooza, Governors Ball Music Festival, and in San Francisco, Outside Lands.

ALTAMONT

Altamont Speedway, 17001 Midway Rd., Tracy

Altamont. For many the name itself signifies the end of the '60s, a bloody disaster where hippie met hubris and Hells Angels, and people died.

Headlined by the Rolling Stones, the free concert held at Altamont Speedway on

"We are doing a free concert in San Francisco. . . . And the location is not Golden Gate Park, unfortunately, but, it's somewhere adjacent to it, which is a bit larger. It's creating a sort of microcosmic society. You know, which it sets an example to the rest of America as to how one can behave in nice gatherings."

—MICK JAGGER OF THE ROLLING STONES DURING A PRESS CONFERENCE IN NEW YORK CITY ON NOVEMBER 26, 1969

December 6, 1969, was originally meant to take place in San Francisco's **Golden Gate Park**. The Stones were looking for an event that would serve as the climax to their 1969 US tour, which was being documented on film by the Maylses's brothers, Albert and David, and Charlotte Zwerin. The musical landscape had changed significantly since the last time the Rolling Stones had toured the United States in the Summer of 1966, and much of the

world's attention was focused squarely on San Francisco.

There are numerous stories about what happened, countless articles and a few books— including Joel Selvin's excellent *Altamont: The Rolling Stones, The Hells Angels, and the Inside Story of Rock's Darkest Day*—but as the concert didn't turn out to be a Woodstock West, few people involved have ever taken credit or blame. As such, the attempt here to summarize Altamont will likely feel incomplete as it's drawn from numerous sources with decidedly different accounts.

The Rolling Stones reached out to the Grateful Dead in the fall of 1969 to discuss the possibility of a free concert in Golden Gate Park, which the San Francisco group had plenty of experience with. With a date set for December 6, Stones road manager Sam Cutler began working on the details of the event, which would feature the two bands and other popular groups, like Jefferson Airplane, Santana, the Flying Burrito Brothers, and the newly minted Crosby, Stills, Nash & Young. The Dead's past experience dealing with the City of San Francisco led them to conclude that the only way to secure a permit for the concert was to not announce the Rolling Stones as its headliner until December 5. By the time of the Stones's press conference in New York City on November 26, Golden Gate Park was apparently already off the table.

Sears Point Raceway (29355 Arnold Dr., Sonoma) was very nearly where the concert happened, a site with easy access and suitable facilities for a large scale event. Work was already underway at Sears Point when on December 4 the deal fell through, reportedly over an escrow deposit and the property's owner, Filmways, Inc., being denied by the Rolling Stones distribution rights to the tour film. Altamont Speedway owner Dick Carter volunteered his financially struggling racetrack in the hopes of establishing the property as a legitimate festival site, and with a little over a day to spare, the crew began moving its operations from Sears Point to a gloomy, relatively remote area roughly 80 miles southeast, where an estimated 300,000 people would soon arrive.

The short turnaround in preparing at an unsuitable site was only part of why Altamont is remembered today, though even in the best of circumstances a short stage at the bottom of a steep hill might have resulted in injury. But there was also the presence of the Hells Angels, who depending upon who's telling the story were either hired with $500 worth of beer to work security or to just help keep people off the stage. As the day wore on, violence began erupting near the stage, flare-ups by most accounts involving Hells Angels.

Santana played first, a seven-song set that was followed by Jefferson Airplane, a group that was no stranger to speaking up and speaking out. Two songs into the set, Airplane singer Marty Balin had had enough of seeing violence unfold in front of the stage and began yelling at the Angels to cool it, and one of them named Animal strode across the stage and hit him in the face. Not long after, Balin jumped into the crowd to try and stop the fighting and was knocked unconscious. Balin was dragged inert backstage, where he reportedly yelled "Fuck you!" at a contrite Animal, who responded by knocking the singer out. Balin would recover in time to rejoin the group onstage for their final number, "Volunteers."

Also battered backstage by Animal was Rex Jackson, a biker who rode with the Hells Angels and also served as a member of the Grateful Dead crew. Seeing the toughest guy in their inner circle brutally laid out was the last straw for the Dead, who left Altamont without playing a note.

The Flying Burrito Brothers played their seven-song set of country rock in an atmosphere of relative calm, but by the time Crosby, Stills, Nash & Young took the stage, there were once again amplified pleas for the fighting to stop. Some Angels were armed with pool cues, some only their fists. But unlike much of the crowd, the bikers were accustomed to mixing it up, and as the long, drunken afternoon slipped into the evening, the violence escalated.

What happened after the Rolling Stones took the stage has been reported exhaustively. The original trailer for *Gimme Shelter*, the documentary of the entire tour, is almost exclusively comprised of terrifying moments from Altamont, a stage crowded with angry Hells Angels, and Jagger jiving around them in a swirling satin blouse, an incongruous image of celebration in the midst of calamitous mayhem. Jagger had earlier been punched squarely in the face by a kid moments after stepping off the helicopter that carried the Stones to the racetrack, but as he was unable to prevent that from happening he was also incapable of stopping the violence unfolding directly in front of the stage.

Meredith Hunter was an 18-year-old Black kid from Berkeley, an art student who was at Altamont with his white girlfriend, Patty Bredehoft, and had reportedly had racial slurs

"Hey, people. Sisters. Brothers and sisters. Brothers and sisters. Come on, now. That means everybody just cool out! Will you cool out, everybody. I know. Everybody, be cool now. Come on. Alright? How are we doing over there? Alright? Can we still make it down the front? Is there anyone there that's hurt, huh? Everyone alright? Okay? Alright. I think we are cool. We can go. We always havin' something very funny happen when we start that number."

—MICK JAGGER, ONSTAGE AT ALTAMONT SPEEDWAY, AS THE ROLLING STONES ATTEMPT TO START "SYMPATHY FOR THE DEVIL."

yelled at him as a result. During "Under My Thumb," roughly midway through the Stones's set, Hunter climbed atop a speaker box next to the stage, where he was confronted by a few Hells Angels, who reportedly chased him into the crowd to beat him up. Hunter returned a few seconds later; in chilling footage seen in *Gimme Shelter*, it appears that Hunter has drawn a .22 caliber revolver from his jacket, and is then stabbed twice in the back by Angel Alan Passaro. Though not captured on film, Hunter was reportedly stabbed five times in the

PRIMUS

Originally formed in El Sobrante in the mid-'80s, the now classic lineup of Les Claypool (bass, vocals), Larry LaLonde (guitar), and Tim Alexander (drums) came together in 1989, blending progressive elements of funk, metal, and nursery rhymes into a sound solely its own. Primus have toured the world, but as principal lyricist Claypool has often shown, El Sobrante and the East Bay are never too far away from their hearts.

Checker Gas (521 Appian Way, El Sobrante): Now a United Gas and Food, Checker Gas was where "Fatty" liked to hang out with friends in the 1993 song "The Air Is Getting Slippery."

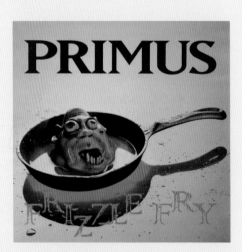

Richmond Fire Department Station #63 (5201 Valley View Rd., Richmond): This fire station was referenced in the lyrics of "Jerry Was a Race Car Driver" from the band's 1991 album *Sailing the Seas of Cheese*. The song also references "El Sob," aka El Sobrante.

De Anza Jig: The lyrics to the banjo-laden "De Anza Jig" off of Primus's 1995 album *Tales from the Punchbowl* squeeze in numerous local references in a relatively short song. **Shell (3621 San Pablo Dam Rd., El Sobrante), Jack in the Box (4080 San Pablo Dam Rd., El Sobrante),** and **Taco Bell (4068 San Pablo Dam Rd., El Sobrante; now Cam Hong Deli)** were all real places visited by the song's Ol' Flouncin' Freddy.

Barrington Hall (2315 Dwight Way, Berkeley): A former student housing cooperative, the graffiti-covered Barrington Hall was known in the '80s for its occasional "Wine Dinners," which included an LSD-laced bowl of punch. *Frizzle Fry*, the debut album by Primus, along with its title track were about the debauchery at Barrington Hall, a theme Claypool revisited with the song "Barrington Hall" on *Purple Onion*, a 2002 album by his side project, Colonel Les Claypool's Fearless Flying Frog Brigade.

upper back, then stomped on while lying on the ground. Some reports also say efforts to bring Hunter backstage for medical treatment were thwarted by Hells Angels. Passaro was later charged with murder, but was acquitted on grounds of self-defense after the footage of the incident was shown in court.

Hunter's wasn't the only death at Altamont. Leonard Kryszak was one day shy of 19 on December 6, when shortly before the music started he climbed a fence by the California Aqueduct, ignored pleas from a state police officer, flipped the cop the bird, slipped into a fast-moving canal for a swim and was swept away by the current; his body was found two hours later in a filter trap a few miles away from where he entered the canal. After the concert, as the crowds inched their way home, some travelers decided to stop and rest, with campfires springing up along the side of the road. Richard Salov and Mark Feiger, two New Jersey natives in their early 20s living in Berkeley, were killed by a hit-and-run driver who was never caught.

Altamont Speedway remained open under the condition that it no longer hosted concerts, and that it limited attendance at other events to 3,000. The racetrack closed for good in 2008.

IVY ROOM
860 San Pablo Ave., Albany
A popular neighborhood bar since the '40s, the Ivy Room has for the past few decades also

hosted live music on its intimate stage, with everyone from the Avengers, the Moore Brothers, the Tet Holiday, Jawbreaker, Meat Puppets, Tarnation, and Green Day side-projects the Coverups and the Longshot all performing there.

EDENVALE ELEMENTARY SCHOOL
285 Azucar St., San Jose
On February 19, 1976, Rick Stevens, former lead singer of Tower of Power, surrendered to police on the playground at Edenvale Elementary. According to the *New York Times*, Stevens was "convicted of killing three men in a drug-addicted haze" over a period of two days, serving 36 years of a life sentence in prison before being paroled. Stevens died of lung cancer in September 2017.

PACIFIC RECORDERS/PACIFIC RECORDING
1737 S. El Camino Real, San Mateo
Opened in the mid-'60s by New York City Columbia Records expats Fred Catero and David Rubinson, Pacific Recording was the first Bay Area studio to install the Ampex MM1000 16-track recorder, attracting local groups like Santana, who cut their eponymous debut album there. The Grateful Dead, the Doobie Brothers, and the Elvin Bishop Group all recorded there as well.

CHATEAU LIBERTÉ
22700 Old Santa Cruz Highway, Los Gatos
A rock and roll biker joint with a swimming pool, a bar cut from timber and an eclectic clientele, Chateau Liberté was a crucial venue through most of the '70s for groups like the Doobie Brothers, Quicksilver Messenger Service, and the reunited Moby Grape.

Crispin Kott

THE DOOBIE BROTHERS

One of the signature groups of the '70s, San Jose's Doobie Brothers had two distinct identities: the original band featuring co-founder Tom Johnston, and the Michael McDonald-led edition that emerged in the late '70s. Both produced some of the best-loved hits of the era, including "Listen to the Music," "China Grove," "Black Water," and "What a Fool Believes."

Guitarist Tom Johnston was studying at **San Jose State University (1 Washington Square, San Jose)** when he moved into a house at **285 South 12th Street** in San Jose in 1969. Through Moby Grape's Skip Spence, he met drummer John Hartman, and the duo added Pat Simmons (guitar), and Dave Shogren (bass) to form Pud, which rehearsed in the 12th Street basement and played extensively throughout the South Bay area for several months before evolving into the Doobie Brothers in 1970.

Their first album, *The Doobie Brothers* (1971) was recorded at **Pacific Studios (1737 S. El Camino Real, San Mateo ⊘)** and was released to little notice. The band continued to tour aggressively, however, and several Bay Area venues proved pivotal to building a following, including **The New Monk (2119 University Ave, Berkeley), Keystone Korner (750 Vallejo St., San Francisco), Bimbo's 365 Club (1025 Columbus Ave., San Francisco),** and the **Fillmore West (10 S. Van Ness Ave., San Francisco).**

Later in 1971, Shogren was replaced by Tiran Porter, and a second drummer, Michael Hossack, was added. The next album, 1972's *Toulouse Street*, partially recorded at **Wally Heider Studios (245 Hyde St., San Francisco),**

was a smash, yielding the hits "Listen to the Music" and "Jesus Is Just Alright," bringing the group to national prominence. Their third album, *The Captain and Me* (1973) proved even more successful, containing hits "China Grove," and "Long Train Runnin'." *Captain* also introduced Steely Dan alum Jeff "Skunk" Baxter to the roster, and his guitar playing would be an integral part of the group for the next several years.

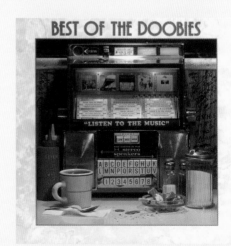

THE DOOBIE BROTHERS

MINUTE BY MINUTE

In 1976 chronic health issues forced Tom Johnston to the sidelines and he was replaced by another Steely Dan veteran, Michael McDonald, whose distinctively soulful vocals brought the Doobies even greater success. *Minute by Minute* (1978) became the group's first album to hit #1 on Billboard's album chart, and the single "What a Fool Believes" hit #1 on the Billboard singles chart. This version of the Doobie Brothers ultimately disintegrated in 1983, but would reunite in various forms many times in the ensuing years. On September 12, 2018, Tom Johnston, Pat Simmons, and John McFee, a veteral of the McDonald era Doobies, fronted the group which played both *Toulouse Street* and *The Captain and Me* in their entirety at the **Masonic Auditorium (1111 California St., San Francisco).** In 2021, a 50th-Anniversary tour is planned, uniting Johnston, McDonald, Simmons, and McFee.

SITTIN' ON THE DOCK OF THE BAY
Waldo Point Harbor, Sausalito

Otis Redding's posthumously released chart-topping single "(Sittin' on) The Dock of the Bay" was inspired by a relaxing stay on a houseboat docked at Waldo Point Harbor. Redding, in town to play a run of shows at **Basin Street West (401 Broadway, San Francisco)**, began writing a song based on what he saw and felt as he watched the world across Richardson Bay.

THE SYNDROME
1310 Old Bayshore Hwy., Burlingame

Opened in 1966 by Joe Gannon, the former road manager of the Kingston Trio, The Syndrome was one of many short-lived clubs to crop up across the Bay Area attempting to stretch the San Francisco sound to the suburbs. Most notable among the acts to play the Syndrome was Luminous Marsh Gas, a group that lasted about as long as a cup of coffee featuring former members of the Frantics, who would go on to form Moby Grape. The Syndrome lasted for about one year before closing.

THE TRIP
4301 El Camino Real, San Mateo

"A Journey Through LSD (Lights, Sounds and Delicious Pizza)." The Trip was opened in 1966 by Yvonne Modica, an entrepreneur who had just recently founded the Big Beat Club in Palo Alto. The Trip was one of a great many teen clubs that attempted to stretch the San Francisco sound into the suburbs of the Bay Area in the mid-'60s. Quickie faux-psychedelic cash grabs would soon become de rigueur in mainstream advertising, but for a couple of years it was suburban club owners who saw the moneymaking potential in trying to tap into youth culture. In Modica's case it didn't pay off for long: By 1968, The Trip had been rebranded as an R&B-themed club Souled Out.

CHUCK'S CELLAR
4926 El Camino Real, Los Altos

Opened in the late '60s, this surf and turf spot is best known as the birthplace of the Eagles after Linda Ronstadt put a backing band together featuring Glenn Frey, Don Henley, and Randy Meisner for a weekend gig in 1971.

THE TRIDENT
558 Bridgeway, Sausalito

Opened in the mid-'60s by the Kingston Trio, this restaurant and bar with views of San Francisco and the Golden Gate Bridge was a popular getaway for the era's musicians and associated counterculture. Bands recording at the nearby **Record Plant (2200 Bridgeway)** frequently visited The Trident to decompress. The Rolling Stones were honored with a private party at The Trident organized by impresario Bill Graham in celebration of the start of their 1972 tour. A few years later, comedian Robin Williams spent three consecutive summers at The Trident as a busboy. The Trident is also renowned as the home of the modern version of the tequila sunrise. Closed in 1976 and reopened four years later as Horizons, the popular tourist destination was renamed The Trident in 2012 and is still in operation.

TARPAN STUDIOS

1925 E. Francisco Blvd., Suite L, San Rafael

Dubbed the "Motown of Marin," Tarpan Studios has seen artists like Carlos Santana, Whitney Houston, Mariah Carey, Curtis Mayfield, Aretha Franklin, and Stevie Wonder come through its doors since 1985.

Index

Acknowledgments

My family has been a source of constant support, especially my daughter Alison, always a ray of sunshine on a cloudy day. My parents, Ron and Judith Katz, Dan and Ellen Brown, Marian Brown, Marcy, Mark, and Stephanie Rothenberg, and Adam Zaid. Special thanks to Rebecca Pieken for making the move westward possible. Many others also provided important moral and/or material support, including Billy MacKay, Simon Astor, Nicholas Sinisi, Kate Krader, Will Murphy, Tony Van de Walle, Richard Ory, Ron Koury, Mary Bahr, Hilary and Davis King, Michael Longshore, Rosemary Marotta, Sean Byrne, and Lenny Kaye. Of course, ultra-special thanks to coauthor and rock and roll soulmate Crispin Kott. How we keep pulling this off I'll never know.

—Mike Katz

All love to my family and friends for sticking with, and often encouraging, my rock and roll nerdiness: My extraordinary wife Eve Levine; our coolest ever kids, Ian and Marguerite Kott; my mom and stepdad, Claudia and Paul Andreassen; my dad and stepmom, Gary and Karyn Kott; my mother-in-law, Suzanne McCombs; Nathaniel Kressen, Jon Herzog and the core members of the Greenpoint Writers Group (RIP); Chris Marron; Jenny Raven and Eric Johnson; Andrew Ledford; Legs McNeil; and my old comrade and writing partner Mike Katz, without whom none of this would have been possible. Our shared love of musical minutiae and talking one another off the metaphoric ledge and out of the desperately lonely fog of academic rock and roll research is now available in book form for a third time. On to the next chapter…

—Crispin Kott

Amy Lyons, Sarah Parke, Rick Rinehart, Katie O'Dell, Kristen Mellitt, and everyone at Globe Pequot Press; Joel Gion; Andi Sumpter and Amy Chase; Neal Schon; Penelope Houston; Corbett Redford; Chris Appelgren; Naut Humon; David Rathod; Corry Arnold; Dave Seabury; Jonathan Burnside; Jodi Haddon; Tom George; Murray Bowles; Mike Murphy; Richard McNeace, Jason Kincade; San Francisco Public Library; Oakland Public Library; Berkeley Public Library; Monterey County Free Libraries, Palo Alto City Library, New York Public Library, Brooklyn Public Library, Nassau Library System

—Mike and Crispin

About the Authors

Mike Katz was born in Atlanta, came of age in New Orleans, and eventually made his home in New York City. He is a rock historian, voracious reader, veteran bookseller, photographer, and father to a much smarter daughter, Alison. He currently lives in Monterey, California.

Crispin Kott was born in Chicago, raised in New York, and has called everywhere from San Francisco to Los Angeles to Atlanta home. A music historian and failed drummer, he's written for numerous print and online publications, and has shared with his son Ian and daughter Marguerite a love of reading, writing, and record collecting. As a longtime Brooklyn resident and recent returnee to the Bay Area, Crispin has been able to indulge in his love of Rock and Roll of the past, present, and future.

Mike Katz and Crispin Kott also coauthored *Rock and Roll Explorer Guide to New York City* (Globe Pequot, June 2018) and *Little Book of Rock and Roll Wisdom* (Lyons Press, October 2018).